Business Process Implementation
Building Workflow Systems

ACM Press Books

This book is published as part of ACM Press Books – a collaboration between the Association for Computing Machinery and Addison Wesley Longman Limited. ACM is the oldest and largest educational and scientific society in the information technology field. Through its high quality publications and services, ACM is a major force in advancing the skills and knowledge of IT professionals throughout the world. For further information about ACM contact:

ACM Member Services
1515 Broadway, 17th Floor
New York NY 10036–5701
Phone: + 1 212 626 0500
Fax: + 1 212 944 1318
e-mail: acmhelp@acm. org

ACM European Service Center
108 Cowley Road
Oxford OX4 1JF
United Kingdom
Phone: 44 1865 382338
Fax: 44 1865 381338
e-mail: acm-europe@acm.org
URL: http://www.acm.org

Selected ACM titles:

Software Requirements and Specifications: A Lexicon of Software
Practice, Principles and Prejudices   *Michael Jackson*

Bringing Design to Software: Expanding Software Development to
Include Design   *Terry Winograd, John Bennett, Laura de Young, Bradley Hartfield*

The Object Advantage: Business Process Reengineering with Object
Technology 2nd edn.   *Ivar Jacobson, Maria Ericsson, Agneta Jacobson, Gunnar Magnusson*

Software for Use: A Practical Guide to the Models and Methods of
Usage Centered Design   *Larry L Constantine, Lucy A D Lockwood*

CORBA Distributed Objects: Using Orbix   *Sean Baker*

Software Reuse: Architecture, Process and Organization for Business
Success   *Ivar Jacobson, Martin Griss, Patrik Jonsson*

Intelligent Database Systems   *Elisa Bertino, Gian Piero Zarri*

Internet Security   *Dorothy E Denning, Peter J Denning*

Business Process Implementation
Building Workflow Systems
Michael Jackson
and
Graham Twaddle

Harlow, England • Reading, Massachusetts • Menlo Park, California
New York • Don Mills, Ontario • Amsterdam • Bonn • Sydney • Singapore
Tokyo • Madrid • San Juan • Milan • Mexico City • Seoul • Taipei

© 1997 by the ACM Press, a division of the Association for Computing Machinery Inc. (ACM)

Addison Wesley Longman Limited
Edinburgh Gate
Harlow
Essex CM20 2JE
England

and Associated Companies throughout the World

The right of Michael Jackson and Graham Twaddle to be identified as authors of this Work has been asserted by them in accordance with the Copyright, Designs and Patents Act 1988.

Cover designed by Odb Design & Communication, Reading
and printed by The Riverside Printing Co. (Reading) Ltd.
Typeset by 30
Printed and bound by Biddles of Guildford.

First printed 1997

ISBN 0–201–177684

British Library Cataloguing-in-Publication Data
A catalogue record for this book is available from the British Library

For my father.
M.J.

For Millar Raeside.
G.T.

Foreword

We are acutely aware from our daily lives that the pace of change in the world is unrelenting. The way that we work today compared to twenty years ago involves significant changes in the inter-action between customers and business organizations. The most successful organizations have been adept at handling these changes in their dealings with clients, and in the development and change of their business processes to support these changes. Other organizations, while being successful, have had to concentrate resources in not just improving client relationships, but on supporting the additional work required to make up for deficiencies in their business processes, business systems and, in some cases, both.

The changes over the next twenty years for business organizations cannot be predicted with any certainty. The structure of organizations, and the business systems that support those, therefore need to have a level of flexibility beyond that which has historically been achievable. We also now move in a world where the flow of information is both greater and more timely. With shorter timescales for the provision of information the accuracy of that information has to be greater as there is less opportunity to audit it before its release. We are therefore faced with the development of systems which need to provide increasing flexibility at reduced costs, and greater accuracy. This places a burden on business people to understand the nature of their organizations, the processes that are employed and the handling of change. For our Information Technology personnel it requires the analysis and development skills which they have acquired to be transferred to the business community in a form which is understandable and usable. The business community cannot seek to develop companies and help develop systems to support these companies without understanding information flows and the power of technology.

In this book Michael Jackson has described methodologies which were used at Century Life in the development of a new life and pensions administration system. I consider that the book is compulsory reading for those involved from both Information Technology and the business community who are involved in projects of a similar nature. The book deals with some very complicated issues but seeks to reduce them, as quoted by Michael Jackson, so 'that everything should be as simple as possible'.

Our own experience of the methodology put forward within this book is that it requires radical thinking on behalf of the business community but that the benefits of the approach are significant and are worth the time involved in understanding the concepts behind the methodology.

John V. Deane, FIA BSc
Century Life plc

Preface

This book is a description of a system development method. But it is, above all, a description of practical experience. The method has evolved from the experience gained by Sherwood International in building and installing many successful systems in the financial services industry in the United Kingdom and several other countries.

Sherwood is a financial software company with offices in Glasgow, London and other cities. In the past few years, Sherwood has developed and installed a series of successful systems for financial services companies. These systems are based on Sherwood's LogicWare and Amarta products. Amarta is an application framework aimed originally at the life and pensions industry and capable of being tailored to a wide variety of financial applications. LogicWare is a development toolset and run-time environment that supports Amarta and other application frameworks based on the same ideas. It has been implemented in two major environments: Informix and Oracle. It has also won a British Computer Society merit award.

Relationship to Business Process Re-engineering

The ideas underlying Amarta and LogicWare, and the systems built on them, have many business advantages. The recent surge of interest in Business Process Re-engineering has focused attention on a view of a business as a complex of processes both within the business organization itself and in the outside world of its customers, suppliers, regulators and other stakeholders. The task of the process engineer is to choose to adapt or devise business processes to meet the needs both of the people who work in the business and of the people and organizations in the world outside.

LogicWare's approach to this problem allows both of these needs to be explicitly and separately analysed and served. The conduct of the business – the business interactions with customers and others – can be expressed with the clarity necessary for good communication during system development and good understanding in operational use. Design of the workflow – the internal management of the office – can focus on considerations of internal efficiency and job satisfaction, and on giving the best level of service.

Flexibility and Responsiveness

The financial industry is very competitive. New products are constantly being designed, and companies must be able to respond quickly to support the new products with new systems or new facilities in existing systems. The LogicWare approach takes an old idea to a new level of effectiveness. Software developers have known for a long time that data is more easily changed than a program. A discount policy built into the logic of the accounting programs is expensive and difficult to change. The same policy expressed as a table in a database can be changed quickly and easily when the need arises.

In the LogicWare approach everything is treated in this way. In effect, not just financial product definitions, but the whole way of doing business – the life-cycles of business entities, the rules governing business interactions and the rules governing the internal management of the office – are captured in database tables and made as easily changeable as they can possibly be.

This flexibility is a huge advantage in an installed system. It is also a huge advantage when a new system is to be built. Existing business models and frameworks are much more easily changed and adapted to the requirements of a new system. Some of Sherwood's customers have been able to build and install new systems in a remarkably short time by exploiting the flexibility of an existing business model. Suppliers of tailorable systems often find that they must place limits on the tailoring that is possible. A major part of the system logic is hard-wired into program texts, whether in C++ or in a 4GL. Changing these program texts is too expensive and too dangerous to the integrity of the system. In the LogicWare approach, almost nothing is hard-wired.

Ownership and Responsibility

This approach of expressing the system behaviour in data has another important advantage. Within the business itself, ownership and responsibility for different levels of the system data can be realistically and clearly allocated. At one level, operational staff own the *production data* – the records of the business' current interactions with its customers – and are responsible for its integrity and correctness. At another level, strategic staff own the *plan data* – the definitions of the company's products and its current way of doing business. At a third level is the *feature data* – the definitions of the low-level calculations and procedures of which the product definitions are ultimately composed – owned by staff who are expert in the detailed intricacies of the business and the system. This ownership and responsibility is very effective in breaking down the walls that too often separate the information system builders from the information system users.

Time's Arrow

In the financial industry, but not only there, the progression of time down its one-way street presents serious problems. Business obligations and customer relationships – especially in life insurance – often endure for many years or even decades. During this time there will be many changes in the rules governing these relationships. Tax laws will change. Regulatory bodies will impose different restrictions. Products evolve. But in many cases the business must continue to handle old relationships under the rules that applied when they were established. A life assurance policy is a lifetime contract, whose terms must continue to be observed long after the company has ceased to offer contracts written in those particular terms.

Even where the rules are unchanged, inevitable delays and mistakes can give rise to the need to go back in time. The broker who fails to implement a client's order correctly may have to go back and rerun the relationship from the time the mistake was made, calculating what would have happened if the order had been correctly implemented.

By keeping so much of the system behaviour in data, the LogicWare approach allows this time travel to be handled more easily. Effectively, the system is capable of running several different versions of itself simultaneously, to cater for the needs of different relationships.

Efficiency and Parallel Lifecycles

The process modelling ideas of Logicware are unusually powerful. Their basis is conventional. They are based on the idea of entity lifecycles (sometimes called entity life histories). The basic idea of entity lifecycles is that the order of events in the life of an entity – possibly over many years or even decades – should be explicitly described and directly modelled in the system. This idea goes back to the JSP program design method of the early 1970s, and has been adopted by most system development methods – object-oriented and others – since then.

In some workflow systems, the lifecycle of an entity has only one thread. That means that the entity, so to speak, can only be in one place at any one time. The effect is very similar to the traditional workflow based on paper files. If a contract file is in the New Business department it cannot also be in the Underwriting department. Underwriting must wait for New Business to complete their work. This is a severe restriction on the efficiency of the workflow. Tasks that could easily be carried out now must wait until the file – whether a paper folder or a database record – arrives at the right desk.

In the LogicWare method an entity may be simultaneously engaged in several lifecycles, and each lifecycle can have several simultaneously active threads. This simultaneity allows the greatest possible flexibility and efficiency in managing the operational work of the business. The method and the lifecycle notation can express, in a readily understandable form, the high degree of parallelism that can be achieved in this kind of system.

Technology and Method

This book was written to capture the method behind the success of the LogicWare approach. It focuses on the conceptual framework of the approach, not on the implementation of technology. LogicWare systems are usually implemented in a client–server environment, but this book is not about client–server systems. They can use an infrastructure based on an intranet; they can use the Web and html documents; they can use Lotus Notes; LogicWare systems are now being developed that exploit the power of software agents. But this book is about none of those things.

Instead, it aims to explain the basic ideas as they are found in the data and process models of Amarta systems. These ideas in themselves are partly very standard and partly somewhat unusual. The process modelling ideas are unusual in their ability to express and exploit parallelism. They do not use the conventional notations of state transition diagrams; instead they use specialized notations to capture the task structure and coordination needed for workflow systems.

The data modelling ideas are unusual in their simplicity, and also in the way they are used to describe powerful concepts of roles and classification. They are easily understood by the system's clients and users, and are very effective in cutting away complexities of data modelling that are not needed for this kind of system. They are also designed to be immediately and easily implemented in a relational database, which today is still the standard database foundation for business systems.

Scope of the Method Description

This book does not aim to cover the whole lifetime of a system, from an initial suggestion through all the stages of requirements analysis, development, testing, installation, acceptance, maintenance and eventual retirement. Its ambition is more modest. It aims only to describe the development approach, starting from a point at which the requirements are reasonably well established. Chapter 9, which discusses project structure, does have something to say about the process of discovering and capturing the system requirements, but this is not a central topic of the book.

Throughout, the central topic is the conceptual nature of systems built using the LogicWare approach, and how that nature is expressed in the data and process models and in the treatment of the workflow within the business. This is the foundation on which the success of these systems has been laid.

Structure of the Book

The book is intended for people who are interested in system development, either from a chiefly business perspective or from a professional information systems perspective. They may be business people becoming involved in a RAD or JAD (Rapid Application or Joint Application Development) team, or systems analysts or designers, or development managers who want to understand the content of the development they are managing.

Chapter 1 is an introduction. It defines and discusses the kind of system – office workflow systems – for which the method is appropriate. Chapter 2 gives an overview of the method, explaining the main development stages of data and process modelling and workflow definition. The following chapters, Chapters 3 to 8, are more technical. Readers who want only an outline of the method could skip straight from the end of Chapter 2 to Chapter 9. Chapter 9 is about project structure, about risks and goals, and the broader context in which development takes place.

The basic ideas of data and process modelling are discussed in Chapters 3 and 4, and workflow is discussed in Chapter 7. All of these chapters are intended to be readable by people with some interest in technicalities – but not necessarily an interest in the finer points and subtler concepts of the method – who want to understand how the system is built and how it works. For readers with a stronger technical bent, Chapters 5 and 6 give more technical detail on data and process modelling and on some of their advanced aspects. Chapter 8 explains the approach to database implementation and shows how the database is structured to make the system easy to change.

Each chapter ends with a summary of its main points and a set of questions. The questions can be ignored, used as topics for discussion or treated as an opportunity to strengthen and deepen the reader's critical understanding of what has been said.

A full glossary of terms is given in Appendix 1. Appendix 2 gathers together the diagrammatic notations used in the book. Appendix 3 gives a brief account of the LogicWare development toolset and environment, and a full index appears at the end of the book.

Contents

CHAPTER 1

Introduction

This book is about a method for developing computer systems. But only some computer systems: not all.

The systems we will be concerned with are office workflow systems. These systems are at the heart of many commercial and administrative enterprises; they are a particular category of what used to be called business data processing systems. In this chapter we will describe and explore their identifying characteristics, and distinguish them from other kinds of system.

Chapter 2 provides an overview of the development method. Subsequent chapters describe the method and its techniques in detail.

Purposes, Systems and Methods

There are many different kinds of computer system. Computers are used in every imaginable application area, and in every possible context. They serve all kinds of purposes and fulfil all kinds of functions. CAD systems are tools for technical design and drafting. Avionics systems control aeroplanes in flight. Banking systems maintain accounts and control the operation of automatic teller machines. Switching systems are at the heart of telephone exchanges and of the nodes of the global telephone network. Desktop publishing systems allow books, magazines and all kinds of publications to be designed and laid out on a personal computer, and colour separations and other necessary materials prepared for volume printing.

These systems are all very different. An avionics system is no more like a switching system than an aeroplane is like a telephone. The system for running the National Lottery and a manufacturing control system have not much more in common than the fact that they both use computers. Even a word processing system and a CAD system have remarkably little in common. The behaviour of their users, the functions they provide and their underlying conceptual foundations are very different.

Different systems demand different development methods. The characteristics and shape of the method must be adapted to the characteristics and shape of the system, of its context, of the way it is used, of the functions it provides, and of the problems it solves. To choose a method, or to be confident that a given method is appropriate for the development of a particular system, we must identify and understand these system characteristics.

The essential constituent techniques of this method are of wide applicability: data and process modelling, the scheduling of program execution, and an implementation in terms of an underlying database. What is specialized about the method is the way in which these techniques are sharply focused on the particular needs of these systems, and the way in which the development concerns are separated in the earlier stages of development and brought together in the later stages.

The System Context

To understand the nature and character of a system development problem the first thing to do is to look at the system context. The context is made up of those parts of the world that affect the system and are affected by it; the parts of the world that you would eventually look at to judge whether the system is fulfilling its function and serving its purpose successfully.

Office workflow systems are found in many areas of administration and business, in which the central function and purpose of the system is to support the work of people in an office who interact with people and organizations in the world outside. For an office workflow system the most important parts of the context are the office itself and the outside world. We can show this in a context diagram (see Figure 1.1).

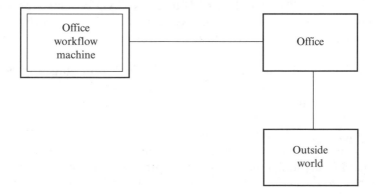

Figure 1.1   *Context diagram for an office workflow system.*

This is a context diagram showing the main parts of the context for an office workflow system. The double rectangle represents the *machine* – that is, the computer, including its attached printers, screens, keyboards, optical scanners, network links, and other devices, and the software that will make it behave as we require. We call this part of the context the 'machine' rather than the 'system', because we will often need to distinguish this part of the context – the computer hardware and software – from the surrounding environment and procedures of the office and the outside world. Although we are talking about it here in the singular, as one machine, it may in fact consist of several computers, possibly placed in different locations and linked by communication channels.

The *office* is the part of the world whose work the system must support. It is an important part of some *enterprise*, which owns and pays for the system. The people working in the office have direct access to the machine through the screens and keyboards of its attached terminals, and through the other input and output devices that are available for their use, such as printers and optical scanners.

The work of the office is to engage, on behalf of the enterprise, in what we may broadly call *business* with people and organizations in the *outside world*. It is business in the narrow sense, covering systems that are used in commercial applications such as insurance and other service industries; and in a broader sense, covering the kind of administration that is the business of some government departments.

The Users

As Figure 1.1 shows, the people and organizations in the outside world have no direct contact with the machine. Their contact is with the people in the office, with whom they communicate, typically by telephone and letter. We will call these people who work in the office the *users* of the system. More precisely, we should call them the *operational* or *production* users. Their job is to undertake the direct work of the business.

As we shall see later in the book, there are other kinds of user. There are *strategic* users, whose job is to set the strategies by which the enterprise conducts the business. And there are *expert users* of various kinds, whose job is to look after the technicalities – both business and computer technicalities – of the system. One of the benefits of the method is that it makes the system equally accessible to all kinds of user, and makes it easy to give the different users different responsibilities appropriate to their skills and their jobs.

Most often, when we talk of users we mean the operational users who carry on the business. Although, as we shall see later in this chapter, there are some direct contacts between the machine and the outside world – for example, by special network links, by use of the World Wide Web, or by electronic data interchange – they are exceptions to the basic pattern shown in the diagram in

Figure 1.1. This basic pattern is important, because it emphasizes a fundamental characteristic of the systems we are concerned with: they support the work of the operational users.

The Business of the Office

The business of the office, then, is mainly conducted by interaction between users in the office and other people and organizations in the outside world. These other people and organizations may be, for example, customers or clients, suppliers of goods or services, agents or intermediaries, banks, government departments or regulatory bodies. Interaction chiefly takes the form of conversations between people and the sending and receiving of letters, preprinted forms, contracts and other documents. Some direct interactions may bypass these channels, but they are still subject to the same kind of business rules.

All of these interactions reflect and serve the contracts and mutual obligations that arise in any business relationship of the kind we are concerned with. Some of these obligations are obviously central to the business. In the insurance industry, for example, the central obligations are concerned with policies: agreements by the insurer to reimburse policyholding customers if they suffer certain kinds of damage or loss, and corresponding agreements by the customers to pay for this service in the form of insurance premiums. In a tax office the central obligations are concerned with the taxpayer's legal duty to pay taxes on income and capital gains, and the office's duty is to assess and collect this tax in accordance with the law.

This kind of business is concerned with relatively long-term relationships. Life policies and pensions – *assurance* in the industry terminology – are obviously long-term. Insurance policies typically provide cover for one year, but are renewed in successive years: the basis for renewal – for example, in the case of a No-Claims Bonus on a motor policy – is often the past history of many years of business between the customer and the office. And claims can arise against a one-year policy many years afterwards: claims for industrial injuries such as asbestosis are often made after several decades. Similarly, the tax office maintains taxpayer records over many years, carrying forward information about overpayments or about capital losses made in one year that can be offset against capital gains in a later year.

Although we are stressing the long-term nature of these obligations and interactions, what characterizes an office workflow system is not that the timescale of obligations is measured in lifetimes or decades or years. What matters is that the obligations pass through several stages, each of which lasts significantly longer than the time for which one person can give it their undivided attention. This has an important effect on the nature of the system. It becomes necessary for the machine to store a considerable amount of information about the history of obligations and interactions, to maintain this information during periods of inactivity, and to make it available to the users in the office when further activity occurs. For example, when a motor insurance policy is in force, the single annual premium has been paid and no claim is currently being made, the system must store a lot of information about the policy, the policyholder and the car. If a claim is made, this information must be made available to the user in the office who will deal with the claim.

Trivial Interactions

Consider, by contrast, the work of a small food shop. There are obligations and interactions that arise from people coming into the shop, taking coffee and frozen peas and other goods from the shelves, and paying for them. But these obligations and interactions have very short lives: certainly no more than the time the customer is in the shop. The cashier deals with one customer at a time, and the complete interaction with each customer is concluded in a minute or two. Once the customer has paid and left the shop, there is nothing to be remembered on either side. A system to support the work of the cashier in a small food shop may be an interesting system. But it is definitely not an office workflow system in our sense; its interactions are too trivial and its obligations too short-lived.

Perhaps, we may think, the small food shop is involved in long-term obligations because customers may later claim that food bought at the shop gave them food poisoning. But this would be outside the scope of any reasonable system: food shops do not keep records of individual cans of beans and their purchasers.

We may also consider that the shop allows customers to order items that are not in stock. Many small food shops do this. The order would then create an obligation over a longer term, perhaps as long as a week or even a month. Would this not convert the system into a workflow system?

No, it would not, unless the handling of such orders became the central form of business, and the orders themselves became far more complex than a request for half a pound of an unusual kind of tea. In analysing the characteristics of a system with a view to choosing a development method, we must always pay attention chiefly to the central, high-volume activities and not be diverted by exceptional cases. One swallow does not make a summer.

Interaction Sequences

We have been discussing the business activity in terms of interactions arising from contracts or obligations. But this is too much of a simplification for an office workflow system. The business is more complex than this, and a significant part of the development method is devoted to handling this greater complexity.

We can capture the flavour of this greater complexity in the idea of an *interaction sequence*. An interaction sequence takes place over a period of time longer than one person's undivided attention span. It consists of a number of related actions by users in the office and people or organizations in the outside world, usually acting alternately. So the simplest interaction sequence might consist of an office user sending one letter to a customer, and the customer eventually replying by letter or telephone. A more complex interaction sequence might be a fire damage claim on a buildings insurance policy. The policyholder telephones the office; the office sends a claim form; the policyholder completes the form; the office sends a loss aduster to inspect the damage; the loss adjuster sends a report to the office; the office pays the adjusted claim.

An interaction sequence is characterized, above all, by a set of related events occurring in some predefined order. The claim must be made before the loss adjuster is sent: the loss adjuster's report must be received before the office will pay the claim. But not all claims involve a loss adjuster. In some cases the insurers will pay on the basis of the claim form alone. So although there is a predefined order, there is some variation in the actions that make up the sequence.

Although the events in an interaction sequence, like the kind we are concerned with, may vary, their ordering is always quite tightly constrained. Some constraints come from simple commercial prudence. A life assurance company will not issue certain kinds of policy until all necessary medical checks have been completed. No sensible retailing enterprise will dispatch a valuable consignment to an unknown new customer without prepayment or a careful credit check. Other constraints come from customary business practices established between agents and principals, or from statutory obligations. For example, customers for certain kinds of financial contract must, by law, be given a 'cooling-off-period' of 30 days, in which they are free to change their mind and repudiate the agreement. Other constraints come from simple common-sense properties of the world around us. An order cannot be cancelled before it is placed, and a letter cannot be received before it is written.

An office workflow system is characterized by the richness of its interaction sequences, and the richness of the relationships among them. At any time, many interaction sequences are in progress, and it is possible for several of them to concern the same client, or the same contract, or the same agent. The policyholder of an assurance policy on the lives of a husband and wife, for example, may be simultaneously engaged in paying this month's premium, making a claim on the death of one of the assured lives, and negotiating a surrender value for the assurance on the remaining life. These are three distinct interaction sequences, each with its ordering of events. All involve the same policy, which of course will be associated with yet another, longer-term, interaction sequence of its own, running from initial proposal to final cancellation or termination.

Business Requirements

The system must support the users in their interactions with the outside world. One aspect of this requirement is that the information stored in the system must be capable of faithfully reflecting the outside world as it affects the business. The users will depend on the system for this information, and they cannot conduct their business if it is inaccurate, arbitrarily restricted, or insufficiently precise.

Part of this information is about the contracts and the people and organizations in the outside world with whom the business is conducted. If the system is capable of storing only one address for each customer, it will be hard to send all the customer's invoices to one address and all the goods ordered to another. If it can store only one Life Assured for each policy, it will be impossible to deal properly with policies on the joint lives of a husband and wife. If a mail-order system cannot pay out a cheque without a valid supplier number, it will be impossible to make refunds to customers – unless they happen also to be suppliers.

Another aspect of the business requirement is that the system must correctly track the order in which the actions in interaction sequences have occurred, and should occur, so that it can support the office users in making appropriate and timely responses. For example, if a loss adjuster's report has been requested, the system should not allow the claim to be paid before the report has been received and examined in the office. It should be able to prevent a contract document from being finalized before the statutory cooling-off period has elapsed. These constraints on the ordering of actions within interaction sequences may be quite complex. Although each individual sequence is relatively simple, the sequences constrain each other where they involve the same people or the same contracts. For example, if a policy is terminated, by death or cancellation or surrender, at a time when the premium payment interaction sequence for next year's premium is in progress, then clearly the premium payment must not be allowed to proceed: no premium can be paid on a terminated policy.

These constraints, to be applied by the system to the actions taken by users, are a central aspect of an office workflow system. A business in which such constraints are absent would not need an office workflow system of the kind we are concerned with in this book. A business in which they are present, but less important, less conspicuous and less complex, might still use an office workflow system; but it could probably use a different kind of system that in this respect, at least, would be simpler and better suited to its purpose.

Workflow Requirements

The business requirements discussed briefly in the last section impose constraints on the sequencing of users' actions in the office: they must fit into the prescribed orderings of the interaction sequences. But they still leave a considerable freedom in the overall sequencing and management of all the actions in the office, and even of the actions of a single user.

The reason for this is that the office is involved in very many contracts, and in very many business relationships with clients, agents, suppliers and other people and organizations in the outside world. At any one time most of these contracts and relationships will be dormant: no action is currently expected either by the office or by the outside world. But that still leaves a large number of contracts and relationships that are not dormant, and roughly half of them will be await- ing some action by the office. (The other half will be awaiting some action by the outside world.) The individual policyholder has only one buildings insurance policy, and at most one claim outstanding on it. But the office may have tens of thousands of policies, and hundreds of outstanding claims awaiting some action. So the question arises: what should the office do next? And, more particularly, what should the individual user do next? Scrutinize the claim form from Mrs Jones, or write to a loss adjuster about Mr Smith's kitchen fire?

Many choices are available here. Some offices aim above all at operational efficiency, narrowly defined. In those offices users will tend to specialize; so one user may spend the whole working day scrutinizing one claim form after another, while another user does nothing but write to loss adjusters. Other offices try to give individual users the more satisfying work of dealing with a whole matter, at least through one or more of its major stages. So in such an office one user may deal with every stage of a claim up to the final decision on payment, while another may be concerned with all of the early stages of new motor policies, for example.

This freedom of choice in managing the office work is a central characteristic of office workflow systems, and it is a central requirement that the system should support appropriate choices. Most business or administration offices have an established internal organization, and established work practices. An insurance office, for example, is usually organized into departments that deal with particular kinds of interaction sequence. The New Business department deals with the interactions involved in setting up a new policy; the Claims department deals with claims; the Underwriting department deals with assess- ing the risk on a proposed policy and determining an appropriate level of premium; the Commissions department deals with the calculation and payment of agents' commissions. Within each department, particular groups of users may specialize in particular aspects of the department's business.

There are other ways of organizing the work of the office. For example, in some businesses, some offices try to assign each customer to one workgroup or even one user, so that the customer will always be conversing, or corresponding, with someone who is familiar with that customer's affairs. Business Process Re- engineering may lead to changes in established patterns of work, as may the development of new products, especially in the financial services industry.

So an office workflow system must be flexible in the scheduling of work, while at the same time ensuring that the ordering constraints of each interaction sequence are respected. It must be possible for the people in the office to choose general patterns of workflow, and for the system to support those patterns by presenting sets of current outstanding actions, in the chosen order, to the chosen users at their desks or terminals.

A More Realistic Context

Figure 1.1 showed a very simple context diagram containing only the machine, the office and the outside world. The people and organizations in the outside world can communicate only with the office and thus only indirectly with the machine. More realistically, there will be other parts of the world to be considered, and other lines of direct communication. Figure 1.2 shows a more realistic context diagram as it might be drawn for a particular system. In addition to the office and the outside world, this diagram shows three further parts of the world: a *legacy system*, the enterprise's *web site* and *automated bank payments*.

The legacy system is an old computer system for handling one aspect of the business that is not to be handled by the new system – perhaps agents' commissions. The web site allows customers who have access to the web to communicate directly with the machine. They can communicate certain simple transactions that can be handled by filling in a form in a web browser – for example, requesting a quotation for motor insurance. The users in the office can also use the web site through a local network. The automated bank payments part represents another computer system, owned by the clearing banks, that handles Direct Debit transfers and some other bank transactions.

The legacy system is directly connected to the office workflow machine in the sense that data flows between the two systems without any intermediate human

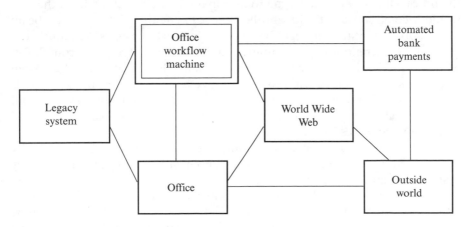

Figure 1.2   *More realistic context diagram for an office workflow system.*

processing. The medium of data flow may be a special-purpose communication link, or it may be as primitive as reels of $\frac{1}{2}''$ magnetic tape moved from machine to machine in each direction. The legacy system is also connected directly to the office: the users in the Commissions department provide its other inputs and handle its other outputs. The automated bank payments system is similarly directly connected to the office workflow machine – perhaps by an established EDI (Electronic Data Interchange) network – and also to the outside world. For example, customers in the outside world issue Direct Debit and standing order instructions to their banks, and it is these instructions that result in the payments arriving from the automated bank payments system.

The additional complexity of this more realistic context imposes some additional complexity on the system, and the development method must deal with this. For example, we must be able to treat the arrival of an automated bank payment, or the receipt of a quotation request at the web site, as an action in an interaction sequence, just as we would treat the arrival of a client's cheque or letter in the post. We must be able to produce the magnetic tape files for the Commission legacy system in the same way as we would produce a batch of new policy documents.

Why People Matter

We must be able to deal with the additional complexity of the more realistic context, both in the finished system and in our method of developing it. But it does not represent a fundamental change to the nature of the system, so long as the mechanized communications with the legacy system, the web site and the automated bank payments system are only a small proportion of the work of the office. Of course, if they came to dominate the work of the office, then we would become concerned with another kind of system, and it would not be an office workflow system. It might be a system in which the users are required to support the operations of the computer, rather than the other way around. But while the mechanized communications are relatively insignificant, the system characteristics are still determined by the three basic parts – the office, the outside world and the office workflow machine – and their relationships and characteristics, and by their structuring of the business as a collection of related interaction sequences.

The difference is between an essentially automatic system and an essentially human system. An office workflow system, even without connections to legacy systems or automated bank payment systems, will contain some automated parts, as we will see later. Reminder letters may be sent automatically to policyholders whose premiums are about to fall due; risks on some policies can be assessed automatically where the policy is standard and the benefit is below some threshold limit; monthly statements may be automatically prepared and sent to customers. But the fundamental purpose of the system is to support the work of the people in the office. Its rhythms are geared to human timescales, not to the speeds of disk drives or network communication links. Essentially, almost everything that comes into the machine, or is produced by it, must pass human inspection either in the office or in the world outside.

These characteristics allow us to emphasize flexibility in the development method and in the systems we will produce. In office workflow systems flexibility is more important than the kind of rigour that is appropriate to many safety-critical systems. In the development of an avionics system to control an aeroplane in flight it is vitally important to evaluate every hazard that can possibly arise in the air, and to anticipate every state that the aeroplane and the control system can get into. This can be done only by a rigour and formalism in development that would be quite inappropriate to an office workflow system. Office workflow is not a safety-critical application. So in our treatment of interaction sequences we will be chiefly concerned to make the development flexible, convenient for the office users and capable of responding to changes in legislation and in industry practice. Anticipating every possible state of the system will be of less concern.

It is worth mentioning that a small element of this attitude is present also in avionics system thinking. An important dispute is currently being waged between those who think that an avionics system should absolutely prevent the pilot from taking action that the system developers have calculated is invalid, and those who think that the pilot must have the ability to override the system. The argument for allowing the override is that the developers can never be sure that they have anticipated all possible circumstances and conditions, and that the final discretion must therefore lie with the pilot. The argument against the override is the real possibility of human error, especially in a situation where things happen as fast they do in a plane in flight.

Fortunately for the developers and users of office workflow systems, it is easy to decide that we can – and must – leave much discretion in the hands of the users. An office workflow system must be flexible, not rigid.

The Focus of This Book

In this book we will focus on a method of developing office workflow systems. The method leads naturally to an implementation centred on a database, in which the machine stores the information it needs to satisfy the business requirement and to support the work of the office.

Although our focus is strictly on office workflow systems, we will sometimes draw examples from other kinds of system and other application areas. Workflow systems have much in common with many other kinds of systems – most notably with other systems that rely on an underlying database implementation.

The main emphasis of this book is on some of the earlier stages of development – what is often called *systems analysis and specification*. For the most part, we will assume that the requirement is already well understood by people in the enterprise for which the system is to be built. In a typical situation, such as that of an insurance company, there is already a system in existence, and the required business interactions are already well established by custom or legislation. The early stages, therefore, do not concentrate on arriving at a conceptual picture of the system as a completely new invention. We will be concerned instead with understanding the information needed to support the business, and recording that understanding in *data* and *process* models. For building these models, the method uses techniques that are particularly tuned to fit the needs of office workflow systems.

The data model is based on recognizing the important entities in the outside world and in the conduct of the business. Some of these entities are customers, agents, suppliers, clients, banks, or statutory bodies – the people and organizations that interact with the office in business relationships. Some are the major contracts and obligations of the business, such as insurance policies and purchase or sale orders. Some reflect subsidiary – but potentially complex – interaction sequences such as those concerning invoices or insurance claims.

The process model is based on the idea of a lifecycle. A lifecycle corresponds to an interaction sequence associated with an entity; so there may be lifecycles for customers, lifecycles for policies and lifecycles for purchase orders. Within a lifecycle there may be smaller interaction sequences, such as those consisting only of sending a letter and waiting for a reply – these smaller interaction sequences are associated with lesser entities, such as letters, that are linked to the entities of the containing lifecycle. The process model is concerned with describing all the interaction sequences that may occur, the relationships among them and the associations of interaction sequences with entities.

The data and process models come together in the database implementation. The database provides the foundation for tying data and process together so that the constraints of the interaction sequences are respected while retaining enough flexibility in the management of the work of the office. This central role of the database is discussed in Chapter 8.

Chapter Summary

This book is about office workflow systems. The defining characteristics of these systems are:

- There is an *office*, staffed by people (*users*), working for an *enterprise* that conducts *business* with the *outside world*.
- The business relationships and obligations are long-term (days, weeks, months, years), not transitory.
- The outside world interacts chiefly with the office rather than with the machine directly.

- Interaction between the office and the outside world is constrained by the permissible interaction sequences.
- The purpose of the system (strictly, the *machine*) is to support the work of the users in the office. This means:
  - providing them with the business information they need;
  - ensuring that only permissible interaction sequences are followed;
  - supporting the chosen scheduling of the work of the office.

Questions

1.1 Draw a context diagram for the system in a local telephone exchange. Its function is to connect local subscribers (those on this exchange) to each other and to remote subscribers on the global telephone network.

1.2 Name the three essential parts of the context of an office workflow system.

1.3 What interaction sequences can you identify in a lottery system? Are they important enough or complex enough for an office workflow system?

1.4 Is the computer system in a lending library likely to be an office workflow system? If so, why? If not, why not?

1.5 Communication by post may involve delays and may even cause letters sent earlier to arrive later. What effect might this have on a workflow system?

1.6 Is what goes on in a High Street bank suitable for support by an office workflow system?

1.7 Describe the interaction sequence involved in a simple telephone call, from the point of view of the person making the call.

1.8 Would you expect a customer's change of address to be regarded as a single event or as an interaction sequence? Why?

1.9 How do you schedule the personal work tasks arising during a week from the letters you receive through the post? For example, do you save them all to the weekend? Deal with all the bills first (or last)? Postpone everything as long as possible?

1.10 How long does the obligation persist of a bus company to each of its passengers? Is it ever more than one journey? How would you decide?

1.11 Could a system to control the operation of a nuclear power station be a workflow system in our sense?

1.12 Could a system for calculating school timetables be a workflow system in our sense?

Overview of the Method

In the preceding introductory chapter we discussed the *context* and the broad characteristics of an office workflow system. At the centre of such a system is the *machine*; and the purpose of the machine is to support the users in the *office* in their business interactions with the *outside world*.

In this chapter we explain the principles and structure of the development method. The development method, in the aspects that are the central focus of this book, is ultimately concerned with developing the machine: that is, to develop its database and its programs. But we cannot start there. We must start from the context, and understand and describe the two fundamental requirements: the information and constraints that the users need to conduct the business properly, and the flow of work in the office that they need to conduct efficiently. Only in the course of making these business-oriented and office-oriented descriptions do we perform the work of developing and building the database and the programs.

Four Phases and a Database

The method can be structured as a fixed sequence of four development phases: *data*, *process*, *tasks* and *workflow*. First we address the need for business information by making a *data model* of the outside world. This data model is based on a recognition of the entities that are significant to the business. Then we address the closely related need to respect the constraints of the business interaction sequences by making a *process model*. In the process model we capture the entity lifecycles through which the entities of the outside world progress, both independently and in the course of their interactions with the office. Then we define the details of the *tasks* within the lifecycles, the points at which some action is taken in the office. An action may be either manual – taken by a user – or automatic – taken by the machine according to a predetermined program. In either case the action must respect not only the permissible interaction sequences, but also the detailed rules by which the business is conducted. Finally, we can determine the *workflow* structure within which automatic tasks are scheduled by the machine and manual tasks are selected for action by users.

The whole system is implemented by menu-driven and background programs operating on an underlying database. The detailed design of this database, to support the business information needs and the workflow structure, may be thought of as a separate, fifth, implementation phase. But this separation is more convincing from a theoretical than from a practical point of view. With the right tools, the database implementation will often be developed gradually as a by-product of the first four phases of the method.

Project Flexibility

In practice, even the simple sequential structure of the four development phases may be too rigid. Development may begin from a previously developed computer system – perhaps a standard system – and proceed by modifying it. Or the business and its requirements may already be very well known and fully documented in data and process models – perhaps as a result of a Business Process Re-engineering exercise. Or demonstrable results may be needed early in the project; so data and process models built in the early phases may be used to provide simple enquiry functionality that will encourage feedback from users to developers. Or the whole system may be built by evolutionary development and delivery, each generation of the evolution delivering further functionality: each generation then has its own four main development phases – data, process, tasks and workflow.

The relationship between method phases and practical project demands, and the way they should come together to form a particular project structure, are discussed in Chapter 9. In particular, that chapter includes a discussion of the process of discovery: that is, of discovering how the business is conducted, what content will be needed for the data and process models, and what business rules are to be implemented in the tasks. This discovery process is not treated as an integral part of the main method summarized in this chapter, because it is essentially an informal process, to be designed in accordance with the local human circumstances of the enterprise and the office. Chapter 9 also discusses a fast-track version of the method, to be used when explicit application of all the phases of the full method is judged unnecessary.

The Method Phase Chapters

Chapters 3 to 7 adhere broadly to the sequence of development phases, with two bites at the more important cherries. The data modelling aspect of business information is introduced in Chapter 3, where we discuss the basic approach to building a data model of the outside world. This is followed by an initial discussion of lifecycle definitions in Chapter 4, and data modelling is taken up again in Chapter 5, when the need for some of its more subtle aspects has been motivated by an understanding of the lifecycle concept. In exactly the same way, some of the more subtle aspects of lifecycle definition are deferred to Chapter 6, along with the treatment of tasks and business rules. The definition of the office workflow is discussed in Chapter 7.

The database implementation is discussed in Chapter 8. Many aspects of the method, including the technique of handling the need for time-dependent processing, and the monitoring and reporting of workflow, depend crucially on the database implementation, and are discussed in that chapter. The method produces a system whose behaviour can be readily changed, especially in respect of the workflow structure. Information to guide changes should be obtained by monitoring the existing behaviour, which is represented in the database records of the lifecycles. Standard techniques of database reporting can be applied to check and report on levels of service, convenience and efficiency.

The Method Phases

We can think of the definition of an office workflow system as progressing through the following phases:

- Entity Model
  In this phase we make a description of the world outside the office. This description is a *data model*, made in terms of *entities*. In addition to describing the world outside, it is also a partial description of the database in the machine.
- Business Interaction Model
  In this phase we make a description of the permissible sequences of business interactions between the office and the world outside. This description is a *process model,* made in terms of *lifecycles*, *lifecycle stages* and *tasks*. In addition to describing the interactions, it also constrains the office to the permissible interaction sequences.
- Business Tasks Definition
  In this phase we further constrain the tasks that can be performed in the office by defining detailed rules governing the nature of each task, the parts of the entity model that concern it and what it must or may do.
- Office Workflow Definition
  In this phase we define the management of tasks to be performed automatically by the machine, or offered to users as manual tasks from which they can choose what to do next at any particular time.

In the following sections of this chapter we explain each of these phases briefly. Then, after a discussion of the database implementation, we explore some of the general principles that are embodied in the method.

The Entity Model Phase

The word 'model' is much used in software development, often meaning no more than the word 'description'. But it has an important meaning of its own. We can say that A is a model of B if A and B share some important properties that we are interested in. This is the meaning we should have in mind when we talk about *data models* or *process models* in software development.

The idea of a data model

In a data model, the data stored in the computer's database is a model of some parts and aspects of the world outside the computer. For example:

In the world	In the database
There is a customer whose customer-ID is 4567	There is a customer record whose CustNo field has the value 4567
The customer whose customer-ID is 4567 has the name 'Jones'	In the customer record whose CustNo field has the value 4567, the Name field has the value 'Jones'
There is an order whose order-number is 1234	There is an order record whose OrderNo field has the value 1234
Order 1234 was placed by customer 4567	In the order record whose OrderNo field has the value 1234, the PlacedBy field points to the customer record whose CustNo field has the value 4567

When we build the data model, we describe the properties shared by the world and the database in a more general way, by giving one description that applies both to the world and to the computer database.

Data model diagrams

A very simple description of this kind, in diagrammatic form, is given in Figure 2.1. The two boxes represent the two *entity classes* ORDER and CUSTOMER. The stripes in the boxes represent the *entity attributes* of the entities in each class. An ORDER has attributes OrderNo and PlacedBy, and a CUSTOMER has attributes CustNo and Name.

When we read the description, we interpret it both as a description of the world of orders and customers, and as a description of the database and its records, just as we did for the little example above with one order and one customer. This phase of the method, in which we make these descriptions, is called

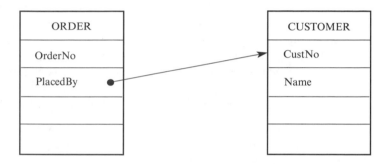

Figure 2.1   *A data model.*

'entity modelling' because the data model we are building is based on identifying and describing the important classes of entity in the world.

It is sometimes convenient to express the same description in an alternative textual form, like this:

CUSTOMER: (CustNo,
                   Name,
                   ...);
ORDER: (OrderNo,
                   PlacedBy: CUSTOMER,
                   ...);

In most data modelling techniques entities and relationships are shown separately in the diagrams – often by using rectangles for entities and diamonds for relationships: hence the term Entity–Relationship modelling. In the method we choose instead to emphasize the entities, and to let the relationships appear in our model as entity attributes. Attributes that express relationships in this way are called *association attributes*. PlacedBy in the ORDER entity is an association attribute.

This simplification is attractive, and it is well suited to the kind of data model that is most often needed in an office workflow system. But sometimes we will be forced to treat a relationship explicitly as an entity. This will happen, in particular, when the relationship between two entity classes is *many-to-many* rather than *one-to-one* or *one-to-many*. Then it is impossible to represent the relationship by an attribute in either of the entities partaking in an association: each of them is associated with many entities, but there is room for only one value of the attribute.

Further aspects of data modelling

In several ways this is a very simple data modelling technique. Techniques of data modelling can be very elaborate, but much of the elaboration is unnecessary for describing the outside world with which the office in an office workflow system interacts. The method discussed in this book follows the principle stated by Einstein: 'Everything should be as simple as possible.'

Then he added: 'But no simpler.' We do need to extend the data modelling technique some way beyond the very simple expression of entity classes, attributes and relationships shown in our example. In particular, we will also be able to use the following additional ideas to describe the world more fully and accurately:

- Only certain *values* are permissible for each entity attribute. For example, if customer entities have an attribute DateOfBirth, then 'Jones' is not a possible value of that attribute for any customer. We must be able to describe these restrictions conveniently: that is, to specify the *domain* of values for an attribute.
- Some entity attributes may have values that are *composite*: that is, they are made up of other values. For example, a date is made up of a day, a month and a year; or an address may be made up of a street address, a post town and a postcode.
- Some entity classes may be *subclasses* of other classes. For example, the CUSTOMER and EMPLOYEE classes may be subclasses of the PERSON class: every CUSTOMER is a PERSON and every EMPLOYEE is a PERSON.
- The association attribute PlacedBy in our example always associates the ORDER with a CUSTOMER entity; but sometimes an association attribute may point to an entity either of one class or of another. For example, the SoldBy attribute of an INVESTMENTPLAN entity may point either to a SALESPERSON entity or to a BROKER entity.

All of these additional ideas must, of course, be properly used and expressed both in describing the world and in describing the computer database. In a project to which fewer or less powerful tools are available, some of the detail of how precisely the model applies to the database may be deferred to a separate database implementation phase.

The Business Interaction Model Phase

In the Entity Model phase we make a *data* model – that is, a *static* model – of the world outside the office. Of course, the world changes: even in our tiny example, the enterprise acquires new customers, new orders are placed and old orders are fulfilled. A static model describes how the world and the database look at any moment when nothing is changing, but it does not describe what changes are possible, and in what order. For that, we need a *process* model – that is, a *dynamic* model – which is the product of the Business Interaction Model phase. Each action in an interaction sequence makes some change, both to the computer database and to the outside world. In this phase we describe the permissible interaction sequences that can take place between the office and the outside world.

Lifecycles and stages

The largest and most important interaction sequences are associated with the entities of the data model. These interaction sequences are called *entity lifecycles*. A lifecycle, rather like a development method, consists of a number of *stages* that occur in order. The stages of the entity lifecycle associated with CUSTOMER entities may be:

- CustomerEntry stage: entering the basic customer information into the database and checking that it has been correctly entered.
- CreditRating stage: checking and recording the customer's commercial credit rating.
- CustomerActivity stage: doing normal business with the customer.
- CustomerAbeyance stage: having ceased to do business with the customer.

The stages of the entity lifecycle associated with ORDER entities may be:

- OrderEntry stage: entering the basic order information into the database.
- OrderCreditCheck stage: checking the customer's current credit against the order value.
- OrderStockCheck stage: finding and picking the goods ordered.
- OrderDelivery stage: delivering the order.
- OrderInvoice stage: invoicing the order.

Figure 2.2 shows diagrams of the entity lifecycles. Each box represents a stage, and the connecting arrows show the sequence of the stages in each lifecycle.

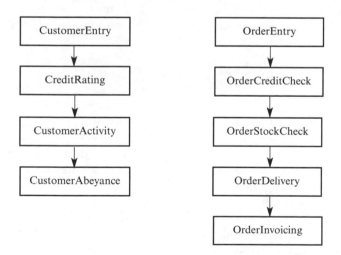

Figure 2.2 *Entity lifecycles for customers and orders.*

Stages and tasks

Each stage of a lifecycle involves a number of tasks to be performed by the office. For example, the CreditRating stage may involve sending an enquiry to a commercial credit rating agency, awaiting a reply and evaluating the information provided in the reply. The OrderDelivery stage may involve interaction with an external transport organization, or scheduling delivery by an internal transport department, followed by informing the customer of the resulting expected delivery date and time. The OrderInvoicing stage will no doubt involve sending the invoice, awaiting payment if necessary, sending reminders to the customer and eventually dealing with the payment in the office accounts department. The content of these tasks will be the subject matter of the next stage in the development method.

Two sides to a task

Because we are building the system to support the work of the users in the office, our primary focus in considering business interactions is on the office end of the interaction. But, of course, the other end of the interaction, in the outside world, is of equal importance for the satisfactory conduct of the business.

In general, we assume in this book that the conduct of the enterprise's business is already well established, and is not being newly invented by the developers of the system. So the adequacy of the defined interactions from the point of view of people and organizations in the outside world is also well established. Where we cannot be sure of this, we must consider the outside world point of view quite explicitly. We will return to this point in discussing discovery processes in Chapter 9.

Lifecycle states

As an entity progresses through its lifecycle we think of it as passing through a number of successive *states*, which we name from the associated lifecycle stages. A customer may be *in* any one of the states: InCustomerEntry; InCreditRating; InCustomerActivity; or InCustomerAbeyance. An order may be in any one of the states: InOrderEntry; InOrderCreditCheck; and so on. There may also be intermediate states, in which an entity is *waiting* to begin a stage: for example, AwaitingCreditRating, AwaitingOrderStockCheck, and so on.

The lifecycle of an order and the lifecycle of the customer who placed the order are obviously interrelated. For example, we may stipulate that the order must not be in the state InOrderDelivery unless the customer is InCustomerActivity. So we can accept an order from a customer before checking the customer's credit rating, but we would refuse to deliver the ordered goods until after the credit rating check. Or, more restrictively, we might stipulate that no order may progress to OrderCreditCheck unless the customer is InCustomer-Activity. And there are other possibilities.

Flexibility and parallel processing

These constraints should reflect the way the enterprise chooses to conduct its business. One important objective is to avoid introducing arbitrary restrictions that are not necessary for the business. The users in the office should give themselves the greatest possible opportunity to progress their interactions with the outside world in the most flexible way that is consistent with the proper conduct of the business. This objective can be expressed in another way: we want to allow the greatest possible degree of *parallel processing* in the office and in the system. Wherever it is possible to allow two lifecycles, or two stages within a single lifecycle, to progress side by side in parallel, rather than forcing one to wait for the other, we should do so.

The technique we will use for describing the relationships between lifecycles is intended to achieve the greatest possible degree of parallelism. We will state the *minimum* dependency of one lifecycle on another. That means identifying the *latest point* in a lifecycle at which it may be forced to wait.

We aim at the same objective in the technique for describing the activity within each lifecycle stage. We think of a stage as consisting of a number of tasks to be performed; within one stage many of these tasks can proceed in parallel.

Consider, for example, the tasks involved in dealing with a completed proposal for a new life assurance policy. The proposal may contain administrative and medical information about the person whose life is to be assured, and information about their bank account. The office must validate this information by obtaining their birth certificate, by obtaining evidence from their medical practitioner and by obtaining a bank reference. There is no reason why these tasks should not be performed in parallel. We can represent them as independent tasks within the lifecycle stage, as shown in Figure 2.3. Just as two lifecycles can proceed in parallel, so can the three tasks within the one ProposalCheck stage of this one lifecycle.

Tasks and subtasks

We are not treating the tasks as separate lifecycles, because we are not thinking of birth certificates, medical evidence and bank references as separate entities in their own right. They are not significant enough in the conduct of the business. But a task can still have its own interaction sequence structure of *subtasks*. Each of the three tasks here has at least two subtasks that must happen in sequence: writing to request the desired information or document, and receiving

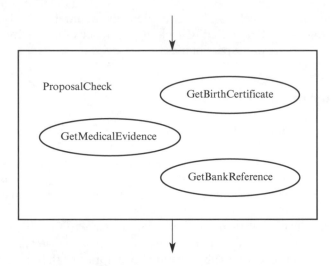

Figure 2.3   *Parallel tasks within one lifecycle stage.*

and inspecting it. And if the inspection shows that something further is needed – for example, supplementary medical evidence – there will be further subtasks again. So the structure of tasks and subtasks within a lifecycle stage must be described and treated with some care.

More about sequencing

The business interaction model has more complexities than we have discussed here. In particular, the method provides for the following modifications to the simple sequence structures of stages within lifecycles and subtasks within tasks.

- An entity lifecycle can be *prematurely terminated* in some circumstances. For example, the result of rating the customer's commercial credit may be to determine that the customer is unsuitable and will never become an active customer.
- An entity lifecycle can be *set back* to an earlier stage in the event of certain failures. For example, an active customer whose payment record is very bad may be set back to the InCreditRating stage. Setting back a lifecycle is called *backtracking*. It is not always possible – the genie can't always be put back into the bottle – and when it is possible it can involve serious complications.
- In certain circumstances, a lifecycle may progress to a later stage while some tasks in an earlier stage are still incomplete. For example, we might decide that the birth certificate is not really essential until the later stage in the life assurance lifecycle at which point the policy is actually issued. We would then describe it as *relevant* at the PolicyIssuing stage. The lifecycle may then be held up waiting for the birth certificate in the state AwaitingPolicyIssuing.

- Subtask structures within tasks are not simple sequences. A single task can *spawn* several subtasks, not just one. Also, a subtask can be a whole group of tasks of which only one will be selected for execution.

The Business Tasks Definition Phase

This is the phase at which we describe the detail of the individual tasks and subtasks. The detail considered here is the detail that is determined by the requirements of the business: the further arrangement and scheduling of the tasks to suit the flow of work in the office is deferred until the next phase.

Task categories

There are several different kinds of individual task. For example, consider the following tasks.

- EnterCustomerData: in this task the information about a new customer is entered into the system. This is a *manual data-entry task*; a user must enter the data into the computer system, creating a new customer record.
- CheckProposalCompliance: in this task a proposal that a certain customer should take out a policy that offers certain tax benefits is checked for compliance with current legislation. This may be an *automatic data-check* task; the data in the existing proposal record, and data in other records for the same client, must be checked against certain business rules.
- RequestBirthCertificate: in this task the proposed policyholder's birth certificate is requested. This is an *automatic letter-writing* task; it is necessary only to select the client's name and address and the proposal reference to be embedded in a standard form letter.
- ReceiveDDPremium: in this task a premium is received by direct debit from an automated banking system and posted to the appropriate account. This is an *automatic event-handling* task; the direct debit payment arrives via a communication network, and is handled without the direct involvement of any user.
- ManualUnderwriteB2: the benefit on a proposed policy is too large for automatic underwriting, and a decision must be made manually by a user in the Underwriting department. This is a *manual decision* task; an appropriately skilled and qualified user must inspect the information available in the system and enter an appropriate decision and authorization code.

Obviously, tasks of different categories will fit into the work of the office in different ways. A manual decision task requires to be presented to a user on a screen, with supporting information already available on the screen or accessible at the user's request. An automatic event-handling task will not be presented to any user, and requires no screen support. The same is true of an automatic letter-writing task. A data-entry task must be presented to a user who will enter the data on a screen and may need assistance in finding some secondary information. For example, data entry of a new order from an existing customer will require the user to find and enter the customer reference.

Task datasets

Each task, whatever its category, concerns some part of the data model. Usually, it concerns more than one entity. For example, underwriting a policy concerns the proposal entity itself and also the associated client entity: the risk depends on both. Determining the price of a customer order concerns the complete order entity, the customer entity, each line entity belonging to the order and the product entity associated with each line of the order. The data concerned in a task is called the *task dataset*.

A task dataset is like a tiny database. It consists of entity records belonging to the system database, extracted according to certain rules, and arranged in a certain structure. It is what is sometimes called a *partial view* of the database. Because an individual task is simple, concerned with one particular element in a larger interaction, the associated dataset is also simple.

The dataset for a task always has a *root entity*. This is the entity in whose life-cycle the task occurs: it forms the starting point for the extraction of the dataset. The root entity of an underwriting task is the proposal entity for the policy to be underwritten; and the root entity of an order pricing task is the order entity. The complete dataset for the task can be assembled starting from the root. For example, the dataset for the order pricing task can be assembled into a multi-level structure, as shown in Figure 2.4.

From the ORDER entity (1), which is the root of the dataset at the top level, the CUSTOMER entity (2a) at the second level can be reached directly by using the PlacedBy association attribute of the order. From the ORDER entity (1) we can also reach, again at the second level, all the ORDERLINE entities (2b) belonging to the order. Each of the order's line entities has an attribute LineOf, which associates it with the order. Although the association attribute is in the ORDERLINE entity, a feature (specifically, the *join* operation) of the database system allows us to reach all the ORDERLINE entities (2b) whose LineOf association attribute points to the ORDER entity (1). From each ORDERLINE entity, the associated PRODUCT entity (3) at the third level can be reached directly by using the ForProduct association attribute of the ORDERLINE entity.

Business rules

The heart of a task definition is chiefly composed of *business rules*. A business rule may specify:

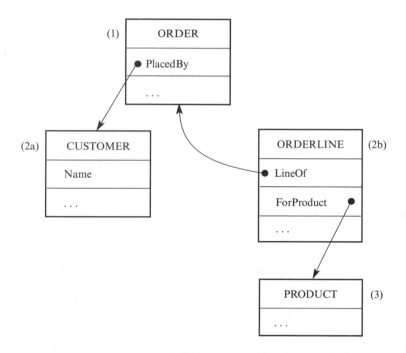

Figure 2.4   *Assembly sequence of the dataset for pricing an order.*

- a *check* that must be made on a relationship among the data in a task dataset: for example, that the relationship between proposal data and the client data conforms to the statutory restrictions on the policy type;
- a value that must be *set* in an entity record: for example, that the customer's available credit must be reduced by the value of the order;
- an *action* that must be performed: for example, the production of a letter to be sent to the client.

A rule may be *conditional*: that is, it may specify a condition under which the rule is applicable. If the condition is not satisfied, then the rule is empty – nothing is checked, no value is set, and no action is performed.

Business rules can refer to any of the entities in the task dataset, to any of their attributes, and to their states with respect to any of their entity lifecycles. Each entity is referred to by the path needed to reach it from the root of the dataset. Thus in the example in Figure 2.4 the customer name attribute is referred to as:

ORDER.PlacedBy → CUSTOMER.Name

This reference can be read as 'the Name attribute of the CUSTOMER entity pointed to by the PlacedBy attribute of the ORDER entity'. Similarly, the product entity is referred to as:

ORDER ← LineOf:ORDERLINE.ForProduct ↦ PRODUCT

This reference can be read as 'the PRODUCT entity pointed at by the ForProduct attribute of the ORDERLINE entity whose LineOf attribute points to the ORDER entity'. Because there is more than one ORDERLINE whose LineOf attribute points to the ORDER entity, the ORDERLINE entity must be regarded as a kind of variable: a particular ORDERLINE entity must be picked out to make the reference specific.

The application of rules in a task produces a *task result state*, which is specified as a part of the task definition. The possible result states of performing a task, and their expected meanings, are as follows.

- Passed: the task was performed successfully. For a *check* rule, the data in the dataset satisfied the checked relationship; for a *set* or an *action* rule, the specified value was set or the specified action was performed.
- Failed: the task performance was unsuccessful. The task contained a *check* rule and the data in the dataset did not satisfy the specified relationship. Rules of the *set* and *action* categories do not cause failure.
- Not Applicable: the task proved not to be applicable to the situation to which it was to be applied.
- Ran: the task was performed, but its performance gave rise to a need for further subtasks involving further rule applications.

Rule application results are important because they determine the results of the tasks and subtasks in which they appear; and task and subtask results, in turn, determine the results of the lifecycle stages to which they belong.

Decision tables

Some business rules are complex in the sense that they must deal with many distinct combinations of varying circumstances. For example, the automatic assessment of risk on a life policy may depend partly on age and partly on the following factors.

- Gender of the assured. Two distinct cases: male and female.
- Smoking habits. There are three distinct cases: non-smoker; 1–10 cigarettes per day; over 10 cigarettes per day.
- Drinking habits. There are four distinct cases: teetotal; 1–5 units per week; 5–15 units per week; over 15 units per week.
- Occupation. There are four distinct cases: no special stress or physical danger (a); stress only (b); danger only (c); both stress and danger (d).

Gender	...	M	M	F	...
Smoking	...	no	1–10	no	...
Drinking	...	1–5	1–5	TT	...
Occupation	...	a	a	b	...
Risk Factor	...	25	30	35	...

Figure 2.5 *Fragment of a decision table for assessing life risks.*

The total number of distinct combinations to be considered is the result of multiplying together all the distinct cases. That is $2 \times 3 \times 4 \times 4$, or 96 combinations. These combinations might be arranged in a table, of which a fragment is shown in Figure 2.5.

Spelling out all 96 combinations may be very tedious. More importantly, it may also be unnecessary. There may be rules that deal with whole groups of combinations: for example, the combination of drinking more than 15 units per week with an occupation in class (d) may place the risk factor at the highest level regardless of gender or smoking habits.

The method uses a technique of specifying decision tables that can take advantage of this kind of structure.

The Office Workflow Definition Phase

Because the office interacts with many people and organizations in the outside world, there are many tasks inviting the attention of users at any one time. The business interaction definition constrains what can happen next in any one lifecycle, but there are very many lifecycles in progress at any one time, and the office is involved in all of them.

So users in the office have potentially very many choices of what to do next. A user is not confronted by an in-tray from which the only possibility is to take the next item in sequence; but rather by a pool of items, any one of which could reasonably be chosen to furnish the next task. Also, each particular task that is waiting for a user may be 'performable' by many different users, all of whom have the necessary skills to deal with it.

The office workflow definition stage is concerned with supporting these choices. It does so in the most flexible way, by maintaining the pool of available tasks in a form that makes them all accessible to all users, subject only to whatever constraints may have been explicitly specified. There is no notion, for example, that the data associated with a task move in a dataflow from one process to another, and can therefore be only in one process at any one time.

Instead, the workflow management technique provides for the greatest possible efficiency, by allowing the maximum parallelism in the performance of the tasks of each lifecycle.

Information support

One obvious area in which support is needed is the provision of information. A user engaged in the task of evaluating a claim on a house contents insurance policy may want to see information about the policyholder's other policies, or other claims, although formally they are not part of the dataset needed for the claim evaluation task. Similarly, a user entering data for a new order may want to see the customer's record and the product records for the line items of the order; not because they are strictly necessary to the task, but merely to find or check the customer and product numbers which the order documentation may have omitted or misstated.

Much of this kind of support can be provided in a very general form. Whenever a reference number or code is required in a data entry task, the program can give the user access to a list of the possible values, or to an easy means of finding the required value. For example, entering the first few characters of the customer's name might show a list on the screen of the customers that may be meant and their identifying customer numbers. This support is so common that it has a special name in the method: *reference help*. This is exactly the feature provided by some graphical user interface environments, and should, of course, be used ready-made if it is available. If not, it can be easily provided. Similarly, simple generalized navigation aids can be provided by which the user can browse in the database by moving from one piece of relevant information to another.

Linked tasks

The interaction sequencing imposed by lifecycle definitions is very loose. Intentionally, it takes no account of some linkages that may be of importance from a practical point of view. A notable example is the linkage among different matters that concern the same customer or client. The office in a marketing-oriented enterprise may recognize that customers are annoyed by having to deal separately with the enterprise on each separate matter. It is slightly annoying, for example, for a bank customer who has three accounts with the bank to receive the monthly statements in three different envelopes. It is considerably more annoying to be forced to deal with three different people in the office on three different current matters arising in connection with one insurance policy. Or, as may often happen, for one taxpayer to be forced to deal with different branches of the Inland Revenue on the taxation of different parts of the same taxpayer's income. From the point of view of the enterprise, even a customer who is not annoyed may represent a lost opportunity for further sales.

There is therefore good reason, in many cases, to provide for this linkage. The user in the office may be presented with all of the currently active matters for one customer in a structure of linked screens and menus.

Workgroup organization

Linking tasks in this way will affect, and be affected by, the organization of the office into workgroups. There are good reasons for the traditional organization of an office into specialized workgroups and departments. Some tasks – such as the assessment of risk involved in underwriting an insurance policy – must be performed by users with highly specialized skills and with the authority to make decisions at the financial level required.

But some restrictions of the traditional organization of the office may be no longer appropriate. The kind of investigation and reconsideration that is involved in a Business Process Re-engineering exercise may reveal many desirable changes. The development of a computer-based office workflow system should support such changes where they are needed.

Scheduling automatic tasks

Many tasks can be performed automatically by the system: that is, they can be performed without involving the attention and effort of any user. These tasks are also to be considered in the office workflow definition stage, because their scheduling can greatly affect the efficiency of the computer system.

Database Implementation

The method discussed in this book is squarely founded on a *database* implementation. To the greatest possible extent, every part and aspect of the system is made explicit in the database. In this section we will briefly discuss some aspects of this strategy. It is more fully discussed in Chapter 8.

Data for lifecycle definitions

An important example of this approach is the treatment of lifecycles and related concepts. The whole description of lifecycles, made in the Business Interaction Model and the Business Tasks Definition phases, gives rise to a separate part of the database. Figure 2.6 shows a model – considerably simplified – of lifecycles, lifecycle dependencies, stages, tasks and their interrelationships.

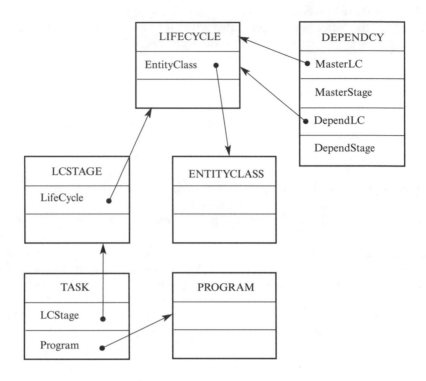

Figure 2.6   *A model of business interactions.*

The diagram shows that each lifecycle definition is represented by a LIFECY-CLE entity. Dependency between two lifecycles is represented by a DEPENDCY entity, which has attributes for the dependent lifecycle and the stage at which it must wait, and for the master lifecycle and the stage for which the dependent life-cycle must wait. Each stage in a lifecycle is represented by a LCSTAGE entity, and each task in a stage by a TASK entity. A TASK entity has attributes that point to its lifecycle stage and to the program that implements the applicable rules. By representing the lifecycle definitions in this kind of way we make it pos-sible for system execution to be largely implemented by very general programs.

Once a dependency between two lifecycles has been defined, a generalized program – the *workflow engine* – can ensure that the dependency is enforced. The developers need do nothing further to enforce the dependency. In the same way, when a lifecycle stage is reached the workflow engine can initiate the asso-ciated tasks, and apply the corresponding business rules.

The workflow engine is generalized in the sense that it enforces general con-straints on the execution of tasks. It depends on no specific constraints about particular lifecycles and their dependencies: only on what it finds in the database.

Entity states and histories

In addition to the lifecycle definitions, it is, of course, necessary to hold information in the database about the progress of each entity of the business data model through each of the individual lifecycles.

This is essentially an addition to the business data model. For each order, we must not only store the attributes PlacedBy and OrderNo, which we defined in the data model. We must also store in the database a *lifecycle instance record* for each order, containing an attribute whose values will be taken from the states of the order lifecycle: InOrderEntry, AwaitingOrderCreditCheck, InOrderDelivery, and so on. The need for these additional records and attributes can be mechanically derived from the lifecycle definitions, and their values can be automatically set and updated by the workflow engine.

For office workflow systems of the kind we are discussing in this book, it is often necessary to maintain detailed historical records, for contractual, commercial, or statutory reasons. By treating the states of each entity as data, and also an entity's progression through the tasks of each lifecycle stage, we make it simple to maintain a complete record of the history of each entity. This history can be kept in the database as long as it may be required: in some cases, only until the lifecycle has reached its end; in others, for the whole lifetime of the enterprise.

Products and plans

In some business areas, especially in the financial services industry, variations on existing products, and even completely new products, are frequently introduced and sold in the market. The speed with which this can be done is often a key factor in the competitiveness of a business.

In the brief discussions in this chapter we have from time to time used life assurance policies as illustrative examples of entities of one class. But these examples have always been greatly oversimplified. All life assurance companies sell many different kinds of policy, often thought of as different kinds of plan. To model a life assurance business with any claim to realism we must certainly have policies as entities, but we must also explicitly represent the different products or plans that the policies exemplify.

Figure 2.7 shows a fragment of a data model, in which each POLICY entity is associated with a PLAN entity. By tying each policy to its plan, and making the detailed properties of each plan explicit in the database, we make it easier to introduce variations and new plans. Of course, the differences between one plan and another may be very significant. In particular, the plan associated with a policy may determine the policy lifecycle: policies of different plans will have different lifecycle definitions. One way to think about this association between policies and plans is to think of the individual plans as *definitions* of *subclasses* of the policy *superclass*.

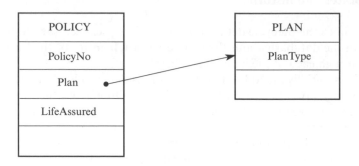

Figure 2.7   *Policies and plans.*

Effective dates

The introduction of new products is not the only way that a typical office work-flow business is changing over time. Agreements defining commercial relationships change – for example, a new commission arrangement is negoti-ated with an agent. And new legislation changes the statutory regulations that must be observed by the enterprise in its dealings with its customers.

These changes introduce a significant complication. It is not enough to ensure that when an agreed or a statutory change takes place it is immediately put into effect in the conduct of the business. In many cases, the new way of doing business must apply only to contracts begun after a certain date. So the old and the new ways must coexist, the old way applying to some contracts and the new way to others. An extreme form of this complication is seen in a tax office, where the tax statutes are changed at least once a year but it takes more than a year – sometimes several years – to determine the tax liabilities of some taxpayers. So the tax office may be involved in interactions to negotiate or com-pute a taxpayer's liabilities from several previous years: each year must then be dealt with differently, according to the statutory regulations that were in force when it was the current year.

Worse still, office workflow systems usually involve a significant degree of *backtracking*. Because much of the communication between the office and the outside world is conducted by post, there are delays and, frequently, errors. Let-ters can cross in the post, or even overtake each other. An action taken in the office, correct on the information available on Tuesday, may turn out on Wednesday to have been mistaken. Even if no mistake is made, people and organizations in the outside world may be permitted to change their minds. For example, a company is permitted by the tax authorities to alter its accounting period with retrospective effect. When this happens, the tax paid or due on earl-ier years must be recalculated on a different basis.

The systems we develop can support this extra complication in its require-ments by marking every record in the database with its effective dates. This *date-effective* marking applies to all records in the database, including the records representing plans and the records representing lifecycle definitions. We will examine the technique, and some of its consequences, in Chapter 8, where we discuss a database implementation.

Chapter Summary

The development method discussed in this book has four main phases.

- The entity model phase: making a data model in terms of the entities of the outside world, and their attributes and relationships.
- The business interaction model phase: making a process model of the business interaction sequences, in terms of entity lifecycles.
- The business tasks definition phase: defining the business tasks that make up the stages of the lifecycles.
- The office workflow definition phase: defining the flow of work in the office.

The method is founded on a database implementation, in which the whole definition of the system is represented in the database. This has a number of advantages, especially in supporting a business in which change is fundamental in every aspect and at every level.

- It gives more flexibility to change the *business products*.
- It allows for a full *historical record* to be maintained of all business interactions.
- It allows *backtracking* over previous interactions to correct the effects of errors or decisions now retracted.

Questions

2.1   Name the four main phases of the development method.

2.2   Is a lifecycle definition a data model or a process model?

2.3   Can an association attribute be used to represent a many-to-many relationship? If so, how? If not, why not?

2.4   Name the possible result states of a task.

2.5   What happens automatically when a task reaches the ran state?

2.6   Suppose that task T is started in stage 1 of a certain lifecycle. In what circumstances can the lifecycle progress to stage 2 before task T is completed?

2.7   What kind of attributes are used to assemble the records of a task dataset?

2.8   What technique is used in the method to handle complex business rules that must deal with many combinations of circumstances?

2.9   Give two reasons why backtracking may be necessary in the lifecycle of an assurance policy premium payment.

2.10 Give two reasons for modifying the simple sequential arrangement of phases of the method in a particular project.

CHAPTER 3

The Basic Entity Model

Building a basic entity model is the first step in modelling the outside world. In this chapter we restate the notion of a *model*, and explain the basic data modelling technique of the method. The underlying database implementation will use relational technology, and the modelling technique is explained in this context.

Entities

We focus particularly on identifying the kind of things – that is, the *entity classes* – that are of interest in the outside world. These entity classes come from a number of sources. Some are the classes of people and organizations, such as customers and agents and suppliers, with which the office interacts in the course of its business. Some correspond to the continuing interactions that this business involves, such as insurance policies, orders for goods or services, tax obligations and long-term contracts. Some are elements in these interactions, such as a single line in an order placed by a customer, or small-scale interactions in contracts, such as an insurance premium payment or a claim. And some arise from essentially technical modelling considerations.

In this chapter we explain how to choose and represent entity classes, the properties or *attributes* of entities, and the various kinds of *relationship* between entities of the same or different classes. We use both diagrammatic and textual representations: these representations are simultaneously descriptions of the outside world and of the relational database that will eventually be built. The chosen representations are simple, but powerful enough for our purposes. Elaborate representations are hard to use. Simplicity, especially in diagrammatic notations, is a considerable virtue.

Further Modelling

As its title suggests, this chapter is concerned only with *basic entity* modelling. There is much more to say about data modelling than appears in this chapter, and several important aspects have been deferred to later chapters. In particular, we say very little here about the concept of an *entity class*, or about the relationships that may exist among different classes. We will discuss these class relationships in Chapter 5. We will also have more to say in Chapter 5 on the subject of *data types*, which is concerned with the values that a particular entity attribute may take.

There are other important aspects of modelling that we will come to in later chapters, after we have begun to consider *dynamic* modelling. Data models may be thought of as static models. They represent the *state* of the world of interest, but they cannot represent the way that state *changes*: for that we need dynamic models. We begin to explore dynamic modelling in Chapter 4, where the concept of an *entity lifecycle* is examined. Then in Chapter 5, when we return to the topic of data modelling, we will be able to discuss some further aspects whose significance emerges clearly only when we can consider the static and dynamic models together.

Some Basic Ideas

The basic entity model that we build in the first stage of development is a description of the world outside the office. Eventually we will need to turn our attention inwards to describe the office itself; but initially our attention is focused on the outside world with which the office conducts its business.

The basic entity model has two purposes. First, to capture our understanding of some of the most important characteristics of the outside world, and to ensure that this understanding is held in common by the developers and the prospective users of the system. Second, to determine what information about the outside world must be held in the computer if the system is to serve the needs of the users in the office. The basic entity model serves both of these purposes. It is a description with two applications: it applies to the outside world; but it also applies to the internal workings of the computer.

Entities and classes

The foundation of our view of the world is that it is populated by *entities*. An entity is a recognizable individual, distinct from all other individuals. A house might be an entity; or an insurance policy; or a commercial company; or a customer; or a motor car; or an air ticket; or a meal. But it is very unlikely that 'houses' or 'some money' could be legitimate entities: they are not recognizable individuals.

In an office workflow system, the important entities will certainly include the people and organizations that the enterprise does business with; it will also include the agreements and contracts that govern that business, such as orders, insurance policies, guarantees, investment plans and licences. There will be many other entities than these, and we will discuss later in this chapter how to recognize them and how to decide which are important enough to include in the model.

It is essential to distinguish an individual entity from the entity class to which the individual belongs. Jane Smith and John Brown are individual entities. If they are both clients, they both belong to the CLIENT entity class. This situation is often expressed by saying that they are *instances* of the CLIENT class.

We group entities into classes so that we can deal consistently with the individuals in each class. We will treat all our clients in the same way, according to the same rules; but we treat our salespeople quite differently. We do make distinctions between individual entities in the same class, but according to general rules consistently applied. Both Jane Smith and John Brown are clients, and we insure both of them against ill health. But there is a general rule relating premiums to age, so John Brown's premium will be higher because he is older.

The basis of this consistent treatment of individuals in the same entity class is to recognize what is common to all individuals of the class, and to recognize what varies from one to another. Both ideas are captured by the idea of entity attributes. Every entity in the CLIENT class has a name attribute and a date of birth attribute. Individual entities of the class differ from one another by having different values of their attributes. John Brown has the value 'John Brown' for his name attribute, and the value '23 October 1932' for his date of birth attribute; Jane Smith has 'Jane Smith' and '7 May 1971' for her name and date of birth.

When we make a data model we deal with the entity classes. We decide which classes there should be, and which attributes each class should have. We do not deal with the individual entities until the system is in operation.

Tables, rows and columns

The information in the computer system will be held in a *relational database*. The information is arranged in *tables*. Each table has a number of *rows* and a number of *columns*. There is one table for each class of entity. For example, we might have one table for clients, one table for policies, one table for brokers, and so on, as shown in Figure 3.1.

In each table there is one row for each entity in the class. When a new entity individual comes into existence – for example, a new policy is created or a new client is acquired – a new row is added to the appropriate table to correspond to the new entity.

The columns of a table correspond to the *attributes* or properties of the entities. For example, each client has a name, an address and a date of birth; so the

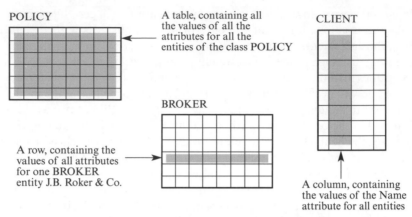

POLICY

A table, containing all the values of all the attributes for all the entities of the class POLICY

CLIENT

BROKER

A row, containing the values of all attributes for one BROKER entity J.B. Roker & Co.

A column, containing the values of the Name attribute for all entities

Figure 3.1 *Tables in a relational database.*

table for clients will have a column for all the names, a column for all the addresses, and a column for all the dates of birth. The row for each client will contain that client's name, that client's address, and that client's date of birth.

Although we add new *rows* to the tables during the operational life of the system, we do not add new *columns*: the number of columns in each table is considered to be fixed when the system is designed. This makes reasonable sense, because we want to store the same attributes for every entity in each class. If we suddenly decide that we want to store an eye-colour attribute for each client, it would be awkward and difficult to go back to all the existing clients, of whom there may be a very large number, and obtain the information. Not impossible, but very difficult. If we think eye-colour is significant, we should have included it in the client attributes in our original model.

The basic decisions in making the entity model are, therefore, as follows.

- What *classes* of entity are significant to the business?
- What *attributes* of each entity in each class are significant to the business?

or, equivalently:

- What *tables* are needed in the database?
- What *columns* are needed in each table?

We will return later in this chapter to a discussion of how these decisions should be made.

Uniqueness of entities

A crucial part of the idea of an entity is that each entity is *unique*. That is, it has a unique identity, or individuality, that distinguishes it, even if nothing else does, from every other entity in the whole universe. You can point to an entity –

perhaps only in a metaphorical sense if it is an abstract entity such as a sales enquiry – and say: 'I mean *this* one, not *that* one.'

In the database, this requirement for uniqueness means that every row in each table must be different from every other row in the same table. Two rows are different if there is any column in the table for which they have different values. So if the only columns in the clients table are name, address and date of birth, then any two rows must have either different names, or different addresses, or different dates of birth. The mechanisms that make a relational database work inside the computer ensure that there are no duplicate rows: if there is ever a situation in which a duplicate row is created, it is automatically removed before it can get into the database and corrupt it.

Because the database is only a *model* of the outside world, it reflects only a small selection of the entities of the world and their attributes: just those that are significant to the business. This restriction of the information in the database can lead to a danger that two entities in the world outside, easily distinguishable in that world, may be indistinguishable in respect of the attributes that are stored in the database. Certainly it is quite possible for two different clients to have the same name and the same birthday and live at the same address. When you meet the real people themselves it is easy to distinguish them: they have different heights and different eye-colours, speak different languages, work at different jobs, and have different parents. But if the clients table columns are only name, address and date of birth, there will be nothing to distinguish each of the two clients from the other.

Keys and IDs

We cannot allow this to happen in our data model. One way to avoid it is to take great care to ensure that each table contains at least one *candidate key*. A candidate key is a column, or combination of columns, that is sure to be different for different rows. If necessary, we can invent such a column, and we often do. So we might give the clients client numbers, and give the policies policy numbers, and so on. Often the problem has arisen long before computers and databases were thought of, and candidate keys of this kind are ready to hand.

But sometimes they are not. When the first major computer system was developed for the British Ministry of Pensions and National Insurance (now the Department of Social Security), it was necessary to give every adult in Britain a unique National Insurance Number. In the process of allocating these numbers, the developers started by trying to find pre-existing candidate keys. The combination of name, address and birthday seemed sure to work.

But they discovered that there were two people, both named John Smith (with no middle name or initial), born on the same day, and living at the same address. The John Smiths were not related to one another. To give each John Smith his allocated National Insurance Number, the department sent an official to visit them in their shared house. Presumably they were distinguished by their parents' names or parents' dates of birth. One wonders what would have happened if they had been identical twins.

A better way to avoid the problem of duplicate rows in the database is to enforce a rule that every row in every table has a hidden key. This key can be a serial number, automatically allocated by the system whenever a new row is added to any table. We can think of it as an ID attribute of the entity that corresponds to the row. The ID of an entity, and its hidden serial number value, can never change, just as one human being can never become another.

The automatic allocation of IDs is not hard to arrange, and it solves the problem completely. All that is necessary when the system is in operation is to ensure that users are always given the opportunity to say whether they are referring to an existing entity or adding a new one. So we will assume that our database has these automatically allocated IDs. Throughout this book, the term 'ID' will mean this unique automatically allocated hidden key.

The advantage these IDs will give us in making our model is that we need never concern ourselves with such questions as: 'How can we distinguish one client from another?' When we come, in a later section of this chapter, to consider the use of the system by users in the office, we will have to return to the subject of candidate keys.

Associations between entities

Some of the attributes we must consider in a data model are properties that concern only the entity they belong to. But some concern *associations* between two entities. For example, a policy has a death benefit amount, a commencing date, a life assured and a policyholder. The death benefit amount and the commencing date are properties that concern only the policy. But the life assured attribute is an association between the policy and a client; and the policyholder attribute is another association between the policy and a client – perhaps the same or perhaps a different client.

We will think of these *association attributes* as having values that are *pointers* to an associated entity. The value of the death benefit attribute of a policy must be a sum of money: say, £10,000. The value of the commencing date attribute must be a calendar date: say, 14 February 1993. The value of the life assured attribute is a pointer to a client, and its value must be equal to the ID of a client; the value of the policyholder attribute must also be the ID of a client, either the same or another client. The value of an association attribute is always an ID.

Treating an association as an attribute with a pointer value in this way is something of a short cut. An association always involves at least two entities, and it is definitely a distortion to make it an attribute of one of them. But it is a small distortion, and one that saves quite a lot of effort. There are usually more kinds of association than there are entity classes; models that show associations separately from entities often become very cluttered. But the short cut is not always possible, as we shall see later in this chapter.

Missing attribute values

A simple data model of CLIENT and POLICY entities may specify that every client has a BirthDate attribute and every policy has a Policyholder attribute. This is clearly true as a description of the world: everyone has a birthday, and a policy is not created unless someone wants it – and that someone is the policyholder.

But it may not be possible to maintain the truth of this description in the database at all times. In particular, the information necessary to give the attribute its value may not be known – for example, because the client has omitted to complete the relevant section of the proposal form. In an office workflow system it is not sensible to refuse to enter incomplete data into the database. Refusal would have two bad effects:

- It would prevent the system from being used in the interaction needed to obtain the missing information. For example, the system could not be used for writing to the client and handling the reply.
- It would often hold up progress unnecessarily. The client's birth date is not needed immediately; there may be other work, such as obtaining a medical report or bank references, that can be done without waiting until the missing birth date has been supplied.

So it is necessary to be able to handle the absence of an attribute value. We may think of an attribute that has no value as having a special *null value*. These null values can cause a lot of difficulty, because it is not always clear what they mean and how they can be used. This is an important matter, especially where we are concerned with pointer-valued association attributes. We will use a special technique for handling null pointer values. It is discussed later in this chapter. For the moment, we will only observe that we should avoid introducing the possibility of null values where they are not absolutely necessary.

Representing the Model

We need a convenient way of showing the entities and attributes of our model while we are building it and when we are discussing it with other people. We will use both entity diagrams, which are a pictorial form, and entity declarations, which are a textual form. The diagrams are better for showing the associations among entities; but the textual form is better for showing the details of entity attributes.

Entity diagrams

We will not use table diagrams like Figure 3.1 to represent the model. They can sometimes be useful, in a slightly different form, when you want to show examples of the contents of the database in discussing technical database issues. But another kind of diagram, like the diagram in Figure 3.2, is more useful for our purposes.

Figure 3.2 is a simple entity diagram. Each box represents an entity class: there are CLIENT, BROKER and POLICY entities. The name of the entity class always appears in capital letters in the top line of the box. The attributes of the entities of the class appear in upper-case and lower-case letters in the remaining lines. An attribute line that has a dot in it is a pointer attribute, and the arrow points to the box for the entity class that is associated by the attribute. So the Life Assured and Policyholder attributes each associate a client with the policy, and the Sold By attribute associates a broker with the policy.

The order of the attribute lines in a box is not meaningful; but it is easier to read the diagram if the line containing the name of the entity class is always the top line in its box. In any particular diagram you can include or omit entity attributes as convenient. In general, it is better to include only the attributes you need for the purpose in hand. If you need to show a complete list of all the attributes of an entity class, the textual form of entity declaration will be more convenient.

Notice that the policy entity class in this diagram has an attribute Policy-Number, which, we may reasonably suppose, is an invented candidate key, and clients and brokers have similar attributes. These are not the hidden IDs that are automatically allocated by the database mechanism. So they are not the values of pointer attributes.

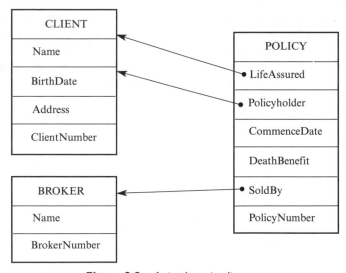

Figure 3.2 *A simple entity diagram.*

Entity declarations

The equivalent entity declaration in textual form is:

```
CLIENT = {Name;
            BirthDate;
            Address;
            ClientNumber};

POLICY = {Life Assured: CLIENT;
            Policyholder: CLIENT;
            CommenceDate;
            DeathBenefit;
            SoldBy: BROKER;
            PolicyNumber};

BROKER = {Name;
            BrokerNumber};
```

The equivalence between the two representations is straightforward. Just as in the entity diagram the order of attribute lines in a box is not meaningful, so in the entity declaration the order of the attributes inside the curly brackets is not meaningful.

There are several features of both notations that are not illustrated or used here. We will discuss them as and when we come to discuss the model features that they represent.

Associations and Pointers

We represented the association between a policy and a policyholder by an association attribute of the POLICY entity, that points to a CLIENT entity. Could we have treated it as an association attribute of the client entity instead? The situation seems symmetrical between policies and clients: each instance of the association involves precisely one policy and one client. But it is not really symmetrical, because although each policy has exactly one policyholder, each policyholder can have more than one policy.

So if we decided that we want to treat the association as an attribute of the CLIENT entity, we would have had to provide for each client to have several values of the same attribute: in effect, the attribute would have to be a set of pointer values instead of a single value. Alternatively, we could provide several attributes: Policy1, Policy2, and so on. A client with six policies would have six of these attributes: Policy1, Policy2, ..., Policy6. For most clients some or all of these attributes would be *null pointers*: Policy6 would point to nothing for any client with fewer than six policies. In general, we try to avoid null pointers. But there is a more serious difficulty.

Fundamental relational database rules

Both of these ideas run counter to established rules of relational databases. The first breaks the rule that each attribute value must be – in some sense – elementary or atomic: it must not be possible to cut it up into smaller pieces that are still meaningful. If we allow a set of pointers as the value of a client attribute, that value would certainly not be atomic or elementary: each pointer is only a part of the value, and is perfectly meaningful taken alone.

The second idea, of having as many attributes as a client has policies, runs counter to a different rule. Each row of a table must have the same number of columns. There must be no *repeated* parts of a row: that is, no parts that are repeated a number of times that varies from row to row. So if the row for one client has six policy pointers, every row in the client table must have six policy pointers, even if the corresponding client has only one policy, or none at all. Of course, if one client then gets a seventh policy the number of columns in the table must be increased. At best, this second idea is going to be extremely inconvenient and inefficient. At worst it is going to be completely impossible to manage.

These rules of relational databases are very restrictive. But the advantages of existing relational database technology for the kind of system we are developing are very considerable. So we are willing to accept the rules, and agree that the association cannot be treated as an attribute of the client entity.

The two rules mentioned here are among the most basic rules of relational databases. The first rule, that attribute values must be atomic or elementary, is the definition of *First Normal Form* (1NF). Some people are working to produce new kinds of relational database technology in which this restriction does not apply.

The second rule, that there must be no variable repetition and each row of a table must have the same number of columns, is even more fundamental: it is an integral part of the notion of a *relation*, whether normalized or not.

Cardinality of an association

The association between a policy and the client who is its policyholder is a *many-to-one* association: there may be many policies associated with each client as policyholder, and each policy is associated with only one client as its policyholder. It is usual to say that *many-to-one* is the 'cardinality' of the association.

The term *many* is being used in a special sense here. It means 'none or one or more'. A particular client need not be the policyholder on any policy: the client may just be the life assured on some policy. And there is no limit to the number of policies one client is permitted to hold.

Sometimes we want to be more precise about the *many* end of the association. When we do, we can write an indication next to the arrowhead of the limits we want to describe. For example, we can describe the association between days and months and years as in Figure 3.3. Each day belongs to

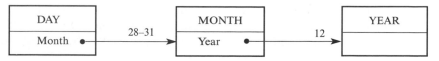

Figure 3.3   *Limits on cardinality.*

exactly one month, and each month has between 28 and 31 days inclusive. Each month belongs to exactly one month. Each month belongs to exactly one year, and each year has exactly 12 months.

It is useful to have a simple convention for writing these cardinality expressions when we want to be more precise. We will use this simple convention.

- A cardinality expression is a list of any number of *ranges*.
- A range is either a single number (like '12') or a lower number and a higher number separated by a hyphen (like '28–31').
- If there is more than one range in a cardinality expression, the ranges are separated by commas. For example, the number of days in a month in a non-leap year is '28, 30–31'.
- In the only or last range of a cardinality expression, the only or higher number can be 'n', meaning an indefinite number. For example, the number of children that one parent can have is '0–n'.

Cardinality in entity declarations

In the text form of an entity declaration, we can write a cardinality expression in parentheses after the pointer attribute name. So the declaration for POLICY would be written:

    POLICY = {LifeAssured: (0-n) CLIENT;
              Policyholder: (0-n) CLIENT;
              CommenceDate;
              DeathBenefit;
              SoldBy: (0-n) BROKER;
              PolicyNumber};

It is important to be clear about the meaning of a cardinality expression in an entity declaration. Because there are no arrows in entity declarations, the association is visible only at the end where it is represented by a pointer-valued attribute. At that end there is always one entity involved. But the pointer points to just one entity at the other end of the association. For example, in the declaration for the POLICY entity above, there is only one CLIENT who is the Life-Assured, one CLIENT who is the Policyholder, and one BROKER that the POLICY was SoldBy.

The cardinality expression therefore specifies how many different instances of the declared entity can be associated with the one entity at the other end of the association. In this case, therefore, the cardinality expressions show that one CLIENT may be the LifeAssured of 0–n POLICY entities and the Policyholder of 0–n POLICY entities; and that 0–n POLICY entities may be SoldBy one BROKER.

Link entity classes

The associations we have considered so far are all *many-to-one* associations. They differ only in the precise meaning of *many*. But some associations are many-to-many, and we cannot represent them by simple pointer attributes with cardinality expressions.

Suppose, for example, that we want to make an entity model of students in a college who enrol for courses. Then the association between students and courses is many-to-many. Each student enrols for many courses, and each course has many students who enrol for it. So we cannot represent this association either by a pointer attribute in the student entity or by a pointer attribute in the course entity. Instead, we must introduce a third entity class, which we may call 'enrolment'. We will refer to this kind of entity class as a link entity class, because its purpose is to link two other entity classes in an association. Figure 3.4 shows how it works.

The link entity has two pointer-valued attributes; one points to the enrolling student, the other to the course on which the student enrols. In any one instance of the ENROLMENT entity, there is exactly one student and exactly one course. The fact that a particular student enrols on many courses is reflected in the number of ENROLMENT entities that have pointers to that student; and similarly the fact that a course is enrolled on by many students.

We can be more precise about cardinality, as before. Perhaps each course is limited to a maximum of 50 students; and perhaps every student must enrol on at least four and no more than seven courses. Then our entity declarations will be:

```
        COURSE = {...};
       STUDENT = {...};
    ENROLMENT = {Student: (4–7) STUDENT;
                 Course: (0–50) COURSE};
```

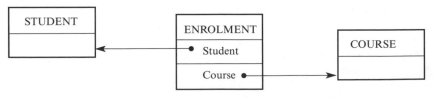

Figure 3.4   *A link entity class.*

Associations of one entity class

There is no reason why an association should not be between two entities of the same class. Every person has a next-of-kin – a nearest living relative; not every person is another person's next-of-kin. Figure 3.5 shows this association.

An association between entities of the same class may involve a link entity class. Figure 3.6 shows the association of marriage.

Attributes and Values

It would be nonsense to say that the DeathBenefit of policy 1234 is 'John Smith', or that the Name of client 4567 is '£10,000'. These are not appropriate – or even possible – values of the attributes. In our data model we need to say something about what values are possible and appropriate for each attribute of each entity. For example:

- The value of the Name attribute of a client must be – naturally enough – a person's name. '£10,000' is not a person's name.
- The value of the DeathBenefit attribute of a policy must be a sum of money. 'John Smith' is not a sum of money. For a British life assurance company it must be a sum of money in pounds sterling.
- The value of the BirthDate attribute of a client must be a date. Something like '28 February 1966' is acceptable; '23 Acacia Road' is not.
- The value of the Gender attribute of a client must be a human gender: that is, 'male' or 'female'. Nothing else is acceptable.
- The value of the Weight attribute of a client must be a person's weight. '10st 5lb' (or perhaps '66kg') is possible; '£103.26' is not.

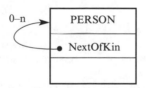

Figure 3.5   *An association of one entity class.*

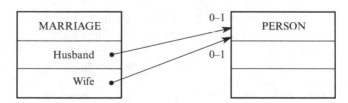

Figure 3.6   *An association of one entity class using a link.*

To deal properly with attributes and their values in a data model we need to consider *domains* and *types*.

Domains

A domain is a set of values of the same kind of meaning. In the examples above we recognized *name*, *money*, *date*, *gender* and *weight* as distinct domains. When a value from one domain is appropriate, a value from another domain will not do.

We can write the appropriate domain for each attribute of each entity class into the entity declarations. So the declaration for the client and policy entity classes may be:

    CLIENT = {Name: *name*;
              BirthDate: *date*;
              Gender: *gender*;
              Weight: *weight*;
              ClientNumber: *clientnum*;
              ... };

    POLICY = {LifeAssured: CLIENT;
              PolicyHolder: CLIENT;
              CommenceDate: *date*;
              DeathBenefit: *money*;
              MonthlyPremium: *money*;
              PolicyNumber: *policynum*;
              ...};

It is now clear that when we declare:

    LifeAssured: CLIENT;

we are saying that the domain of the LifeAssured association attribute is ID (of a CLIENT).

The information that we define in the data model is needed to support the conduct of the business. This means that we must be able to enter new information when new clients and new policies come into being; and to display or print it when it is needed on a document or to help a user to perform some task. So every domain must allow its values to be entered into the database and displayed or printed. (IDs are a special case, which we will return to later in this chapter.)

But we must be able to do other things also with domain values. For example, we must be able to add together two sums of *money* and get another sum of *money*; to multiply or divide a sum of *money* by a *number* and get another sum of *money*; and to divide one sum of *money* by another and get a *number*. We must be able to add a *number-of-days* to a *date* and get another *date*, or subtract one *date* from another and get a *number-of-days*. Given two *dates*, we must be able to determine whether they are equal or which is later.

Not all operations make sense for all domains. In fact, the only operations that make sense for all domains are entering and displaying or printing a value, and comparing two values to see whether they are equal. It makes no sense to add two *names* together, or to multiply a *date* by a *number*. In the kind of system development we are discussing in this book, we need not treat the matter of operations in any formal way: common sense will serve well enough. But it is helpful to remember that when a question of domains or permissible values arises, it may often be clarified by a careful consideration of the operations that are applicable.

Storing values in a database

The value of an entity attribute is stored in the database in the appropriate row and column of the appropriate table. It must be stored in one of the *types* provided by the underlying database mechanism, and there may be only a few of these types. For example, the types provided may be as follows.

- Characters(n): a string of up to n characters. For example, 'John Smith' is a string of 10 characters (including the space between 'John' and 'Smith').
- Integer: a whole number, such as '10,000'.
- Decimal(d): a number with a fractional part of d decimal places. For example, '14.35' is a number with two decimal places.
- Date: a date, such as '15 January 1962'.

The database mechanism allows certain operations on each of these types. For example, integers and decimals can be added and subtracted, multiplied and divided. Integers can be added to dates, but decimals cannot. Two strings each of up to n characters can be joined to give a string of up to $2n$ characters, but they cannot be added together.

The type chosen for a domain must allow at least the operations that are necessary for the domain. It would be wrong to choose Characters(n) for the *money* domain, because the database mechanism would not then support the very necessary arithmetic operations on *money* attributes. But because the number of types is much smaller than the number of domains, it is not possible to choose a type for each domain that supports all the necessary domain operations and no others. The type Integer may be chosen for both the *weight* and *height* domains. The operations of adding two *weights* together and adding two *heights* together are then supported. But so too, unfortunately, is the nonsensical operation of adding a *height* to a *weight*.

Restrictions to avoid nonsensical operations cannot usually be imposed in the data model. They must be implicitly observed when we come to define the user tasks that will manipulate and change the attribute values in the database. Not very satisfactory. But the best we can do.

Domain declarations

We say what type we have chosen for each domain by writing a domain declaration. In form, a domain declaration is very like an entity declaration. For example, we might declare some of the domains we have been discussing like this:

> *name* = {Character(20)};
> *money* = {Decimal(2) [£.pp]};
> *gender* = {Character(1)[M/F]};
> *clientnum* = {Character(8)};
> *weight* = {Integer [number of pounds]};

The comments in square brackets added to some of the domain declarations explain how the values of the domain are represented. For example, without the comment in the declaration of *weight* we would not know whether the integer is a number of pounds or a number of hectograms (0.1kg units).

Domain declarations do not appear in entity diagrams. In an entity diagram we are chiefly concerned with the relationships among entity classes, not with the detail of the entity attributes.

Datagroup domains

One established rule of relational database systems which we encountered earlier in this chapter is that each attribute value must be elementary or atomic. But it is often very useful – and sometimes necessary – to treat some group of data as a single attribute even though it is clearly not atomic. We do so by declaring a *datagroup domain*. Here is a declaration of a *postaddress* domain appropriate for UK postal addresses:

> postaddress =   {*addressline1*: Character(30);
> *addressline2*: Character(30);
> *posttown*: Character(20);
> *postcode*: Character (8)};

By making this declaration we reconcile two apparently conflicting purposes. First, we can use the *postaddress* domain in entity declarations just as conveniently as if it were an elementary domain. For example:

> CUSTOMER = {CustomerName: *name*;
> DeliveryAddress: *postaddress*;
> InvoiceAddress: *postaddress*;
> CustomerNumber: *custnum*;
> ... };

Second, we can still refer separately to each part of each address. We do this by imagining that domain declarations had been made just for the individual parts of the address, like this:

> *addressline1* = {Character(30)};
> *addressline2* = {Character(30)};
> *posttown* = {Character(20)};
> *postcode* = {Character (8)};

And that the entity declaration had been written like this:

> CUSTOMER = {CustomerName: *name*;
> DeliveryAddress.addressline1: *addressline1*;
> DeliveryAddress.addressline2: *addressline2*;
> DeliveryAddress.posttown: *posttown*;
> DeliveryAddress.postcode: *postcode*;
> InvoiceAddress.addressline1: *addressline1*;
> InvoiceAddress.addressline2: *addressline2*;
> InvoiceAddress.posttown: *posttown*;
> InvoiceAddress.postcode: *postcode*;
> CustomerNumber: *custnum*;
> ... };

The rule, then, is this. If an entity attribute (such as DeliveryAddress or Invoice-Address) has values in a datagroup domain, then each part of the value is referred to by writing the entity attribute name, followed by a dot, followed by the part name.

Unfortunately, it is necessary to use something like the cumbersome declaration of the customer entity shown above when we are describing the customer table, so that a standard relational database mechanism can handle it. Essentially, the declaration of each table must list all of its columns explicitly. But it is desirable to hide the cumbersome form behind the more convenient and simple form of a datagroup domain declaration.

In principle, there is no reason why the parts of a datagroup domain should not themselves have values in another datagroup domain. So we might declare:

> *postaddress* = {*addressline1*: *streetaddress*;
> *addressline2*: Character(30);
> *posttown*: Character(20);
> *postcode*: Character (8)};

and:

> *streetaddress* = {*housenumber*: Integer;
> *streetname*: Character(25)};

Then we could refer to the customer entity attributes:

DeliveryAddress.addressline1.housenumber

and:

DeliveryAddress.addressline1.streetname

In practice, in typical office workflow systems, these extra levels are unlikely to be needed, and even more unlikely to be supported by the development software environment. One level of datagroup domain declaration is usually enough.

Choosing Entity Classes and Attributes

We are discussing the development method in terms of four phases, to be carried out one after the other. Making the entity model is the first of these four phases: the central decisions of the entity model are choosing the *classes* of entity, and the entity *attributes* in each class, that are significant to the business. To some extent we can carry out this task before we progress to the next phases, in which we make the business interaction model and define the business tasks in detail. But in practice we cannot expect to make a perfect entity model before we begin to consider the interactions and tasks. Development must be to some extent iterative: we will need to return to the entity model after we have explored the business interactions and tasks.

But the central choices of entity classes and attributes are usually ready to hand. In the early phases of developing an office workflow system we concentrate on capturing details of the outside world and how it currently interacts with the office. We are not inventing it from new. The kind of system we are concerned with is usually tightly constrained by the practices of an already established business or administrative sector. In this kind of system, a Business Process Re-engineering exercise will have its chief impact inside the office: the business requirements that determine how the office sees the outside world and how it interacts with it will remain relatively unchanged. It is these requirements that we are concerned with in making an entity model.

Physical entities

We have already said that the significant entities include the people and organizations with whom the enterprise conducts its business: clients and customers, agents, brokers, suppliers, distributors, sales representatives, students and lecturers. These are *physical* entities, in the sense that they can be directly seen and touched in the outside world. Depending on the business, the enterprise may be concerned with other physical entities. For example, an insurance company may be concerned with particular houses, particular works of art and particular cars that it insures. All of these physical entities are individuals, in the sense that they have distinct identities. The distinction between different individuals is fundamental.

People and organization entities have attributes that the enterprise must record and use in communicating with them. Names, addresses and telephone numbers are almost universal examples. Other attributes characterize entities within the same class in ways that are important for the business. For a life assurance company the date of birth and the profession of a client are of the utmost significance if the client's life is to be assured. The replacement value and engine size of a car, or the rebuilding cost and location of a house, partly determine the risk of insuring it. For a sales organization a customer's credit rating is crucial. A tax office is concerned with a taxpayer's date of birth, PAYE tax code and residential status, among other attributes.

Attribute categories

All of these attributes describe the entities they belong to, but in different ways. We can classify these ways, partly to help our understanding, and partly as a checklist of sources of significant attributes. The classification is based on distinguishing attributes with fixed values from attributes whose values can vary over time; and on distinguishing attributes whose values are determined by the outside world from attributes whose values are determined by the office. The four resulting classes are as follows.

- Attributes fixed by the outside world. A client's date of birth is a fixed attribute: it cannot change in any circumstances. Its value is fixed by an event in the outside world. Of course, the BirthDate in the database may be subject to change if the original information supplied about the client was wrong and must be subsequently corrected. The correction would merely repair a failure of the database to reflect the outside world correctly.
- Attributes fixed by the office. The essential attributes of an investment plan offered as a financial product are fixed by the office. They cannot be changed, because they immediately become contractual obligations to the clients who invest in policies or pensions defined by the plan. A plan with different values for any one of these attributes would be a different plan entity.
- Attributes variable by the outside world. A client's address is a variable attribute: a client can move house. This attribute is varied by the outside world, in the sense that the client's decision to move house is not made in the office. Similarly the rebuilding cost of a house changes according to current economic conditions, and the colour of a car according to its owner's whim.
- Attributes variable by the office. A sales organization may decide that some customers are to be allowed special discounts on all their purchases. The tax office sets each taxpayer's PAYE tax code.

The first three categories are straightforward. The last category, of attributes variable by the office, needs a little more care. The essential point is that the office has some discretion in determining these attribute values. There may be established general rules for allowing special discounts, but the users retain some discretion. Perhaps customers who are habitually late in paying are not allowed to have special discounts for which they would otherwise qualify; perhaps a much sought-after customer may be allowed a special discount as an inducement. Similarly, the PAYE tax code for each taxpayer is usually determined by the taxpayer's current tax allowances according to the applicable statute. But it may also be affected by considerations such as tax unpaid from previous years, and the effect of these considerations may be to some extent negotiable between the taxpayer and the tax inspector.

Derived attributes

The category of variable attributes changed by the office includes only those for which there is some discretion, however small. It does not include what are often called *derived attributes*: that is, properties that can always be calculated with absolute certainty and precision from other attributes of the entity or of associated entities. For example, it does not include the client's age-last-birthday, which can be calculated from the client's BirthDate attribute and the current date; or the customer's total-sales-last-month, which can be calculated from the associated order entities. The office has no discretion in determining the value of age-last-birthday or of total-sales-last-month.

We will return to the subject of derived attributes, but not until we come to consider the detail of business tasks. We will then treat derived attributes as *definitions* that are used in business tasks rather than as entity attributes belonging to the data model. We regard this treatment as more appropriate, even if it is possible – as it may be – to arrange for the database mechanism to calculate the value of a derived attribute automatically, either whenever it changes or whenever we need to refer to it.

Obligation entities

The business proceeds on the basis of contracts and agreements, and the working out, through interaction between the office and the outside world, of the *obligations* that arise from them. These contracts and agreements must be entities in the data model, because information about them and their progress, about the discharging of the obligations, is central to the conduct of the business. So there will be entity classes for policies and pensions, sales and purchase orders, negotiated terms-of-trade, building contracts, tax assessments and mortgages. We may call them *obligation entities*.

It is characteristic of these entities that they arise only because of the conduct of the business. The physical entities of the outside world – the customers

and suppliers, the motor cars and buildings – would still exist even if the enterprise and its business did not. But the contracts and agreements reflect and
capture the conduct of the business through business interactions.

Obligation entities will always have pointer-valued attributes to associate
them with the people, organizations and things that are involved in the obligation. So a buildings insurance policy will have attributes that point to the
policyholder and to the insured building; a customer order will have attributes
that point to the customer who placed the order and to the goods ordered.

They will also have attributes that capture other details of the obligation
entered into. So a motor insurance policy entity will have attributes such as
Excess (the amount of each loss that the insured must pay), AnnualPremium
and Restriction (whether only the insured is allowed to drive the car).

Link entities

We have already seen an example of a class of *link* entities: the enrolment entity
that linked students to courses in the section Link entity classes earlier in this
chapter. It is possible for a link entity to arise wherever there can be several
simultaneous values for what would otherwise have been a simple pointer
attribute. It is then always necessary to decide between introducing a link entity
and having a fixed number of pointer attributes in the original entity.

For example, if a certain kind of life assurance policy has precisely two
assured lives, we must decide between these two possibilities.

- Introduce a link entity, with one pointer to the policy and one to one of the
  two clients whose life is assured on the policy.
- Replace the single LifeAssured attribute by two pointer attributes. For example, FirstLife and SecondLife.

The two possibilities are shown together in Figure 3.7.

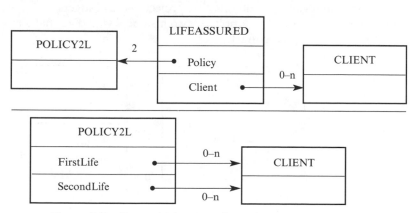

Figure 3.7   *Two model fragments for policies with two lives assured.*

The first choice, the use of a link entity, is always possible. But the second choice is possible only when the number of pointer attributes is fixed. A joint-lives policy of the kind considered here always has precisely two assured lives. If it can sometimes have only one, then some of the entities would have null pointer values for the SecondLife attribute. (Remember that, in general, we try to avoid null pointer values.)

A link entity is often a vestigial obligation entity. It might be that a life policy on several assured lives pays out a different benefit for each life. The benefit would then be an attribute of the link entity, and the LIFEASSURED entity would have a PayableBenefit attribute. Similarly, in the enrolment example, we might enlarge the enrolment entity by adding further attributes beyond its two pointer attributes Student and Course. For example, we might add Enrolment-Date and CourseGrade.

Associations of more than two entities

A link entity class is absolutely necessary when an association involves more than two entities. The classic database example is this. There are supplier, part and project entity classes. Suppliers may be authorized to supply particular parts to particular projects. So, for example, supplier ABC may be authorized to supply (only) widgets to project X and (only) gadgets to project Y (project X also uses gadgets, but obtains them from another supplier).

We must represent this association by a link entity with three pointer attributes, as shown in Figure 3.8.

The crucial point here is that this association cannot be represented by associations involving only two entities each. Suppose, for example, that we break it into the associations shown in Figure 3.9.

- One association SP between suppliers and projects: two instances would be that supplier ABC is authorized to supply to project X and to project Y.
- Another PP between projects and parts: two instances would be that project X uses widgets and gadgets, and one that project Y uses gadgets.
- A third PS between parts and suppliers: two instances would be that supplier ABC supplies widgets and gadgets.

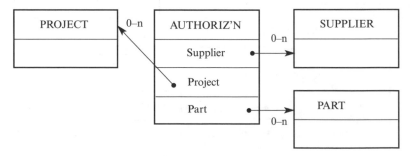

Figure 3.8   *A three-way association.*

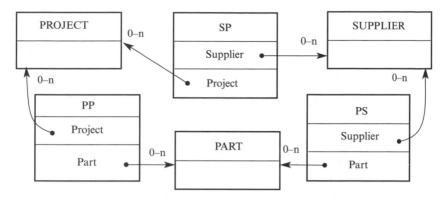

Figure 3.9   *A three-way association misrepresented as two-way associations.*

Now we have lost some information. There is no way to record the information that supplier ABC is *not* authorized to supply gadgets to project X or to supply widgets to project Y. So we must represent this three-way association by a link entity with three pointer attributes, as shown earlier in Figure 3.8.

Dependent entities

The relational database rule forbidding repetition of table rows has another effect beyond the need for link entities. It may also make it necessary to introduce *dependent entities*.

Consider, for example, the usual form of a customer order. A customer may order several groups of items in the same order: 20 widgets, 36 gadgets and 12 fidgets. Because the number of item groups that can be ordered is not fixed – in fact, it is not even limited – the item groups cannot be treated as attributes of the order entity, even if we use a datagroup domain. We cannot avoid treating them as a separate entity class, which we may call ORDER-LINE, as shown in Figure 3.10.

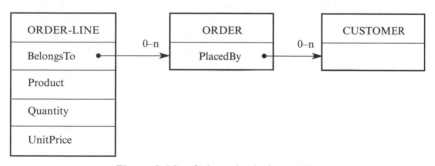

Figure 3.10   *Order and order-line entities.*

No link entity is needed here, because each order-line belongs to precisely one order, just as each order is placed by precisely one customer.

An order-line is definitely an obligation entity in its own right, although it cannot occur independently of the order entity it belongs to. It has its own attributes, such as Product, Quantity and Unit Price. And, as we shall see in Chapter 4, it can have its own lifecycle of interaction. We may choose to deal separately and independently with the different order-lines, depending on the different circumstances relevant to each one. The gadgets are in stock, and will be delivered tomorrow. The widgets are also in stock, but are very bulky, and cannot be delivered until next week. The fidgets are not in stock, and have been ordered from the supplier.

Although the order-lines may have independent lifecycles, they are all dependent on the order for their existence. It is conceptually impossible to have an order-line that does not belong to any order. This is why entities of this kind are called dependent entities.

Null values and the UNKNOWN ID

Although it makes no sense for a dependent entity to exist in the world without the entity on which it depends, it may still be appropriate to allow its record to exist in the database without the record on which it depends. Although this is an anomaly, in the sense that it cannot be a faithful representation of the world, it may well be a very useful temporary intermediate stage in data entry.

For example, it makes no sense to have a premium payment that is not associated with a policy. But if the office receives a premium payment by cheque whose policy cannot be identified, it makes perfectly good practical sense to enter it in the database to await the eventual completion of the data. The question immediately arises: What is the value of the Policy association attribute in the premium record? There is no real policy with which it can be associated – yet – and no real policy record in the database.

So long as the policy has not yet been identified, the value of the association attribute in the premium record would be a pointer to a special policy entity record whose policy ID is UNKNOWN. It's important to understand that this special policy entity record is really present in the database. The technique here is quite different from the traditional relational database technique of using a *null value*. A null value doesn't point to anything. A pointer to the record with the UNKNOWN ID points to that special record. This technique simplifies a number of difficulties in database design and implementation – the difficulties arising from null values are notorious – and can be extended to embrace other special entity records such as ANY and ALL. We will return to this subject in Chapter 5.

Shared datagroup attributes

Datagroup domains were discussed above. We looked at the example of the domain postaddress, whose domain declaration was:

postaddress = {*addressline1*: Character(30);
$\qquad\qquad$ *addressline2*: Character(30);
$\qquad\qquad$ *posttown*: Character(20);
$\qquad\qquad$ *postcode*: Character (8)};

In some cases we might decide to make what could be a datagroup domain into an entity class. If client entities have an attribute PostAddress, we might decide to make postaddress an entity class, as shown in Figure 3.11.

The reason for treating what could have been a datagroup domain as an entity class is simply to avoid duplication. If we have many clients who share a postaddress with at least one other client, then by making postaddress an entity class we avoid storing the same values of AddressLine1, AddressLine2, Post-Town and PostCode more than once. We also avoid the need to enter them more than once: after the first entry of a particular postaddress it is necessary only to enter a reference to the existing postaddress entity.

This example is less implausible than it may seem at first sight. Many enterprises that deal with private clients or customers often have to deal with different customers living at the same address. This is especially true in the financial services industry, where a husband and wife, or a parent and child, are very likely to be different clients living at the same address.

Of course, in a system for handling mortgages, or for the work of an estate agency, or for householder buildings insurance, address may at first sight seem to be an entity class in its own right. But more properly that entity class would be DWELLING. For a mortgage company, an estate agency or a buildings insurer, an address is simply the geographical location attribute of a dwelling.

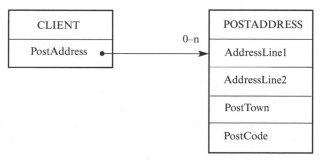

Figure 3.11 *A datagroup domain treated as an entity class.*

Dependent interaction entities

In principle it is possible that a single event might require to be treated as an entity. More often, we will need to make an entity out of a dependent interaction within a larger obligation entity. This happens when the dependent interaction is complex enough to need its own lifecycle.

Consider, for example, the payment of an insurance policy premium. In the simplest possible case, the premium merely falls due on a certain date, and is paid. But there may be a number of complications. The premium may normally be paid by direct debit or standing order from the client's bank account. If the direct debit or standing order is not paid by the bank on the due date, the insurance company will start an interaction with the client to determine why the payment was not made. This interaction may involve exchanges of letters or telephone calls, both with the client and with the bank. A premium may be eventually returned to the client on cancellation of the policy. A premium may be paid in error: for example, because the policy had been surrendered but the client's bank paid the premium before receiving notification that it should cease. These cases will give rise to further interactions.

The information to be stored about these interactions is information about the particular premium – the premium due on 1 July on policy LP1234 – not about the policy or the client. So it must be associated with a PREMIUM entity.

Similar examples arise out of almost any complex obligation. Customers order goods, and may then return them after delivery. Insurance policies give rise to claims. Students in an examination may be entitled to appeal, and even to have their papers marked a second time if they believe they have been given an unjustly low grade.

It is not too far from the truth to say that almost every event that at first sight appears only to be a simple event, atomic and instantaneous, may turn out to be a complex interaction requiring to be treated as an entity in its own right. Many of these interaction entities will emerge only at the next stages of the development, when we consider business interactions and tasks. But it is good to be aware of their possible emergence from the outset, while the basic entity model is being made.

Entity Keys

We have stipulated that every row of every table in the database will have a unique identifier. This is its automatically allocated ID: whenever a new entity record is created in the database, it receives a unique ID. All pointer attributes have IDs as their values. So there is no difficulty in ensuring that every entity in every class can be unambiguously identified.

In the usual terminology of relational databases, the automatically allocated ID is a *key*. This means that in the table whose rows it identifies, its values uniquely distinguish each row from all other rows of the table. Since there may be other unique identifiers for the same table, the ID is said to be a *candidate key*: that is, it is one of a number (possibly only one) of keys for the table. So, for example, the hidden ID for customer entities is a candidate key in the customer table.

Foreign keys

In any table, an association attribute pointing to a CUSTOMER entity has a value which is the value of the hidden ID for the customer. That attribute is a *foreign key*. It is called a foreign key because it is a candidate key to some table row, but it is not a key of the row in which it appears.

Of course, the value of a foreign key attribute might happen to be the same as the value of a candidate key of the entity whose attribute it is. For example, suppose that in some system there are PERSON entities, and that each person has a financial adviser, who is also a person. The Adviser attribute of each person points to the person's financial adviser. There is no reason why a person should not be his own financial adviser. For such a person the value of the Adviser pointer attribute would be the same as the person entity's hidden ID. But the Adviser attribute is still called a foreign key of the person entity record.

Essentially, each association attribute is a foreign key.

Hidden keys

In the entity model the IDs are hidden. An ID is not shown as an attribute of the row that it identifies; and the domain of a pointer attribute is always written as the name of an entity class. So if order entities have an attribute PlacedBy, which points to a customer, we write the entity declarations like this:

        ORDER = {PlacedBy: CUSTOMER;
                    ... };
    CUSTOMER = {...};

and not like this:

        ORDER = {PlacedBy: ID (of a CUSTOMER);
                    ... };
    CUSTOMER = {Identifier: ID;
                    ...};

User keys

These automatically allocated hidden IDs solve the problem of unique reference to entities within the database. But we must also consider the database from a user's operational point of view, and from the point of view of the people and organizations in the outside world with whom the users communicate.

The problem of finding unique identifiers for individual entities is an old one. The usual solution is to allocate an arbitrary identifier and insist on its use. So the insurance company allocates policy numbers and claim numbers and client numbers, the Department of Social Security allocates National Insurance numbers, local authorities allocate dwelling numbers, and commercial organizations allocate customer numbers and invoice numbers and product numbers. (Of course, these numbers are not always purely numeric. They often have alphabetic characters in them, and are really just character strings rather than numbers.)

We are all well accustomed to these identifiers. Users of the computer system in the office will expect to see them on the screen, and clients and agents and customers and suppliers will expect to see them on documents. They are an important factor in reducing misunderstanding and error in communication between the office and the outside world.

Combining user keys and hidden IDs

There is no difficulty in combining the use of hidden IDs with the use of user keys.

From the point of view of the entity model the user keys can be treated exactly like other attribute values of the entities to which they belong. Clients have names, and they also have client numbers and National Insurance numbers. An insurance company would expect to print all of these on a formal document. Similarly, to find the information stored in the system about a client, the user in the office may enter any of these pieces of information. The system should be designed so that if the information entered is not enough to identify the client – in this example, if it is only the client's name – then a list is displayed of clients whose attributes match the information entered. The user then decides which is intended.

Primary keys and hidden IDs

A user in the office, looking at the attributes of a policy entity on the screen, may very probably need to know which client is the policyholder of this policy. But the Policyholder attribute is a pointer-valued attribute, and its value is a hidden ID. This value has no meaning to the user: it is purely internal to the database. It would be more convenient if the client number were displayed instead.

The client number would be more convenient not only because it is a user key, but also because it is the *primary key* for client entities. That is, it is the key chosen as the most important from the user point of view. Primary keys can be indicated in an entity declaration by underlining, as in:

ORDER = {<u>Order Number:</u> ordernum;
     ... };

This is the traditional way of indicating the primary key of a row of a relational database table. We can make use of this declaration of the primary key to improve the display of information to the user when we come to define the details of the business tasks and the programs that will support them. Because it is the primary key, the appropriate Order Number can be displayed whenever an order entity ID would have been displayed otherwise.

Composite user keys

Quite often there is no single attribute that can act as the user key for an entity class. This is particularly true of link entity classes. For example, the ENROL-MENT link entity that arises from the many-to-many association between students and courses seems to need a composite key consisting of both the Student attribute and the Course attribute of the enrolment. To identify an enrolment entity we must give the values of both the Student and the Course attributes.

But this composite key is not really satisfactory. To see why, consider what would happen if a student were to enrol on a particular course in one term, abandon the course, and then enrol again in the following term. We would presumably want to count this as two distinct individual enrolments. But even the composite key is not enough to distinguish these two individuals.

We might, perhaps, decide that the ENROLMENT entity class should have another attribute EnrolDate, which is the date on which the enrolment takes place. Now we may use the composite key consisting of all three attribute values: EnrolDate, Student and Course. The problem is solved – at least until we discover that one student may enrol twice in the same day for the same course.

Essentially we must regard composite user keys as informal and unreliable paths to human identification of individual entities. The formal and reliable identification within the system must rest on the hidden IDs that the system allocates automatically. That is why we have them. In practice it will often be clear that there must also be a primary user key, if necessary specially constructed. For example, the enrolment office would be well advised to assign an EnrolmentNumber to each new enrolment; it may save a lot of trouble.

The Limitations of a Data Model

The entity model that we build is a data model. That means that it describes both the database in the computer and some aspects and properties of some part of the world outside the computer. The description is only of *static* properties: that is, it describes the state of the database and of the world, but it does not describe how that state changes.

Omitting dynamic properties

Suppose, for example, that we declare MaritalStatus as an attribute of person entities; and that MaritalStatus can have the values Unmarried, Married, Widowed and Divorced. Then we do not attempt in the basic entity model to specify that a person can change MaritalStatus only in the following ways:

- from Unmarried to Married;
- from Married to Widowed;
- from Married to Divorced;
- from Widowed to Married; and
- from Divorced to Married.

It is not possible to change directly from Unmarried to Widowed or Divorced. We leave this kind of dynamic model until a later stage in the development.

Limited expressive power

It is not only dynamic properties that we must omit from the entity model. There are static properties also that we must omit because we choose to use a language that is not powerful enough to express them. For example, in our entity model we cannot say any of the following things.

- A person cannot be their own NextOfKin.
- Any student who enrols on the Physics course must also enrol on the AdvancedMaths course.
- The Gender attribute of a person playing the role of Husband in a marriage entity must be 'male'.
- Only one month in any year can have exactly 28 days.

This does not mean that we cannot impose these restrictions on the system. We can impose them when we come to define the programs for the business tasks. But we cannot impose them in the data model. And for the data model of this kind of system we should not try. Especially, we should not add more elaborate notations to the entity diagrams or declarations to represent these restrictions. Notations should always be kept as simple as possible.

Chapter Summary

We have discussed basic aspects of the entity model.

- It is a static data model both of the database and of the outside world with which the office conducts its business.
- It is based on recognizing classes of entities. Entities are individuals that have attributes reflecting their properties and states.
- Each individual entity has a unique, hidden, automatically allocated identifier called its ID.
- The values of attributes are restricted to appropriate domains. Domain values are represented in the database by types such as character strings and numbers.
- Datagroup domains have non-elementary values.
- Associations among entities are represented by association attributes or by link entities.
- An association attribute is an attribute of one of the entities in an association, and its value is the hidden ID of another entity in the same association.
- A link entity represents an instance of an association between two or more entities. It has a pointer-valued attribute pointing at each of the associated entities.
- The hidden IDs can be used in combination with user keys, which can be displayed in place of IDs for better readability.

Questions

3.1   Draw an entity diagram showing that every *person* has a mother and *father*, each of whom is also a *person*.

   Can you think of a reason why it might be difficult to store the table for this person entity class in a database without at least some distortion?

3.2   What kind of attribute is a No-Claim-Bonus on a motor insurance policy? Is it fixed, variable by the outside world, or variable by the office? Or is it a derived attribute?

3.3   Would you treat Discount as an attribute of an order entity or of an order-line entity? What would determine your decision?

3.4   What might be the user primary key for a marriage entity? What if two people marry, divorce and then remarry?

3.5   Draw an entity diagram showing that a BOOK has an AUTHOR, an INTRODUCTION, a number of CHAPTERs and a PUBLISHER.

3.6 Modify the entity diagram of Question 3.5 to provide for joint authorship of a book.

3.7 Modify the entity diagram of Question 3.5 to provide for republication of the same CHAPTER in more than one BOOK.

3.8 Is it possible to show in an entity diagram or an entity declaration that all the BOOKs of an AUTHOR must be published by the same PUBLISHER?

3.9 Write a set of entity declarations equivalent to the entity diagram of Question 3.6.

3.10 Write a domain declaration for a composite domain *formalname*, consisting of a title, a forename, a middle initial and a surname. The title is always Mr or Ms, and forenames and surnames are limited to 25 characters each.

CHAPTER 4

Initial Lifecycle Definitions

In this chapter we begin to examine the business interaction dynamics of a system. Our starting point is the concept of an *entity lifecycle*, which is the basis of the interaction dynamics between the office and the outside world. A lifecycle is ultimately composed of tasks to be performed by users in the office, often in response to events in the outside world. Further aspects of this business model are discussed later, in Chapter 6, where we also discuss how to represent the rules and the programs that define each task within the system.

The organization and scheduling of tasks, subject to the constraints imposed by the entity lifecycles, is the concern of the office workflow design. Office workflow is discussed in Chapter 7.

Lifecycle Stages

A lifecycle is a sequence of major *stages* in the life of an entity, through which it progresses in the defined order. For example, a new life assurance policy may progress through the stages of proposal entry and validation; underwriting, where the risk is assessed and the premiums fixed accordingly; acceptance by the client; and, finally, issue of the policy document to the client. Similarly, a customer order may progress though the stages of checking the customer's credit; checking the availability of stock; pricing; delivery; and invoicing.

These lifecycle stages are not invented by the system developers; nor are they the product of any kind of top-down design. Usually, each stage of a lifecycle is the responsibility of one *workgroup* of users in the office: the New Business department, the Underwriting department, the Credit department, or the Transport department. So they are a direct reflection of the known practices of the organization. They may also reflect standard practices in the industry or business sector, or even – especially in the financial services industry – procedures imposed by legislation.

Flexible Sequencing

The fixed sequential structure of one lifecycle is too simple to reflect the full range of possible orders in which things can happen in a workflow system. The necessary flexibility and power come chiefly from three sources.

(1) The lifecycle for a particular entity may be ended prematurely, or even set back to an earlier stage. For example, if the client does not accept the premium quotation the policy is not proceeded with any further.
(2) Each stage of a lifecycle has an internal structure of *tasks* and *subtasks*. The tasks of each stage proceed in parallel, and a task may give rise to one or more subtasks if it cannot be completed in the simple standard manner. For example, underwriting of life policies below £10,000 may be performed *automatically* by the system, while larger policies are passed on to a task of *manual* examination and decision by a user in the underwriting department.
(3) Related entities have related lifecycles, and an entity may therefore be involved in more than one lifecycle at one time. For example, an order entity may be involved both in its own lifecycle as sketched out above and in the smaller lifecycles of checking and picking the stock for each line of the order.

The resulting structure of lifecycles, stages, tasks and subtasks constitutes an initial *process* model – a *dynamic* model – of the interactions between the outside world and the office. Just as for the data – the *static* – model, we will use a diagrammatic notation that is simple, but sufficient. It will allow us to represent the structuring of lifecycles into stages, and stages into tasks and subtasks.

Office Tasks

Tasks are the fundamental building blocks of business interactions. Because we are concerned to support the work of users in the office, we will look at everything that happens in terms of office tasks. When a customer pays an invoice by cheque, that is an event in the world outside the office. But we will be concerned with the tasks arising in the office – matching the cheque and payment advice against the invoice, posting the payment to the customer's account, writing to query any discrepancy, and so on.

In this section we discuss a three-dimensional categorization of office tasks.

Task initiative

There is, of course, an obvious and important difference between events caused or initiated by people and organizations in the outside world, and events caused or initiated in the office. We will categorize tasks in several ways. One important classification is according to how they are initiated. The initiation of a task determines essentially whether it must be waited for, and for how long. The categories are:

- *X-tasks* are eXternally initiated. Dealing with a cheque payment by a customer is an X-task, because the customer takes the initiative to make the payment. So is dealing with a policyholder's decision to surrender the policy. So is entering the information concerning a new order received from a customer. All X-tasks are associated with the arrival of some kind of input from the outside world, announcing the event (payment, policy surrender, order placing) that has occurred and must be dealt with by the office.
- *T-tasks* are initiated at a predetermined Time. The task of dealing with the arrival of the 65th birthday of pension client is a T-task. So is the task of dealing with the lapse of a 30-day cooling-off period in which a client who has bought an investment policy is permitted to revoke the purchase. So is the task of calculating the capital value of a policy on each anniversary of its commencement.
- *P-tasks* are initiated immediately following a Preceding task. If we separate – as we do – the task of validating the information entered for a new order from the task of its original data entry, then the validation task is a P-task. The task of writing a letter to a life assurance client's medical practitioner is a P-task following the task of checking the proposal. A P-task is initiated immediately after the preceding task has been performed, but is not necessarily performed immediately. There may be some delay because of the way work is scheduled in the office. But there is no constraint in the business interaction to prevent it from being performed immediately.
- *I-tasks* are initiated Internally, in the office. If it is decided that all customers who currently pay by cheque should be invited to change to payment by Direct Debit, then writing the letter of invitation may be an I-task. (Alternatively, it may be a P-task following the I-task of identifying the customer as one who currently pays by cheque.) I-tasks are not associated with the arrival of input to the office from the world outside, because they are not responses to individual events in the world.

Categorization by task initiative is only one dimension of our scheme. Every task must be in one of the initiative categories, and also in one of the performance and content categories described in the next two sections.

Task performance

A second important dimension of categorization is the distinction between a task that can be performed automatically, by the computer system, and a task that must by its nature involve a human user. The categories are simply:

- *A-tasks* are performed Automatically, by the computer system. For example, deciding to write a standard letter to a customer requesting payment of an overdue invoice may be an A-task. All the information necessary is in the database, and the credit manager may have decided that there is no discretion to be exercised. Subsequently, the formatting and printing of the letter can also be done entirely automatically, and it is therefore another A-task.

- *M-tasks* cannot be performed automatically. A prototypical M-task is the Mannal task of underwriting an unusual risk: that is, determining what premium is an appropriate price for covering the risk. Another M-task might be dealing with a request by a bank customer for a moratorium on interest payments on a loan. Human discretion is necessary to evaluate the circumstances and decide whether the request should be allowed.

An important concern in any office workflow system is to move tasks from the M-task to the A-task category. Underwriting the simplest standard cases can become an A-task, provided that the rules for those cases are well enough understood to be formalized in a computer program. As we shall see, a common pattern is to handle standard cases by an A-task, leaving the more difficult non-standard cases for a following M-task. The same pattern can be seen in many data entry tasks. Entering payment details from a direct-debit record (properly, acceptance of a direct-credit) delivered by an automated banking system is an A-task. Entering the same details from a cheque received in the post is an M-task.

The distinction we are making here, as in all the dimensions of our categorization, is made from the point of view of computer support of the work in the office. So it is important not to be misled by this last illustration. The question is not whether input for a task arrives automatically, but whether the system can deal with it automatically.

When we want to use both dimensions, we simply concatenate the category prefix letters. So we can speak of a task, for example, as an XA-task or a TM-task. Entering details of a direct-credit record is an XA-task. Dealing with the interest moratorium request is an XM-task.

Task content

The third dimension of task categorization concerns the content of the task: what it consists of, from the office point of view. We will recognize these five categories:

- *E-tasks* are data-Entry tasks. We define these to be the entry of new records into the database, rather than the updating of existing records. Given our view of the data model, which we base on the idea of entities, E-tasks are the entry of information about new entities. So the entry of the information for a new client or a new taxpayer or a new order or a new enrolment of an existing student on an existing course is an E-task.

- *K-tasks* are tasks that checK the consistency or completeness of the information in the database, or its conformity to business rules. A typical K-task is to check that the address entered for a new customer contains a valid postcode. As we shall see, there are good reasons to separate this checking task from the data entry task itself.
- *U-tasks* are tasks that Update the information in the database, but do not add new entities to the existing data model. So entering a client's change of address, and entering a revised quantity on an order line, are U-tasks. U-tasks do not involve decision making, whether automatic or manual. Essentially, they either update entity attributes that are variable by the outside world, or else correct errors or omissions of fixed attributes.
- *D-tasks* are tasks that consist essentially of making a Decision. An underwriting task is a D-task, and determining a taxpayer's PAYE tax code is a D-task. A D-task may be an A-task or an M-task. The result of a D-task may be to create or update information in the database: obviously, for example, the result of determining a taxpayer's PAYE tax code must include the update of the TaxCode attribute of the taxpayer's record. Some decisions will result in setting the value of an attribute fixed by the office – for example, deciding what withdrawal notice will be required on a new investment account.
- *O-tasks* are tasks that produce Output. Producing a policy document, printing a letter, generating a financial report, or creating a direct-credit output record for an automatic banking system, are all O-tasks.

Task simplicity

As before, the content categorization can be combined with the other dimensions. Here are three simple examples.

- Printing a standard demand for an overdue payment is a *TAO-task*. It is initiated at a predetermined time (ten days after the payment's due date); it is automated; and it produces output.
- Entering information for a new customer is an *XME-task*. It is initiated by the customer in the outside world; it is manual; and it creates a new customer entity record in the database.
- Deciding whether to allow a certain simple type of claim on a householder's contents insurance – for the theft of a camera or some similar insured article – is a *PMD-task*. It is initiated immediately following the preceding task of receiving the claim; it is manual, because it must be done by a user in the Claims department; and it is a decision task.

In each dimension, the categories are mutually exclusive and exhaustive. So each task can be categorized by giving its three prefix letters. The letters have been chosen so that no letter appears in more than one dimension, so it is permissible to give just one, or just two prefix letters if that is enough for the purpose in hand.

The scheme reflects the simplicity and small scale of each task. We want to keep the tasks small so that their management and scheduling will be as flexible as possible; so that task definitions will be reusable in more than one context; and so that we can generate as much as possible of the necessary computer programs by mechanized techniques.

Our general approach, then, is to avoid tasks that are even slightly complex, by breaking them into two or more simpler tasks. This does not mean that a user in the office must be faced with a plethora of tiny tasks. As we shall see when we come to consider the office workflow, separate tasks can, where appropriate, be combined into larger jobs. But in structuring business interactions into entity lifecycles we will build on a foundation of tasks that are very small and simple.

In the diagrams that we will draw for lifecycles, we will represent a task by an oval, with the task name written within the oval. If we wish to, we can add the task categorization after the task name, as shown in Figure 4.1.

Starting a Lifecycle

In this chapter we will be chiefly concerned with the structures of lifecycles, and with tasks as the ingredients from which lifecycles are built. Lifecycles are linked to entities, and tasks within lifecycles are linked to those same entities. For example, the task of underwriting a policy is a part of a lifecycle linked to that policy; the task of printing a request for overdue payment is a part of the lifecycle for the invoice; the task of deciding whether to allow a claim is a part of the lifecycle linked to that claim.

Freestanding tasks

Not all tasks are positioned within lifecycles. Some tasks are *freestanding*, outside lifecycles, and can occur at any time. This is true, especially, of some of the tasks that start new lifecycles. So, for example, the task of entering the information about a new CLIENT entity is not a part of any lifecycle. In particular, we will not regard it as a part of the lifecycle linked to the client, because the CLIENT entity does not exist in the database at the time the task falls to be performed: the whole point of the task is to create a new client, and to start off the client's lifecycle.

Figure 4.1   *A task.*

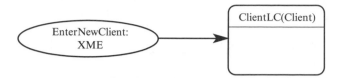

Figure 4.2 *A task starting a new lifecycle.*

The creation of the new lifecycle is shown in Figure 4.2. The lifecycle is represented by a rounded rectangle with a horizontal stripe. The name of the lifecycle is written in the stripe, with the name of the linked entity class in parentheses. The line from the task indicates that the task has an important effect on the lifecycle. The arrowhead indicates that the task starts the lifecycle (as we shall see, a task can also halt a lifecycle).

Data entry tasks

The pattern of a data entry XME-task starting a lifecycle is very common. It occurs whenever the enterprise starts a new business relationship with a person or organization in the world outside, or starts a new obligation within an existing business relationship. So it occurs for a new customer, a new policy, a new product, a new supplier, a new purchase order, a new sales order, and so on.

The data initially entered in the XME-task may well be incomplete, erroneous, or possibly just incorrectly entered. It is important in an office workflow system not to allow this incompleteness to hold up progress more than is absolutely necessary. So the definition of an XME-task should always be as permissive as possible, allowing work to proceed on the basis of whatever good information is available rather than waiting until all the data is perfect.

Checking the data entered is, therefore, not a prerequisite of starting the lifecycle, but rather one of the first tasks to be performed in the lifecycle. Anticipating the topic of a later section of this chapter, we can show the common pattern in Figure 4.3.

The first stage of the ClientLC lifecycle is concerned with tasks that check the data entered by the EnterNewClient task. As we will see later, the checking

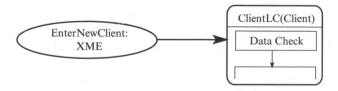

Figure 4.3 *A task starting a new lifecycle that checks the data entered.*

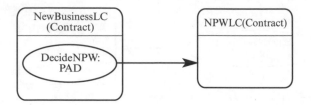

Figure 4.4   *A task within one lifecycle starting another lifecycle.*

can be separated into checks that must be passed immediately for any further progress to be possible, and checks that can be satisfied either immediately or at a later stage.

Starting a lifecycle from a lifecycle

New lifecycles can also be started by tasks within other lifecycles. Figure 4.4 shows a task within the NewBusiness lifecycle of a CONTRACT entity. The task starts an NPW (Not Proceeded With) lifecycle for the same contract.

There are many situations in which a task within one lifecycle must start another lifecycle. Usually, they are situations in which the expected normal progress of a lifecycle is broken or interrupted by an external event that causes a deviation from the main line of the interaction. In this case, the external event may be the repudiation of the contract by the prospective policyholder.

When we show a task starting (or halting) a lifecycle, as in Figure 4.4, we mean that it is possible for that task to start (or halt) that lifecycle, not that it will always do so. When we want to show the relationship between lifecycles without being specific about the tasks, we can represent the task as a small unnamed oval, as in Figure 4.5.

Lifecycles and Entities

Lifecycles are linked to entities. It's worth being a little more precise about this.

The descriptions we make in the data model are descriptions of entity *classes*. When we describe entity attributes and domains and types, we are

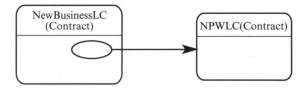

Figure 4.5   *An unnamed task starting a lifecycle.*

describing the classes of entities in the world. The world is populated by *individual* entities, and each individual entity belongs to – that is, it is an *instance* of – one entity class.

Similarly, the descriptions we will make of lifecycles in the process model are descriptions of classes of lifecycle. When we come to describe the structure of a lifecycle in terms of stages, and the structure of a stage in terms of tasks, we are describing the classes of lifecycle – of business interaction – there can be in the world. The task descriptions, of course, are similarly descriptions of task classes. What actually happens in the world is *individual* tasks, and structures of individual tasks composing individual lifecycles.

When we say that lifecycles are linked to entities, we mean two things. First, that each class of lifecycle is linked directly to just one entity class. The NPWLC class of lifecycle is linked only to entities of the contract class. And second, that each individual lifecycle is linked to an individual entity; there cannot be a lifecycle that is not linked to any entity. Naturally, the individual entity linked to an individual lifecycle must be of the entity class appropriate to the class of lifecycle.

Each individual entity may be involved in several lifecycles both consecutively and simultaneously. There must be at least one lifecycle concerned with the beginning of the entity's business existence. For example, the NewBusiness lifecycle is concerned with the beginning of a contract's existence. If the contract is not proceeded with, then the NPWLC lifecycle follows the NewBusiness lifecycle for the same contract.

Lifecycle versatility

In fact, it is too simple to say that each lifecycle class is linked to just one entity class. As we shall see in the next chapter, when we come to discuss some further aspects of the entity model, entity classes are more complex than we have so far acknowledged.

A lifecycle class may be more restricted or less restricted in its linking with entity classes. A *polymorphic* lifecycle class may be linked to more than one entity class – in the extreme case, with all entity classes. And a lifecycle class that is linked to an entity class – say, life policies – may in fact be linked only to a more restricted subclass – say, life policies adhering to a particular plan of payments and benefits. These ideas are closely related to ideas found in object-oriented development. In the method discussed here they are specifically adapted to the needs of workflow systems.

Multiple lifecycles for one entity

An important entity such as an insurance policy will be potentially involved in several overlapping lifecycles. For example, the client may be in the process of surrendering the policy at the same time as a premium is being paid, an endorsement is being added, a claim is being made, and the policy is in the course of an annual valuation. Some of these lifecycles are linked to the policy only indirectly. For example, the claim is probably a separate entity in its own right. Tasks in the claim lifecycle involve the policy because the claim is a claim on that policy: the claim entity has a Policy attribute that associates it with the policy entity. For the same reason, the claim lifecycle also involves the policyholder.

So although each individual lifecycle is linked to an individual entity, it may also involve other entities that are associated with the linked entity. We will return to this point later in this chapter.

Lifecycles and Stages

The large structure of a lifecycle is essentially a sequence of *stages*. In an office workflow system, the stages of an entity lifecycle are often roughly recognizable from the entity's journey through the office departments. Each stage represents a period of time in which the entity 'is in' a department, in an almost physical sense.

Sometimes the sense is definitely physical. If you take your car to the local distributor for a major service, the lifecycle describing what happens to the car may look something like Figure 4.6.

The first stage is Reception, in which the car is parked in the customer reception area. It then proceeds to the Servicing stage, being driven into the workshop where the service work takes place. Finally it is driven to the customer collection area for the booking out stage.

In the figure, the stages are represented as rectangles, and the sequence of the stages is represented by the connecting arrows. The stages are shown here inside the rounded rectangle that represents the whole lifecycle. When we know which lifecycle we are talking about, and are concerned only with the stages, we can omit the rounded rectangle and show only the stages and their connecting arrows.

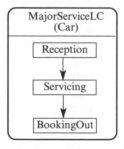

Figure 4.6   *Lifecycle for a 25,000 mile service.*

Stage sequencing

The stages of a lifecycle follow one another consecutively. The MajorServiceLC lifecycle always begins with the Reception stage. If the lifecycle is not prematurely halted, it proceeds from Reception to Servicing and from Servicing to BookingOut. A stage can never be omitted. So it is not possible to proceed from Reception to BookingOut without passing through the Servicing stage.

This sequencing is an important key to defining lifecycles and how they fit together. Suppose that we judge the stage sequencing of the MajorServiceLC lifecycle to be too restrictive. We want to say that a car can proceed straight from Reception to BookingOut. Then we should consider the following possibilities.

- In fact the car does always pass through the Servicing stage, but the task performed in that stage may be very simple for some cases. Perhaps it is no more than a visual check carried out by a fitter.
  - Our conclusion then is that the stage sequencing is correct. We were misled by the fact that the Servicing stage may be very small and simple.
- The car does not always pass through the Servicing stage because at the Reception stage it may be decided that Servicing is not appropriate. The car then passes straight to the BookingOut stage. The BookingOut stage is performed as normal, although it may be simpler because there has been no Servicing.
  - Our conclusion is that Servicing is a separate lifecycle in its own right. The relationship between MajorServiceLC and ServicingLC is shown in Figure 4.7.
- The car does not always pass through the Servicing stage because at the Reception stage it may be decided that the MajorScrviceLC lifecycle has failed. Perhaps, for examplc, the customer is refusing to pay the current charge for the service. In this case, neither the Servicing nor the BookingOut stages will be performed. Failure of a lifecycle in this kind of way requires no special notation, as we shall see later in this chapter.
  - If the failure is due to a cause that requires special procedures – say, the customer's credit card proves to be stolen – then we may conclude that those procedures constitute another lifecycle, as shown in Figure 4.8.

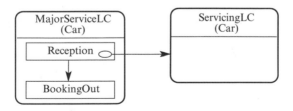

Figure 4.7   *Two lifecycles for a 25,000 mile service.*

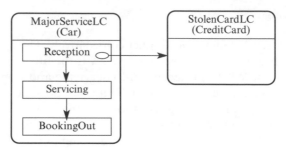

Figure 4.8   *Two lifecycles for a 25,000 mile service.*

Lifecycle states

If the service manager asks about the progress of a particular car brought in for servicing, the answer may be that it is 'in Reception', or 'in Servicing', or 'awaiting Booking Out'. These are states of the car with respect to the lifecycle in which it is involved. Or, looking at the same answers from the point of view of the lifecycle, they are states of the individual lifecycle linked to the particular car.

Once an individual lifecycle has been started, directly linked to an individual entity, there is always exactly one state that describes the progress that has been made so far in the lifecycle. We can think of these states chiefly as indicators of the place in the diagram of lifecycle stages where the entity is currently engaged.

As we shall see, it is sometimes possible for the lifecycle to proceed to a later stage although some tasks of an earlier stage are still incomplete. In the Major-ServiceLC lifecycle, the car may be transferred to the workshop while the customer is still discussing certain charging details with the receptionist. These details must be settled before BookingOut can begin, but they need not hold up the Servicing stage. The paper seat and floor covers, intended to protect the upholstery and carpets from workshop grease, are normally removed in the Servicing stage. But it is still possible to do this in the BookingOut stage, after the car leaves the workshop to proceed to the customer collection area.

States in relation to a stage

The effect of this partially simultaneous performance of some stages is that it may be necessary to pause in the lifecycle, waiting to start a later stage because a minor task of an earlier stage is not yet complete. We must also remember that a stage can fail, so terminating the lifecycle prematurely, and that a lifecycle can be halted.

So the states describing progress through a lifecycle can be:

- In StageN. StageN is currently being performed. StageN+1 has not yet been started. So the car might be in the state InReception, InServicing or InBookingOut.

- FailedStageN. StageN has failed, because some task in it has failed. No further activity will take place in this lifecycle. The car might be in the state FailedReception, FailedServicing or FailedBookingOut. Because a later stage can start while a minor task of an earlier stage is incomplete, it is possible, for example, that a car in the state FailedReception – perhaps because the car has been discovered to be stolen – had in fact already started its Servicing stage. It would then have gone from the state InServicing to the state FailedReception.
- AwaitingStageN. StageN cannot yet be started because some task from StageN–2 or from an earlier stage is not yet complete. The car might be in the state AwaitingBookingOut. It cannot ever be AwaitingReception, because when any lifecycle is started its first stage starts automatically. And it cannot be in the state AwaitingServicing, because if a Reception stage task is not yet complete the car would then simply be InReception.
- HaltedStageN. The lifecycle was halted while StageN was being performed.

An individual lifecycle, once it has started, is in exactly one such state at any time.

Lifecycles and Tasks

Within a single lifecycle stage the tasks can be performed in parallel. This means that there is no business interaction constraint that requires one task to be performed before another in the same stage. If there is such a constraint between two tasks, then they should not appear within the same stage: one should be in a later stage than the other.

We show this potential for parallel or simultaneous execution of tasks within a stage by representing them as disconnected ovals within the stage rectangle, as in Figure 4.9.

The tasks can be executed in parallel or simultaneously in the sense that there is no business requirement to perform one before another. The actual scheduling of their performance in any particular case will depend on practical considerations within the workshop. If there is only one fitter, then no doubt the tasks will be done consecutively, in some order that the fitter finds convenient. If there are two fitters, then perhaps one will do the ignition and engine while the other does the brakes and tyres.

The analogy with an office workflow system is quite exact. The office users are like the fitters. The order in which they perform the tasks in a lifecycle stage will depend on practical considerations of managing the office work conveniently and efficiently. These practical considerations will be the subject of a later chapter, when we come to consider the workflow aspect of the problem. For now we are considering only the business interaction aspects.

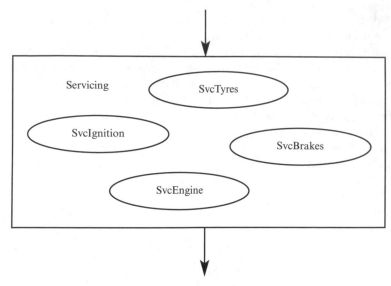

Figure 4.9   *Tasks in a lifecycle stage.*

Tasks and subtasks

The tasks we have been considering so far are *original tasks*. The original tasks of a lifecycle stage are all started when the stage is started, and they can all be performed in parallel.

In some cases a task may spawn a subtask. This will happen when the task is unable to complete its work and must delegate the completion. For example, consider the task of determining a taxpayer's tax code. For the simplest cases this may be an automatic decision; for a slightly more complex case it may require a manual decision; for a still more complex case it may require writing to the taxpayer for further information on which to base the decision. We regard the whole process as having the structure shown in Figure 4.10.

The original task is the AD-task EasyCode. If this task is performed and can decide the code according to the specified rules, that is the end of the matter. But if it determines that the code cannot be decided automatically, it spawns the MD-task HardCode.

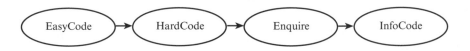

Figure 4.10   *Tasks spawning subtasks.*

The arrow connecting the two tasks shows that HardCode may be spawned by EasyCode *in some cases*: it does *not* mean that every EasyCode task will necessarily spawn a HardCode task. To find out which cases will involve HardCode and which can be settled finally by EasyCode we must examine the internal description of EasyCode. (The internal definition of tasks is discussed in a later chapter.)

Just as EasyCode may spawn HardCode, so HardCode in turn may spawn Enquire. Enquire is an automatic task which writes a letter to the taxpayer asking for further information as specified by the HardCode task. It always spawns the InfoCode task, which is an XMD-task: when the information is received from the taxpayer, a user in the office uses this information to decide the code. Figure 4.10 does *not* show that Enquire always spawns an InfoCode task: again, we must examine the internal description of the Enquire task.

We will say that HardCode is a *child* task of EasyCode, and the *parent* task of Enquire. Most tasks have only one parent task. We will also say that Easy-Code is an *original* task, and that all of the others are *derived* tasks.

Task states

Each task that could be performed in a lifecycle has a state. There are six possible task states. One is a null state; one is an initial state; and the other four are result states. The six states are as follows.

- *null* A task that has not been started – and perhaps may never be started – is in the *null* state.
- *start* When a lifecycle stage is started, all of its original tasks are started – that is, they are automatically placed in the *start* state. So when the Servicing stage of Figure 4.9 is started, all of the tasks SvcIgnition, SvcTyres, SvcBrakes and SvcEngine are placed in the *start* state. A task in the start state is ready to be performed as soon as possible by the system (if it is an automatic task) or by a user (if it is a manual task). If it is an X-task, depending on an event in the outside world, it will, of course, remain in the start state at least until the appropriate event occurs.
- *passed* A task that succeeds places itself in the *passed* state. So if the Easy-Code task finds that the code can be determined automatically according to the criteria, it does so and places itself in the *passed* state. A task in the passed state does not spawn any child tasks, so if EasyCode has passed then none of the other tasks shown in Figure 4.10 will be performed at all.
- *ran* A task that has been performed, but has not succeeded in carrying out the required action, places itself in the *ran* state. So if the EasyCode task finds that the tax code cannot be determined automatically according to the specified criteria, it places itself in the *ran* state. A task that has run – that is, has placed itself in the *ran* state – automatically spawns all of its child tasks. So when the EasyCode task has run, the HardCode task is spawned. That means that the HardCode task is automatically placed in the *start* state.

- *failed*   A task that has been performed, and has determined that the required action is impossible, places itself in the *failed* state. For example, a K-task (a checking task), may *fail* if the information found in the check does not satisfy the criterion against which it is being checked. It is appropriate for a task to fail only when the failure cannot be remedied within the current lifecycle. As we shall see, failure of a task causes failure of its stage and so of its lifecycle.

- *n/a*   A task places itself in the *n/a* (not applicable) state when it has determined that it is not applicable to the case in hand. For example, the SvcIgnition task in the Servicing stage of Figure 4.8 would prove to be not applicable if the car has an electric engine instead of an internal combustion engine. A task in the *n/a* state does not spawn any of its child tasks.

The possible state transitions of a task are shown in Figure 4.11. As the figure shows, a task that has reached one of the four states *n/a*, *ran*, *passed* or *failed* can make no further transition.

Relevant stage

As we saw in the case of the MajorServiceLC, a task belonging to one stage may not become critically important until a much later stage. Certain details of the arrangements for charging for the service are dealt with at the Reception stage – say, by a ChargeDetail task – but do not become critically important until the BookingOut stage. We will then say that the ChargeDetail task is *relevant* at the BookingOut stage. The BookingOut stage cannot begin until the ChargeDetail task has been successfully completed. This is the origin of a lifecycle state such as AwaitingBookingOut.

The stage at which a task is relevant may be specified independently for each task in each stage of a lifecycle. It makes no sense to specify that a task is relevant at its own stage, or at an earlier stage. And if no stage of relevance is specified it is assumed that the task is relevant at the next stage, the stage immediately following the stage to which it belongs.

The purpose of specifying a relevant stage for a task is to allow the lifecycle to proceed without waiting for a task whose performance has not yet become necessary to progress. Consider, for example, the task of obtaining a birth

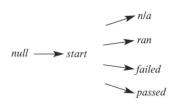

Figure 4.11   *Possible state transitions of a task.*

certificate for the LifeAssured in a life assurance policy. A BirthDate has already been given in the completed proposal form, so the assessment of risk can proceed on the basis of the date given. The birth certificate is needed as formal confirmation of the date, but it is not strictly needed until the point is reached at which the policy is about to be issued. At that point the assurance company must insist on seeing the formal evidence supporting the given date of birth, because it would be a serious commercial mistake to issue a policy on what could prove to be erroneous information.

Assigning tasks to stages

Why, then, not simply wait until the policy issue stage to set about obtaining the birth certificate? Once posed, the question answers itself. Obtaining the birth certificate may take some time, and it is sensible to start it as early as possible. It can then proceed in parallel with many of the other tasks that make up the lifecycle.

The basic principles, then, of assigning tasks to lifecycle stages are as follows.

- Each task should be placed as early as possible in the lifecycle: that means, as soon as its input information is available.
- Its relevant stage should be as late as possible in the lifecycle: that means, the latest that its output information output is needed.

An obvious application of the second principle is to the data checking tasks that follow a data entry task that starts a lifecycle. The checking should always be split into separate original tasks according to the stages at which the different parts of the checked data become absolutely necessary to further progress in the lifecycle.

By applying these two principles we can allow the maximum possible time for the completion of each task. However, there are two further considerations that should be taken into account.

- If a task is expensive to perform, it may be wise to delay it until it is definitely known to be necessary. This is why a wise house buyer does not instruct a lawyer until agreement has been reached with the seller.
- If the failure of a task will make it necessary to reverse the effects of some subsequent task, and that reversal is expensive, difficult or perhaps even impossible, it may be wise to make it relevant to the stage to which the subsequent task belongs. This is why an automatic cash machine does not count out the cash until the last stage in the transaction, after the card number, PIN code and bank account have been checked. Once the cash has been counted, even if it has not yet been dispensed to the customer, it cannot be returned to the store of notes available for subsequent transactions.

Task states and stage states

The lifecycle stage states are, naturally, determined chiefly by the task states. The determination is as follows.

- When the lifecycle is started, its state is InStage1.
- A lifecycle in the InStageN state remains in the InStageN state until one of the following situations holds of the task states:
  - Situation 1: Some task of the lifecycle, in StageN or an earlier stage, has reached the *failed* state.
  - Situation 2: No task of the lifecycle has reached the *failed* state; and every task of StageN that is in the *start* state is relevant to a stage later than StageN+1.
- From situation 1 (a task has failed) the lifecycle progresses to the state Failed-StageF, where the task that failed belongs to stageF.
- From situation 2 (all the starting tasks of stageN are relevant to a stage later than stageN+1) the lifecycle progresses either to the state In stageN+1 or to the state AwaitingStageN+1.
  - If any task from a stage earlier than stageN is in the *start* state and is relevant to stageN+1, the lifecycle is said to be *waiting for a task*, and progresses to AwaitingStageN+1.
  - If any lifecycle dependency (see 'Lifecycle stage interaction' later in this chapter) prevents stageN+1 from starting, the lifecycle is said to be *waiting for an external lifecycle*, and progresses to AwaitingStageN+1.
  - If the lifecycle is neither waiting for a task in one of its own stages, nor waiting for an external lifecycle, it progresses to the state In stageN+1.

This sounds more complicated than it really is. In fact, it corresponds well to a simple intuition about progression through a structure of partly parallel tasks.

Subtask Structures

Figure 4.10 showed a simple subtask structure in which the original task Easy-Code has one child task, HardCode; that in turn had one child task, and so on. If a task places itself in the *ran* state, its child tasks are automatically spawned: each of them is placed in the *start* state. The relationship between a parent and child task is not like the relationship between an assembly and one of its parts; it is more like the relationship between a runner in a relay race handing on the baton and a runner to whom it is handed. The child task is not in any sense a part of the parent: once the parent task has placed itself in the *ran* state, it is complete as a task, although the required work is not yet complete.

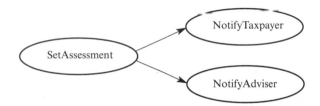

Figure 4.12 *Mutually independent child tasks.*

Independent child tasks

A task may spawn more than one child. The children of a task can be related to each other in either of two very different ways. Often, they will be mutually independent, just as the original tasks of a stage are mutually independent.

When the parent task places itself in the ran state, all the children are placed in the *start* state and progress from there as if they had been original tasks. This is illustrated in Figure 4.12.

When the SetAssessment task places itself in the *ran* state, both of its children are placed automatically in the *start* state, and will then be performed independently. If there are no failures, both of the tasks NotifyTaxpayer and NotifyAdviser will be performed.

Task selection groups

Sometimes, a certain group of tasks should be related to each other by a relationship of mutual exclusivity. Only one of the group can be performed. We will call such a group of tasks a *selection group*. The tasks in a selection group must all be child tasks of the same parent. A selection group is represented in Figure 4.13.

The parent task, SendContract, is an AO-task that sends a contract to a client. The client, by law, may cancel the contract at any time within the following 'cooling-off' period of 30 days. If the client does not cancel, then the office sends the client a confirmation of the contract. The SendContract task has two children: Wait30Days and ClientCancel. Wait30Days is a TA-task that effectively counts

Figure 4.13 *A selection group.*

down the cooling-off period and then spawns a child task to send a confirmation letter to the client; ClientCancel is an XM-task that receives the client's notice of cancellation. By placing the Wait30Days and ClientCancel tasks in a selection group we ensure that only one of them is performed.

The precise rule for tasks in a selection group is as follows. When the parent rule places itself in the *ran* state, all of the child tasks in the selection group are automatically placed in the *start* state. Then, as soon as one of them places itself in the *ran*, *failed* or *passed* state (but not the *n/a* state), all of the others are automatically placed in the *n/a* state. If one child task in the group places itself in the *n/a* state, the others are unaffected.

So when the SendContract task places itself in the *ran* state, both of the tasks Wait30Days and ClientCancel are automatically placed in the *start* state. Then:

- If the 30-day period runs out without the client exercising the right to cancel, the Wait30Days task places itself in the *ran* state. At this point the Client-Cancel task is still in the start state, and is now automatically placed in the *n/a* state. The SendConfirmation task is automatically placed in the *start* state.
- If the client cancels within the 30-day period, the ClientCancel task places itself in the *ran*, *failed* or *passed* state, according to its internal definition. At this point the Wait30Days task is still in the *start* state, and is now automatically placed in the *n/a* state. The SendConfirmation task remains in the *null* state, and is not performed.

Multiple parentage and task loops

A task may have more than one parent task. There are two kinds of common situation in which this is useful. First, the two parents may be independent but may both require a certain subtask. Consider, for example, an underwriting stage in a policy lifecycle in which a medical examination may be required either because of the proposer's age or because of the proposer's occupation. The subtask structure may be as shown in Figure 4.14.

Naturally, the purpose of this structure is to ensure that either or both of the CheckAge and CheckOccupation tasks can spawn a RequestMedical task; but

Figure 4.14   *A task with two parents.*

only one medical examination is to be requested. We handle this situation by specifying a maximum number of times that the RequestMedical task may be performed. In this case, the number is one. When a task is spawned, but has already been performed the maximum number of times, it is placed in the *n/a* state.

Another situation in which multiple parents are appropriate is in the construction of a task loop. One obvious case is the potential need to iterate over a sequence of two tasks: Correction and CheckCorrection. If the CheckCorrection task places itself in the *ran* state rather than the *passed* state, another iteration of the sequence is needed. Again we must specify a maximum number of times the Correction task may be performed. The subtask structure is as shown in Figure 4.15.

When CheckCorrection places itself in the *ran* state, a further instance of the Correction task is spawned.

An original task is not allowed to have any parents at all – having no parents is the distinguishing characteristic of an original task. So it cannot be in a loop.

Interacting Lifecycles

Although lifecycle classes are directly linked to entity classes, and individual lifecycles to individual entities, there are usually further associated entities involved. Lifecycles of associated entities are not completely independent: they interact with each other.

For example, progress through the lifecycle of a customer order entity affects, and is affected by, progress through the customer entity lifecycle. If the customer's credit is not good, the order may be refused. If the order is accepted and delivered, the customer's account balance is altered. The order entity also affects, and is affected by, progress through the lifecycles of its order-line entities. If the order is cancelled by the customer, then all of its lines must also be cancelled. If none of the line items is in stock, then no delivery can be made for the order. If one of the lines is cancelled, the value of the complete order is reduced.

Lifecycle stage interaction

Progress through one lifecycle may depend on progress through another. The method provides notations for specifying this kind of lifecycle interaction.

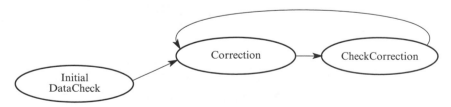

Figure 4.15   *A task with two parents.*

Consider, for example, the treatment of a customer order. It may go through the lifecycle stages of NewOrder, CreditCheck, StockCheck and Delivery. We will assume that the nature of the business is such that each order is for one item only, and that the Delivery stage includes picking the item from the warehouse as well as delivering it to the customer.

We must ensure that goods are delivered only to customers in good standing, whose credit is good. That means that we must not allow the order to progress to its Delivery stage unless the associated customer has reached the Customer-Activity stage. We can represent this interaction between the lifecycles as shown in Figure 4.16.

The arrow pointing from the CustomerActivity stage of the CustomerLC lifecycle to the connection between the StockCheck and Delivery stages of the OrderLC lifecycle represents a *lifecycle dependency*. The OrderLC lifecycle depends on the CustomerLC lifecycle. It cannot progress to the state InDelivery unless the CustomerLC lifecycle is either:

- in the InCustomerActivity state; or
- in the InStageX state, where stageX is a later stage in the CustomerLC lifecycle than the CustomerActivity stage; or
- in the AwaitingStageX state, where stageX is a later stage in the Customer-LC lifecycle than the CustomerActivity stage.

When an OrderLC lifecycle completes its StockCheck stage, but is unable to progress to its Delivery stage because it is waiting for the CustomerLC lifecycle, it enters its AwaitingDelivery state.

There may be, of course, many order entities associated with one customer entity. The dependency shown applies to each order entity separately. The direction of the dependency is important. In this example, we will say that the dependency is of the type *many-depend-on-one*. The progress of each order depends on the progress of the customer, but not vice versa.

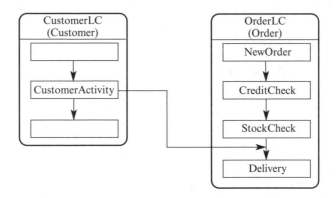

Figure 4.16   *A lifecycle dependency (many-depend-on-one).*

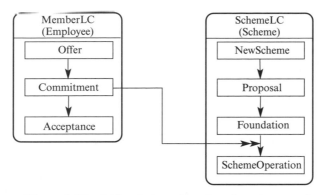

Figure 4.17   *A lifecycle dependency (one-depends-on-many).*

It is entirely possible that the CustomerLC lifecycle will fail while some OrderLC lifecycle is in the Delivery stage. This failure would prevent any further orders that had not yet reached their Delivery stage from doing so; but its effect, if any, on orders that had previously reached their Delivery stage would be handled by a task interaction.

A lifecycle dependency may be the other way around. It may be of the type *one-depends-on-many*. Consider, for example, a group pension scheme that can be established only if every employee of the company joins the scheme. Then the dependency may be as shown in Figure 4.17.

The double-headed arrow shows that this dependency is of the *one-depends-on-many* type. The lifecycle for one scheme depends on the lifecycles for many employees. In a *one-depends-on-many* dependency, the rule is that all of the many lifecycles must be in the appropriate state for the one lifecycle to progress.

So in this example, the SchemeLC lifecycle cannot progress to the state In-SchemeOperation unless every one of its associated MemberLC lifecycles is either:

- in the InAcceptance state; or
- in the InStageX state, where stageX is a later stage in the MemberLC life-cycle than the Acceptance stage; or
- in the AwaitingStageX state, where stageX is a later stage in the MemberLC lifecycle than the Acceptance stage.

When the SchemeLC lifecycle completes its Foundation stage, but is unable to progress to its SchemeOperation stage because it is waiting for one or more MemberLC lifecycles, it enters its AwaitingSchemeOperation state.

Lifecycle task interaction

A lifecycle can also interact with a task in another lifecycle. We have already seen how a task in one lifecycle can start another lifecycle. It is also possible for a task in one lifecycle to halt another lifecycle. An example is shown in Figure 4.18.

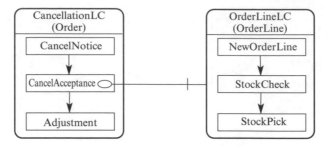

Figure 4.18   *A lifecycle task interaction.*

In this example an order has many lines, each of which has its own Order-LineLC lifecycle. It is possible for a customer to cancel an order, the cancellation being treated in the CancellationLC lifecycle. If the cancellation is accepted, the CancellationLC lifecycle progresses to its CancelAcceptance stage, in which one of the tasks halts all of the OrderLineLC lifecycles.

When a lifecycle is halted, no further task execution takes place in that lifecycle.

A less dramatic, but more common, interaction between a lifecycle and a task in another lifecycle is that a task may refer to the lifecycle states of entities associated with the entity to which it is directly linked. We will return to this subject when we discuss the definition of task detail in Chapter 6.

Chapter Summary

In this chapter we have begun to examine the dynamic behaviour of entity life-cycles and how they are defined.

- A lifecycle is structured as a sequence of stages. The stages in a lifecycle occur in a fixed order.
- A stage consists of tasks. Tasks are considered from the point of view of the users in the office, because the purpose of a workflow system is to support their work.
- Tasks may be classified according to the way they are initiated, according to whether they require human involvement or can be performed automatically, and according to their content.
- A lifecycle is started by a task, either a freestanding task or a task in another lifecycle.
- A lifecycle is linked to an entity, but may involve other associated entities.
- The state of an entity's progress through its lifecycle is defined in terms of the lifecycle stages. The possible states are: *in* a stage; *failed* at a stage; and *awaiting* a stage.
- Within a stage the original tasks are executed in parallel.

- A task may spawn further tasks, which are then executed either independently or, if they are in a selection group, by choosing only one of the group.
- A task may have more than one parent task. A maximum number of task performances may be specified for a task.
- One lifecycle may depend on another. One form of dependency is that a certain stage in one lifecycle may not be started until a certain stage of the other lifecycle has been reached. Another form of dependency is that a task in one lifecycle may halt another lifecycle, or may make a decision that depends on the state of another lifecycle.

Questions

4.1 Name the possible states of a task. What is the state of a task that has spawned subtasks?

4.2 A lifecycle has stages S1, S2 and S3. What are its possible states?

4.3 What is the state of a task that has been spawned but cannot be executed because it has already been performed the specified maximum number of times?

4.4 Sketch a lifecycle for the repair of a domestic appliance such as a washing machine.

4.5 A task selection group contains three tasks. What must their result states be when the whole group has been executed?

4.6 Task B is a child of task A. Describe three different circumstances in which task A is performed but task B is not performed.

4.7 In the Payment stage of a lifecycle for an invoice, the first task is to send out the invoice to the customer. Then one of three things may happen. The customer may pay within 14 days by automatic bank transfer; the customer may pay within 14 days by sending a cheque through the post; or the customer may fail to pay within 14 days. In the last case a LatePaymentLC lifecycle must be started. Sketch a possible task structure for the Payment stage, and show how it interacts with the LatePaymentLC lifecycle.

4.8 In chasing late payments, the first task is to send an initial letter. If no response is received in 10 days, a polite letter is then sent. If no response is received to the polite letter in another 10 days, another polite letter is sent. The process is repeated until no response has been received 10 days after sending the fourth polite letter. Then an angry letter is sent. Describe this task structure as a single lifecycle stage.

4.9   What is the definition of an *original task*? When is it started?

4.10 The process of making super coffee is as follows. The coffee beans must be placed in the grinder and ground; the water must be boiled; the milk must be heated; the ground coffee must be placed in the water in the jug, and allowed to settle; the filter plunger must be pushed down after the coffee grounds have settled; and the coffee poured into the cup first, followed by the milk. Describe this process in such a way that you allow the greatest possible parallel execution of the tasks.

CHAPTER 5

Further Entity Modelling

The basic entity model described in Chapter 3 was limited in a number of ways. Some of the limitations are fully acceptable for the specialized purposes of workflow systems. But some are not.

Further Topics

This chapter discusses further modelling ideas that overcome those limitations and give additional flexibility and power. That additional flexibility and power will be exploited when we come to discuss the detailed definition of tasks and lifecycles in Chapter 6 and the following chapters.

Entity classes

There are often important complexities in the relationships among *entity classes*. In the basic entity model we treat the entity classes as *disjoint*: that is, no entity can be a member of more than one class. However, we often need a more flexible and powerful class structure than this, in which we recognize at least one level of the *subclass* relationship. For example, we may want our model to include both a POLICY class and three subclasses: LIFE-POLICY, HEALTH-POLICY and PENSION-POLICY. A simple but effective technique of achieving the desired class relationships is explained and discussed in this chapter.

Entity roles

Another similar complexity arises from the fact that entities of the same class may play different *roles* in the outside world, and entities of different classes may play the same role. For example, we may define the two entity classes

PERSON and COMPANY. Entities of the different classes will have different attributes. But the entity that plays the role of SellingAgent for a POLICY may be either a PERSON or a COMPANY. The same problem arises in the other direction when we consider the entities that play the two different roles Life-Assured and Beneficiary in a LIFE-POLICY: both may be PERSON entities, but the model needed for a LifeAssured is different from the model needed for a Beneficiary. Again, in this chapter we discuss a simple but effective technique for dealing with this problem.

Datasets

We have already seen in Chapter 4 that entities of different classes may be related by shared or interdependent lifecycles. A task in which stock is picked for a line in a customer order may involve the customer, the order, the line and the product. Tasks in lifecycles, then, are associated not merely with individual entities, but with structures of related entities. In terms of the underlying database we may view these structures as *datasets* or *partial views*. Such a dataset consists typically of one or two *hierarchies* of database records that may be formed by the *join* operation of the relational database engine. In this chapter we will discuss how these datasets may be defined, and how their hierarchical structures may be represented both diagrammatically and textually.

Special attribute values

Finally, we will discuss the treatment of null attribute values, especially of association attributes, and other special values that are explicitly recognized in the method's approach to data modelling.

Entities and Classes

We base our data modelling on the concept of the individual *entity*. An individual entity is distinct from all other individual entities – that is what *individual* means. It has attributes – Name, Weight, Address, Owner, Price – that have particular values at particular times. It is involved in events that result in changes to its attribute values, but while the attribute values may change over time the entity persists in its distinct individuality.

   To see the world as populated by individual entities is fundamental to our view. Equally fundamental is to see those entities as members of entity *classes*. The members of an entity class are similar in ways that we recognize to be important for our purposes, and we want to treat them all in a consistent fashion. Concerts are for listening to; apples are for eating; and books are for reading.

We can put the same point the other way around. We place in the same class just those entities that we mean to treat in the same way. So in our entity model we may have such classes as customer, employee, client and supplier. We define those classes, and assign individuals to one of these classes, chiefly on the basis of the interactions of entities in the outside world with the office to support whose work we are making the model. When we define such entities as agreements, or policies, or orders, we are going even further. We are making the individual interaction itself into an entity. An entity class here is simply a class of similar interactions. The individuality of such an entity persists because something is fixed and unchanging in the agreement on which the interaction is based.

We classify entities, then, largely according to the interactions we expect to have with them. We define entity attributes for the class according to the information and properties that will be significant in that interaction. That is why DateOfBirth is an important attribute of an employee or a life assurance client but of no interest in the case of a mail-order company's suppliers.

Classification Entities

Unfortunately, a classification system can easily grow to encompass a huge number of classes and so become unworkable. This is especially true in the financial services industry, where competitive pressure requires the continual introduction of new products: new kinds of insurance policy, new investment schemes, new pension plans, new kinds of bank account. Each of these involves a different pattern of interaction with the customer or client, and seems to demand to be treated as a different entity class. But then the number of classes would grow beyond the point where the classification scheme is worth having. If almost every individual policy has its own unique pattern of interaction there is little point in considering it to be a member of a class. A classification scheme in which each class has only one member brings few benefits.

Classification hierarchies

The solution to the dilemma is to recognize that classes overlap. One individual entity may be a member of more than one class simultaneously. We may then consider a relationship among classes, according to whether a pair of entity classes does, or does not, have individual entities in common. A standard approach to this relationship, popularized by object-oriented programming languages, is to regard entity classes as arranged in a hierarchical structure. So, for example, we could arrange insurance policy classes in some structure like that shown in Figure 5.1.

Each class is a *subclass* of the class above it in the hierarchy, which is called its *superclass*. This means that every member of the subclass is also a member of

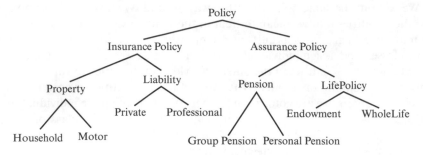

Figure 5.1   *Single inheritance.*

its superclass, and so on up to the top of the hierarchy. So every Motor policy is a Property policy; every Property policy is an Insurance policy; and every Insurance policy is a Policy. Similarly, every Group Pension is a Pension, every Pension is an Assurance policy, and so on.

This arrangement is called *single inheritance*. Inheritance, because each class *inherits* the properties of its superclass; and single, because each class has only a *single* superclass from which it inherits.

Multiple inheritance

A more flexible scheme is *multiple* inheritance, in which each class may have several superclasses. So, for example, we might decide that an important distinction to be made in our classification scheme is the distinction between group and personal policies. We made this distinction in Figure 5.1 in the case of Pensions, but we may decide that we need it also in the case of Household and Professional Liability and perhaps all other policies, and that Group and Personal should be explicitly recognized as policy classes.

Now the inheritance hierarchy will be more complex. A part of it is shown in Figure 5.2. The class of Group Household policies is a subclass both of the

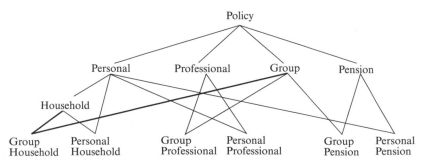

Figure 5.2   *Multiple inheritance.*

Household policy class and of the Group policy class. That is, every Group Household policy is a Household policy and it is also a Group policy.

Of course, we need not stop there. We may also want to classify policies as single premium or multiple premium, and multiple-premium policies as monthly or annual; and we may have Tax-Exempt and Taxable as classes. Potentially every further classification cuts across the classifications we already have, and further complicates the already complicated hierarchical structure as each class acquires more superclasses.

Classification entities

One way of looking at the situation of complicated class relationships is to recognize that there are many properties that an entity may possess, and that possession of one property is – to a considerable extent – independent of the possession of another. In the multiple inheritance scheme we are treating each property as a superclass of the class of entity that may possess it. So Tax-Exempt and Taxable, and Single-Premium and Multiple-Premium, and Group and Personal, and Private and Professional all become superclasses, and every different combination of inheritance gives a different entity class at the bottom of the hierarchy.

Instead of treating all of the properties in this way we can instead treat them as attributes of a *classification entity*. It works like this. We define an entity class which we may call PLAN. PLAN entities have attributes whose values correspond to the different groups of mutually exclusive superclasses. Tax-Exempt and Taxable are mutually exclusive superclasses of policy, so each plan entity will have an attribute TaxStatus whose values will be *tax-exempt* and *taxable*. Similarly Group and Personal are mutually exclusive, so each plan entity will have an attribute Membership whose values will be *group* and *personal*.

The individual entities of the PLAN entity class reflect the different plans. That is, they reflect the different combinations of properties that different individual policies may have. Each policy entity is then associated with a PLAN entity, as shown in Figure 5.3.

We call a plan a *classification* entity because each individual plan entity corresponds to a classification of policy entities – that is, to a subclass of the policy entity class.

Because an individual plan entity corresponds to a subclass of policies, not to an individual policy, there will in general be many policies associated with each plan. It follows that all the attributes that vary from one individual policy to another must still be associated with the policy entity. So, for example, if policies whose plan TaxStatus has the value *tax-exempt* must have a TaxExemptionCode attribute, then that attribute must be an attribute of the policy entity. It cannot be an attribute of the plan entity.

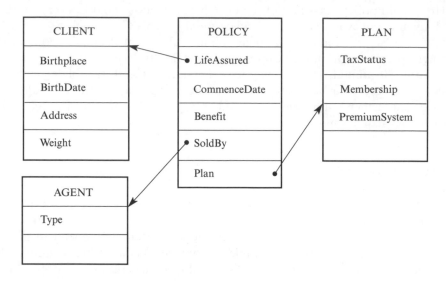

Figure 5.3   *An example of a classification entity class: PLAN.*

It is interesting to note that in Smalltalk, often regarded as the archetypal object-oriented programming language, object classes are themselves objects. So if a particular Smalltalk program has customer objects and supplier objects, then in addition to the individual customers and suppliers there will also be a customer class object and a supplier class object. Our classification entities are somewhat like these class objects.

Using classification entities

As we shall see in a later chapter, a central use of classification entities is in determining the appropriate lifecycle for an individual entity. We can define different lifecycles for different policy subclasses. Thus a tax-exempt policy may have a TaxAccountLC lifecycle that applies only to policies of that subclass; and a group policy may have a different lifecycle from a personal policy.

The classification entity may also play a part in the individual tasks within the entity's lifecycles. Just as the treatment of an order may depend on the attributes of the customer pointed at by the PlacedBy attribute of the order entity, so too the treatment of a policy may depend on the attributes of the plan pointed at by the Plan attribute of the policy entity. The plan entity is associated with the policy entity, and is therefore potentially involved in its lifecycles and in their constituent tasks.

Entity Classes and Roles

We are accustomed to the idea that a single individual person may play several roles in life: parent, manager, employee, householder, customer, amateur musician, investor. These roles may be played consecutively, but also simultaneously. We are also accustomed to the idea that a single class of role may be played by different classes of entity. For example, the role of *vehicle owner* for a motor car may be played by a person or by a company; and the role of *dwelling* may be played by a house or a boat or a caravan.

Exactly the same is true in almost any system, and certainly in any office workflow system. One entity may play more than one role, and the same role may be played by entities of different classes. We must be able to handle this variety conveniently.

Roles

The idea of a role is bound up with the idea of an interaction. An entity that is involved in an interaction is thereby playing a role. An order entity involved in an OrderLC lifecycle is playing the role of 'the order'. The customer entity involved in the OrderLC lifecycle of the order is playing the role of 'the entity that placed this order'. The client entity involved in the PolicyLC lifecycle of a policy for which the client is the life assured is playing the role of 'the life assured for this policy', while the same or another client is playing the role of 'the policyholder for this policy'.

The role of an entity that is only indirectly involved in a lifecycle or a task can be characterized by the attribute that points to it. So we would say that the customer entity is playing the PlacedBy role for the order, and that one client is playing the LifeAssured role for the policy and the other the PolicyHolder role. The case of the policy is illustrated in Figure 5.4.

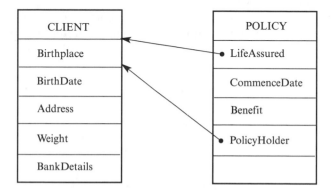

Figure 5.4 *Two roles for one entity class.*

The distinction between the two roles is not simply that the pointer attributes have different names. The distinction is rather that the entities playing the roles must satisfy different expectations. We expect – actually we will insist – that the policy must not be issued without the PolicyHolder supplying full bank details. It is essential to know that the premiums can be paid.

The LifeAssured, on the other hand, need not supply bank details. For the LifeAssured we will insist on details of the place and date of birth and the body weight. It is essential to know the age and body weight of the life assured, because they are important factors in determining life expectation and hence the risk. It is also essential to identify the person who is the life assured beyond any reasonable possibility of mistake; for that identification the person's birthplace and birth date must be known.

Explicit roles

At first sight it may appear that the natural consequence of these different expectations is to assign the different roles to different entity classes. Instead of a single class of client entities, we would then have two classes: a class of life assured entities and a class of policyholder entities.

But this will not do, because the two classes would not be disjoint. There is no reason why the policyholder on one policy should not be the life assured on another. The policyholder and the life assured will very often be the same person. By placing them in different classes we are making them different entities from the point of view of the system, and we will then have to go to a lot of trouble to overcome the difficulties that result. In particular:

- We will have to find some way of storing the fact that the apparently different entities are 'really' the same entity.
- We will have to accept the inefficiency of storing much of the information about the entity twice. For example, both a policyholder and a life assured have names and addresses.
- We will have to ensure that any changes to the stored information are consistent. For example, if the policyholder moves to a different address, then so does the life assured. But the office will surely receive only one notification of the change.

A better approach is to introduce the explicit idea of a *role* into the entity model.

In Figure 5.5 the arrows for the pointers are marked with role names. The role of the LifeAssured client is simply [life] and the role of the PolicyHolder client is [payer]. These names are arbitrary, but they have been chosen to reflect the expectations associated with the roles.

Role names are always written inside square brackets, to avoid any confusion with entity class names.

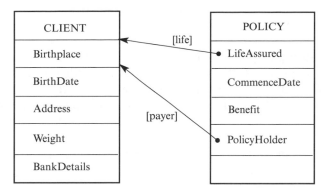

Figure 5.5   *Explicit role names.*

Role definitions

The significance of a role marking on the entity diagram is that it indicates the minimum subset of the entity attributes that must be present. We define this minimum subset in a *role definition*, which we express in a textual form. The role definitions for *life* and *payer* will look something like this:

```
[life] = {          {Name;
                     Birthplace;
                     BirthDate;
                     Weight};
         CLIENT {Name;
                     Birthplace;
                     BirthDate;
                     Weight};
         };
[payer] = {         {Name;
                     Address;
                     BankDetails};
         CLIENT {Name;
                     Address;
                     BankDetails};
         };
```

Each role definition is a selection of the attributes of the client entity class. The [life] role has four role attributes: Name, Birthplace, BirthDate and Weight; when the role is played by a client entity, these role attributes are respectively the client's attributes Name, Birthplace, BirthDate and Weight. The correspondence between each role attribute and the corresponding entity attribute is given by its place in the list. And similarly for the [payer] role. In this example the role attributes have the same names as the entity attributes. But this will not always be so, as we shall see later in this section.

Although in our example these roles are needed only for clients associated with policy entities, they may be needed elsewhere for clients associated with other entities. For example, the [payer] role may be needed in association with an investment bond. For an investment bond entity, the attribute that points to the [payer] is not the PolicyHolder attribute, but the Investor attribute. Roles may also be needed for entities in a context in which they are not associated with any other entity at all. For example, when a task is performed in a lifecycle directly linked to an entity, it will be appropriate to define a role for the entity that it plays in that task. This is why we do not simply call the roles by the names of the attributes that point to them.

Clearly, the values of the Name, Birthplace, BirthDate and Weight attributes must be available for any client who will be playing the [life] role, and the values of the Name, Address and BankDetails attributes must be available for any client who is playing the [payer] role. For a client who is playing both roles, whether for the same or for different policies, both sets of attributes must be available.

Floating roles

Although the [life] and [payer] roles of clients are not necessarily tied to the PolicyHolder and LifeAssured attributes, we have been thinking of them as tied to client entities. But a role need not be tied in this way to an entity class. It is perfectly possible for a role to be played by entities of different classes. We then call it a *floating role*.

Consider, for example, the SoldBy attribute of a policy entity. A policy is sold by some person or organization authorized to sell the policy and – since they will not usually do so without a financial incentive – to receive some commission on the sale. There may be many different people and organizations so authorized, and it may not be convenient or even possible to place them all in the same entity class. Figure 5.6 shows a part of an entity model in which the SoldBy attribute of a policy entity may point either to a broker or to an agent or to a salesperson.

The definition of a floating role is a little more complex than the definition of a tied role. We have to define the attributes required of the [seller] role in such a way that they can be recognized in any entity of any of the entity classes BROKER, SALESPERSON and AGENT.

In the example, let us suppose that the role attributes of the [seller] role are as follows.

• Name is the name by which the seller is known; for a salesperson or agent this is the Name attribute, and for a broker it is the CompanyName attribute.

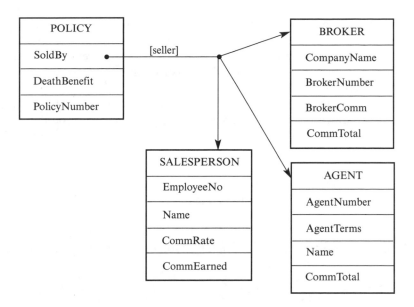

Figure 5.6   *A floating role.*

- PerCent is the percentage commission rate; for a salesperson this is the CommRate attribute; for an agent it is the AgentTerms attribute; and for a broker it is the BrokerComm attribute.
- Cumulative is the cumulative commission earned in the current calendar year. For a salesperson this is the CommEarned attribute; for a broker or agent it is the CommTotal attribute.

Then we can write the definition of the [seller] role like this:

```
[seller] = {         {Name;
                      PerCent;
                      Cumulative};
           BROKER{CompanyName;
                      BrokerComm;
                      CommTotal};
     SALESPERSON{Name;
                      CommRate;
                      CommEarned};
          AGENT{Name;
                      AgentTerms;
                      CommTotal};
          };
```

The role attributes do not always have the same names as the entity attributes. This allows the same role attribute to be provided by differently named entity attributes. So, for example, the role attribute PerCent is provided by the attributes BrokerComm, CommRate and AgentTerms in the different entities. This is an important freedom, because it allows us to name the attributes of one entity class independently of another.

But, of course, the entity attribute *domains* must be the same. That is, their values must be drawn from the same set, and represented by the same type in the database. So if the AgentTerms attribute of the agent entity is declared like this:

> AGENT = { ...
>   AgentTerms: *percentage*;
>   ... };

then the CommRate attribute of the salesperson entity must be declared like this:

> SALESPERSON = { ...
>   CommRate: *percentage*;
>   ... };

The domain of the role attribute PerCent is, of course, *percentage*. It is not necessary to specify domains for role attributes, because they must be the same as the corresponding entity attributes.

Role IDs

A role is essentially an entity. That is, a role class is a class of entities, and an individual role is an individual entity. The significance of roles is as follows:

- Role classes can cut across entity classes. A [seller] may be either a broker or a salesperson or an agent. A client may be a [life] or a [payer].
- Role attributes are a subset of the entity attributes. A [life] does not have a BankDetails attribute.
- Role attributes are renamed. Their names need not be the same as the corresponding entity attributes. The PerCent attribute of [seller] is the CommRate attribute of salesperson.

The relationships among the entity classes and role classes we have mentioned in this section are shown in Figure 5.7.

The entity classes policy, client, broker, agent and salesperson are *disjoint*: no individual entity can belong to more than one of these classes. Entity classes are always disjoint. (If in the real world an agent is also a client, the identity is

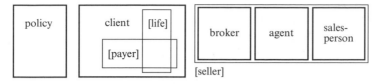

Figure 5.7 *Entity and role class relationships.*

ignored in the database.) The [payer] and [life] role classes are both subsets of the client entity class: every [payer] must be a client, and so must every [life]. The [payer] and [life] role classes intersect: a client may be both a [life] and a [payer]. But a client may be neither a [life] nor a [payer].

We have shown the broker, agent and salesperson entity classes as subsets of the [seller] role class. That is, every broker, every agent and every salesperson is a [seller]. In fact there may perhaps be brokers, agents or salespersons that are not [sellers], but we are assuming that this does not occur.

Unique role IDs

Because an individual role is an individual entity, it must have a hidden ID to identify it uniquely. That is, it must have the hidden ID of the individual entity that plays the role. Just as we do not declare the hidden ID in an entity declaration, or show it in an entity diagram, so we do not declare it in a role declaration.

Earlier in this book, in Chapter 4, we said that hidden IDs must be globally unique. That is, it is not enough that the hidden ID of an individual BROKER is different from the hidden ID of every other BROKER; it must also be different from the hidden ID of every SALESPERSON and every AGENT. The reason should now be clear. Since we cannot be completely sure which roles we may later want to define, we must make every hidden ID in the system different from every other.

Specifying roles in entity declarations

In Figures 5.5 and 5.6 we showed role names in entity diagrams. We must similarly be able to show role names in the textual form of entity declaration.

Because we have explicit role definitions, as discussed in the sections on 'Classification entities' and 'Using classification entities' above, it is straightforward to use role names, written in square brackets, in place of entity class names in entity declarations. So we would write part of the entity declarations for Figure 5.5 like this:

POLICY = {LifeAssured: [life];
              CommenceDate: *date*;
              Benefit: *money*;
              Policyholder: [payer];
              ... };

and for Figure 5.6 like this:

POLICY = {SoldBy: [seller];
              DeathBenefit: *money*;
              PolicyNumber: *policynum*;
              ... };

To determine the entity classes that may be pointed at by the association attributes LifeAssured, PolicyHolder and SoldBy, it is necessary to look at the role definitions for [life], [payer] and [seller] respectively.

Datasets

The performance of a task in a lifecycle involves the entity that is directly linked to the lifecycle. Usually it also involves other entities that are associated with the directly linked entity. To process a task we must assemble all the entities involved. The technique we use is to assemble them in a hierarchical structure.

Hierarchical structures

Consider the entity model shown in Figure 5.8. There are orders, which are placed by customers. Orders have order-lines, each order-line being for some quantity of some product.

Entities in this model might be involved in a lifecycle for a customer, for an order, for an order-line, or for a product. Depending on the starting point – that is, the directly linked entity – we can assemble the entities into four different hierarchical structures, shown schematically in Figure 5.9.

If we start with a CUSTOMER, as shown by the box marked C in structure (a) in Figure 5.9, we can proceed to add to the dataset all the ORDERS PlacedBy that customer. The box marked O* indicates that the orders are identified by their association with the customer, the star '*' indicating that there may be several of them. From each order we can add all the ORDER-LINEs that are a LineOf the order, represented by the box marked L*. Finally from each order-line we add the PRODUCT pointed at by the order-line's ForProduct attribute, as indicated by the box marked P. The last box, of course, is marked P and not P*, because there is only one PRODUCT entity associated with each ORDER-LINE entity.

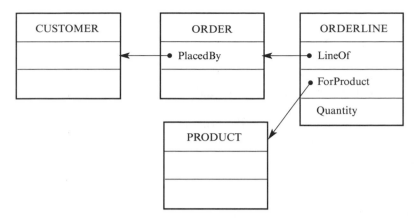

Figure 5.8 *Part of an entity model.*

The other three structures show the results of different starting points. For example, if we start with an order-line, as in structure (d), we can add the product associated with that order-line, and also the order associated with the order-line. From the order we can add the customer. Which of these four dataset structures will be needed will depend on the particular task we are concerned with.

To specify a dataset we specify an entity class from which the starting point is taken, and then we specify successive entity classes in the order in which they are to be added to the dataset.

Comparison with structured programming

The diagrams shown in Figure 5.9 look rather like the diagrams used in structured programming to represent data and program structures. But they are different in major ways.

- They are *navigation* structures, not *composition* structures. The 'children' of a 'parent' can be reached from the parent, and their children can be reached

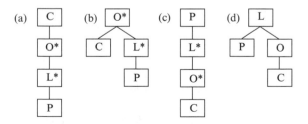

Figure 5.9 *Four dataset structures.*

from them, and so on. In diagram (a), for example, the relationship between the top two boxes is that the Os *can be reached from* the C, not that the Os are *parts of* the C.

- They do not express *sequence* in the structured programming sense. Two boxes in a navigation diagram that have the same parent are *independently* reachable: there is no presumption that the left box must be reached *before* the right box.
- They do not express *selection* in the structured programming sense. There is no way of saying that from X either Y is reachable or Z is reachable, but not both.

Nonetheless, once a dataset has been assembled by starting at the root and adding the records reachable from there and from records already reached, the resulting structure can be regarded as similar to a data structure in the structured programming sense. When treating it as a data structure in an environment associated with a typical database access and manipulation language, two points must be borne in mind.

- By using *cursors* it is possible to traverse the structure quite freely. The essential service provided by a cursor is to save the information that allows the traversal to return to the preceding record.
- Every box in the structure represents either one entity record or zero or more entity records. That is, the useful data is not only at the lowest-level boxes – the *leaves* – but everywhere in the structure.

A textual representation

We can write the structure of a dataset in a textual form, using numbers to indicate the levels of the structure. The four structures of Figure 5.9 would be written like this:

(a)	1 CUSTOMER	(b)	1 ORDER
	2 *ORDER		2 CUSTOMER
	3 *ORDER-LINE		2 *ORDER-LINE
	4 PRODUCT		3 PRODUCT
(c)	1 PRODUCT	(d)	1 ORDER-LINE
	2 *ORDER-LINE		2 PRODUCT
	3 ORDER		2 ORDER
	4 CUSTOMER		3 CUSTOMER

The rule for writing this textual representation is to write each higher-level node immediately before its first child at the next level, and to write the children of a node in order from left to right.

In reading the text, to find the parent node of a node at level N, scan the text upwards to the nearest node at level N–1. To find all the immediate children of a node at level N, scan the text downwards to all the nodes at level N+1, stopping at the next node at level N or at the end of the text.

Choosing a dataset for a task

The choice of a dataset appropriate to a task depends, of course, on the nature of the task. For example:

- To invoice a customer, use structure (a). It allows examination of all the orders for the customer, and all the order-lines for each order.
- Structure (a) may also be used for a task concerned with planning delivery to a customer. It allows delivery to be coordinated across all the order-lines and all the orders.
- For separate invoicing of a single order, use structure (b). It allows all the information about that order to be examined without considering other orders for the same products or other orders placed by the same customer.
- For picking a product to satisfy all current outstanding orders for the product, use structure (c). It allows all order-lines for that product to be examined, and the order and customer for each order-line. Irrelevant order-lines for other products are not considered, even if they appear in an otherwise relevant order.
- Structure (d) is less likely to be useful, because it presumes that an order-line can be a topic of interest in its own right, and can be accessed independently of the ordered product and the containing order. But it would be useful for answering a management query such as: 'What is the highest-value order-line awaiting picking?' or a customer query: 'What has happened to the widgets I ordered recently?'

To access a dataset some reference is needed to the root entity. The slight implausibility of structure (d) is closely related to the difficulty of finding a plausible user key for an ORDER-LINE entity. The hidden ID is not suitable for human use, and the order-lines may have no primary key. So access to the dataset is likely to be by identifying the customer, the order or the product. That would lead to using structure (a), (b) or (c).

Names, roles and pointers

The textual representation allows us to write more information into the structure in a convenient way. In particular, we can write the following.

- A *local name* for each node of the structure. We may want to use a local name when there is more than one node of the structure for the same entity class. We might, for example, have a structure like this:

        1 PERSON
        2 *PERSON

in which the level-1 node is any person entity, and the level-2 nodes are any persons for whom the level-1 person is the financial adviser. We would then want to use local names:

        1 ADVISER: PERSON
        2 *ADVICE-TAKER: PERSON

- A *role* for each node in the structure. In general the performance of a task will not involve all the attributes of an entity, and it will be appropriate to consider each node as involving an individual role rather than an individual entity. So we might write structure (b) as:

        1 MYORDER: ORDER [ord]
        2 THECUSTOMER: CUSTOMER [cust]
        3 *ALINE: ORDER-LINE [line]
        4 LINE-PRODUCT: PRODUCT [prod]

- A *link* for each node in the structure. Each node is associated with the node immediately above it in the structure; but this may not be enough to fix the particular pointer-valued attribute of the association. So in each linked node – that is, every node except the starting node at the top level – we write the name of the association attribute that links it to the node above it in the structure. This association attribute may be either in the linked node, or in the node at the level above. So we need two ways of writing it:

  - If the association attribute is in the linked node, we write it with a trailing '^' character, indicating that it points from this node to the level above.
  - If the pointer attribute is in the node at the level above, we write it with a leading '<' character, indicating that it points to this node.
  - So we might write structure (c) as:

        1 theproduct: PRODUCT [prod]
        2 *aline: ORDER-LINE [line] ForProduct^
        3 itsorder: ORDER [ord] <LineOf
        4 itscustomer: CUSTOMER [cust] <PlacedBy

A link must use the name by which the pointer attribute is known in the role in which it appears.

The provision for no fewer than three names – local name, entity class name and role name – in each line may seem cumbersome. It is not often necessary to use all of them. Names that are not needed may be omitted according to the following rules.

- It is always necessary to write either the entity class name, the role class name, or both.
- Where all the attributes of an entity are potentially involved – or where it is uneconomical to exclude those that are not —the role class name may be omitted. The effect is then the same as if the role class name were identical to the entity class name.

- Where the role is a tied role – that is, the role class is restricted to one entity class – and the role name is written, the entity class name may be omitted. The effect is then the same as if the entity class name were identical to the role class name.
- Local names may be omitted where there is no ambiguity. When the local name is omitted, the effect is the same as if the role class name were used as the local name.

The use of datasets in tasks is discussed further in the next chapter.

Null and Special Values

For reasons briefly introduced in Chapter 3, it may be necessary to provide for situations in which no value is available for some attribute in an entity record. For example:

- The correct value may be unknown. For example, a new employee's home telephone number or date of birth may not yet be known.
- Exceptionally, the attribute may be inapplicable to the entity concerned. For example, an employee who is a foreign national may have no National Insurance number.
- The data model may have treated an association as many-to-one or one-to-one that in fact it is many-to-one-or-zero or one-to-one-or-zero. In database terminology, it has treated as *mandatory* an association that in fact is only *optional*.
- The correct value may be 'anything you like'. For example, a decision table for discount may specify a percentage between 0.0 and 49.9 for the discount depending on quantity, product class and customer status. But if the customer status is *recent-delinquent* then the discount is 0.0 regardless of quantity and product class – quantity and product class can be 'anything you like'.

There is an obvious way of representing these *null values*. Simply use a value that has the correct format but cannot be a real value in the outside world. For example, an unknown telephone number could be given the value 000-0000, an unknown National Insurance Number could be XX-99-99-99-X, an unknown date could be 00/00/0000, and an unknown name could be 'NameUnknown'.

But this approach has some difficulties and dangers. It is often hard to find a value that can never be a real value. Choose £0.00 as the null value for the Price attribute of a product, and soon the company will offer a promotion in which some products are given away free.

Choose 'NONE' as the null value for a car registration plate, and you may suffer the fate of one city in the United States. The police in that city record the registration plates of parking offenders, obtain their addresses from the registration records, and send out notices of parking fines. If an illegally parked car has no registration plate, the police simply write 'NONE'.

Unfortunately, the state in which the city is located allows car owners to choose their own registration plates. One philosophically minded city-dweller chose the registration plate NONE. The philosopher duly received hundreds of parking violation notices, and was easily able to demonstrate to the court that they could not all be valid. The notices were duly cancelled.

Special key values

Standard relational database systems allow a special null value to be defined for each attribute of each entity. They usually stipulate that no null value may be defined for any attribute that is a key, or a part of a key.

The approach taken by the method described in this book is to regard only the automatically allocated hidden ID as a key attribute from the point of view of the database mechanism. So suitable null values may be freely defined – with appropriate care – for such attributes such as NationalInsuranceNumber, ClientNumber and PolicyNumber. The hidden IDs, however, are keys from every point of view, and must always have real values. There is therefore a need to provide real values for the cases in which the actual value of an ID is unknown or missing or otherwise unobtainable.

The solution is to use special values that appear to the underlying database system to be ordinary IDs, but point to records that have special significance in the data model. This is done by defining special entity records in every class that correspond to the required special values. There are special entity records with the following IDs.

- UNKNOWN. For example, any premium record whose policy has not yet been identified is a premium record for the POLICY entity UNKNOWN. This means literally that it is associated with that policy.
- NONE. In an employment data model, every employee reports to a manager. The Manager attribute of each EMPLOYEE entity record points to the record for the employee's manager. But the managing director has no manager. The Manager attribute of the managing director's employee record therefore points to the record for the EMPLOYEE entity NONE.
- ANY. In the database representation of the discount decision table, the ProductClass attribute in the rule about *recent-delinquent* customers points to the PRODUCT-CLASS entity ANY.

Notice that each one of the special entities must be present in every entity class. That is, it must have a corresponding record in every database table. The ID value for a special record, therefore, will vary according to what class of special entity it identifies. The attribute values for these special entity records must be carefully constructed. For example, pointer-valued attributes in a NONE record should themselves usually have the value NONE.

It may also be useful to provide special records for IRRELEVANT and ALL, if these are to be distinguished from ANY.

Chapter Summary

The simple view of entity classes used in the basic entity model is too simple to express everything we need. For several reasons we need to classify entities in more flexible ways. The classification techniques discussed in this chapter include:

- Using *classification entities*. Entities of a broad class, such as policies, can be classified in a finer-grain way by associating each entity with a classification entity that carries more information about its properties.
- An associated classification entity can be used to determine which lifecycle is appropriate for an entity.
- Entities of the same entity class can play different *roles*. The attributes necessary for each role are a subset of the attributes of the entity class.
- Roles can be written on the pointer arrows of an entity diagram, and can be explicitly defined in a textual *role declaration*.
- A role definition defines a subset of entity attributes, and renames them.
- The same role can be played by entities of different classes. The attribute subset drawn from the different entity classes must be consistent with respect to the attribute domains.
- A *dataset* is a hierarchical assemblage of entity roles involved in a task in a lifecycle. A dataset can be represented by a simple diagram, and declared in a textual form.
- Each node of a dataset is linked to its parent by a pointer-valued attribute either in the node itself or in the parent.
- Special ID values, including UNKNOWN, NONE and ANY, must be defined for association attributes. For ordinary attributes a special *null value* of the domain must be defined.

Questions

5.1   Write a dataset declaration suitable for a task in a lifecycle linked to a policy and involving the LifeAssured and the Policyholder of the policy.

5.2   Choose a suitable null value for the domain *money*. What would be the effect of using this value in typical operations on values of the domain – for example, in calculating interest? In calculating a price–earnings ratio, where the money value represents the earnings?

5.3   Draw an entity diagram showing that a CAR has one or more owners, each of whom may be a PERSON or a COMPANY.

5.4   Express the entity diagram of Question 5.3 as a set of entity declarations in textual form.

5.5   Drawn an entity diagram describing a dinner party. There is a host, a cook and some guests, all of whom are PEOPLE.

5.6   In your description of the dinner party in Question 5.5, is it possible for the host to be the cook? If not, why not?

5.7   In traversing the dataset structure (a) shown in Figure 5.9, zero or more lines (L*) can be reached from each of the zero or more orders (O*). Can the order be reached from a line? If so, how?

5.8   To calculate commission on a policy it is necessary to use a dataset derived from the entity diagram shown in Figure 5.6. Both the policy itself and the recipient of the commission must appear in the dataset. Write a textual representation of the dataset.

5.9   Consider the following dataset:

1 WHATSIT
2 THINGUMMY <Attrib
2 *GIZMO Link^
3 DOODAH Assoc^

In what entity declaration would you look for the association between a THINGUMMY and a WHATSIT? A THINGUMMY and a GIZMO? A GIZMO and a DOODAH?

5.10 Is there anything wrong with the following dataset?

1 GADGET
2 *FLANGE <Link

If so, what precisely is wrong? If not, draw an entity diagram from which it could have been derived.

CHAPTER 6

Tasks, Lifecycles and Programs

In Chapters 3 and 4 we discussed the basic entity and lifecycle models of the outside world and its interactions with the office. In Chapter 5 we returned to the entity model to explore further aspects, particularly some aspects concerned with relationships among entity classes and with additional data structuring techniques. Now in this chapter we return to the lifecycle model to look at it in more detail.

Progress Through a Lifecycle

In particular, we will discuss the way task outcomes affect progress through the lifecycle stages, especially where failure of a task leads to the premature termination or failure of an entity lifecycle. At a finer level of granularity, an error such as the inability to obtain a necessary piece of information can also lead to the failure of an entity lifecycle when the stage is reached at which the information becomes essential.

Error or failure may require that a lifecycle be set back to an earlier stage than it has already reached, and in this way frustrate the planned progression through the stages of the lifecycle. Because office workflow systems are not safety-critical, and because the business proceeds on an essentially human timescale in a series of human interactions, it is practical to provide for this kind of backtracking in lifecycles. But backtracking must be handled with care. The side-effects of tasks already executed must be carefully examined and appropriately dealt with according to whether they are beneficent, intolerable or neutral, and whether they are reversible or irreversible.

Programs for Tasks

We also discuss techniques for defining the properties and effects of individual tasks: that is, for defining the programs that are executed by the system when the tasks are performed. In defining programs we are often concerned with *common functions*, which are executed in many different programs, and with *common templates* – common patterns of program execution. These topics too are discussed in this chapter, using forms of the function invocations that are similar to the forms used in the LogicWare software environment.

The programs to be defined are very varied. Some are concerned with data input and the creation of a new entity record, with the accompanying initiation of a new lifecycle. Some embody business rules: for example, rules for calculating discount on a customer order, or rules for determining whether the information necessary for a policy has been correctly completed, or rules for determining eligibility for a particular kind of pension policy. Some produce output to be printed, such as a cheque in payment of a claim, or an invoice, or a letter requesting a policyholder to arrange a medical examination. Some handle mechanized or manual notifications of external events, such as bank payments in accordance with clients' direct debit instructions, or a customer's decision to cancel an order. Some respond to the arrival of regular time points, such as the end of a month; or to the end of a predetermined delay since a previous event – for example, the lapse of a notice period for cancelling acceptance of a policy.

The execution of these task programs fits into the system in many different ways. To some extent the possibilities are determined by the implementation environment: different operating systems and database management systems provide different facilities for program execution. The best choice for each program depends on the nature of the task for which the program is to be executed, and on the intended workflow in the system. Workflow is discussed in Chapter 7.

The Context and Content of a Task

Tasks are not performed in a vacuum. Each task is performed in a certain context, and it has a certain content, expressible in a program.

Task context

Consider the arrival in the office of a customer order. It is from a new customer, so the tasks that will have to be performed, in some sequence and at some time, may include the following.

- Entering the customer details to create a new CUSTOMER entity record in the database, and checking the data entered.
- Entering the order details to create new ORDER and ORDER-LINE entity records in the database, and checking the data entered.
- Checking the customer's credit.
- Pricing the order, including the calculation of any discount.

- Checking the stock position for the ordered products, and informing the customer about out-of-stock items.
- Delivering the order.
- Sending an invoice to the customer and chasing the payment if it is late.

The performance of these tasks, and their effects, will be governed by a number of constraints and rules.

- *Task initiative constraints.* For example, an X-task is externally initiated: that is, the initiative must come from the outside world. The task of entering the order details is an X-task: it cannot be performed unless and until a customer places an order. Similarly, a T-task is initiated at a predetermined time. The task of checking, and if necessary chasing, the invoice payment cannot be performed until an appropriate time has elapsed after the invoice was sent.
- *Lifecycle constraints.* Each task that is not freestanding is positioned in a stage of a lifecycle. It can be performed only when the appropriate stage of the lifecycle is reached. So, for example, there may be a lifecycle constraint that order pricing is not performed until the customer's credit has been checked.
- *Lifecycle effects.* Each task will have some effect on one or more lifecycles. For example, the task of entering the customer details will start a new customer lifecycle; if the credit check task fails it may cause the order lifecycle to terminate.
- *Workflow constraints.* In a business where each order is of relatively low value, the tasks of entering and checking the customer data may be combined with each other and also with the task of entering the order details. In a business where each order is of very high value, the entry of new customer details and the entry of order details may be the responsibility of different workgroups in different departments.
- *Workflow support.* The task of entering an order-line will involve the entry of a product code or identifier. The user performing this task may need support in the form of help, visible on the screen, in finding the user key for the product.
- *Workflow manual constraints.* An M-task is not performed automatically, but involves interaction between the system and a user in the office. The task of pricing a non-standard or very high-value order may require the attention of a user expert in such sales, and cannot be performed until a qualified user is available and willing to undertake it.
- *Dataset context.* Order pricing cannot be performed in the context of the order and its order-lines alone. The price for each line will certainly depend on the price of the product, and the discount will probably depend on the attributes of the customer. This task must therefore be performed in a context in which the current dataset includes the PRODUCT entity record for each line and the CUSTOMER entity record for the order.
- *Data interactions.* Each task interacts with the data in the database. Some tasks create new records; some only read and check existing records; some

update records by setting new values for their attributes. Each task must be able to refer to the relevant data; for example, the task that checks the stock position for each order-line must be able to refer to the PRODUCT entity record for the product ordered.

- *Business rules*. The calculation of the net order price will depend on the discount allowed, and this will depend on the business rules governing discounts. For example, it may be that no discounts are allowed to new customers, or on certain products, or that discounts vary according to product quantity ordered. The rules may be relatively simple, or they may be extremely complicated.

Program functions

The program executed in the computer for each task must combine and give effect to all of these considerations. In this chapter we will examine some of these considerations, and some of the program elements – the program functions – that contribute to the program for the task.

The program aspects concerned with the task initiative and workflow constraints and with workflow support will be postponed to the next chapter. That means that we will not be considering here such matters as the combination of different tasks into one piece of work for a user; nor the combination of tasks into one batch job for the computer.

In this chapter we will discuss the elements of individual tasks, regarded as program functions. We will be concerned with the functions associated with the lifecycle constraints and effects; with the dataset context; with the data interactions; and with the business rules. Where necessary, we will also describe some of the important considerations involved in the use of these functions.

(It is worth noting that the word *function* is used in mathematics with a very specific and precise meaning. To say that $F(x)$ is a function of x means that for each value of x, $F(x)$ defines exactly one value. If the defined value is always an integer, we would say that $F(x)$ is an integer function of x; if it is always a date, we would say that $F(x)$ is a date function of x, and so on. Here we are using the word function in a much looser sense. We just mean any piece of program that can be thought of as a unit and used in the program for a task.)

Function descriptions

In describing a function to be used in tasks we are describing only fragments of the system's functionality. This fragment must be set in its proper context according to the nature of the task itself and the constraints imposed by lifecycle definitions and workflow scheduling.

So a function description is always incomplete, in the sense that we are not describing fully the context in which it will be performed. This incompleteness is not a disadvantage. On the contrary, it is a considerable advantage, because it allows us to exploit what is common among different tasks, describing the common aspects only once although they apply to many tasks in many lifecycles.

In the rest of this chapter, therefore, it should be borne in mind that we are always describing what will often – even usually – be the common ingredients of many different tasks, and the common considerations that govern their description.

Tasks and Lifecycles

The execution of tasks determines the progression through entity lifecycles. A lifecycle can be affected by the results of its own tasks and also by explicit operations in tasks of other linked lifecycles. In this section we will discuss how these results and operations are specified by functions invoked in the detailed description of a task.

Task Results

As we saw in an earlier chapter, when a task is performed it can place itself in any one of four result states.

- *passed*   The task has been successfully completed, and none of its child tasks – if it has any – will be performed.
- *ran*   The task has been performed, but it is still necessary for its child tasks to be performed to complete the required action.
- *failed*   The task has been performed, but did not succeed. Its child tasks will not be performed, and the lifecycle in which it appears has now failed at the stage containing the task.
- *n/a*   The task was started, but it was determined that the task is not applicable to the individual lifecycle in which it occurred. The child tasks will not be performed, and the lifecycle in which it appears is unaffected by the task.

If a task is in a task selection group, then it will automatically be placed in the *n/a* result state as soon as any other task in the group places itself in any one of the result states *passed*, *ran* and *failed*.

A task places itself in a result state by executing the *result function*. We may write the function invocation in the conventional way:

SET_RESULT (*"failed"*) ;

and so on. There is, of course, no need to specify which task is to be placed in the specified result state: it is necessarily the task in which the function invocation occurs.

Starting a lifecycle

A task may cause a new lifecycle to be started for an existing entity – that is, for an entity for which there is already a record in the database. Again, this is done by executing a function:

START_LC (*entityclass, id, lcname*) ;

The parameters of the function are the entity class and the hidden ID of the individual entity for which the lifecycle is to be started, and the name of the lifecycle.

Strictly, it is not necessary to specify the entity class. The hidden ID of an entity is distinct from the hidden ID of every other entity, so it identifies the individual entity uniquely. However, requiring the entity class also to be specified in the parameter list provides some useful redundancy and allows a more efficient implementation.

The lifecycle name *lcname* in the function parameters specifies a *family of lifecycle classes* rather than just one particular lifecycle class.

Lifecycle families and controlling influences

As we discussed in the preceding chapter, classification entities may be used to achieve a more flexible scheme of entity classification. For example, instead of making a hierarchical structure of subclasses of the policy entity class, we may define plan as a classification entity class. Each policy entity has a Plan attribute, which is a pointer to its associated plan entity. The plan entity contains details of the rules by which one of the policy subclasses is governed. The treatment of the policy entity will then depend in a number of respects on the values of its associated plan's attributes; the plan entity may form a part of the entity dataset for many of the tasks in lifecycles linked to policy entities.

Where there is a *family of lifecycles*, the particular lifecycle started for a policy is controlled by an attribute value of its associated plan. For example, the plan entity may have an attribute PremiumSystem. The value of this attribute may be:

- '*dd*'   the premiums are paid by direct debit; or
- '*ap*'   the premiums are paid automatically from the benefits of an associated policy.

The particular lifecycle to be started for an individual policy when another premium is due may depend on the value of this attribute. We would then specify two different lifecycles, both named 'CollectPremium'. In the description of the CollectPremium lifecycle that handles direct debit premiums we would specify the following.

- The entity to which this lifecycle is directly linked is always a POLICY entity.
- The *controlling influence* for this lifecycle is the PLAN entity pointed at by the Plan attribute of the policy.
- The *determining attribute* in the controlling influence is the PremiumSystem attribute.
- The *determining value* of the determining attribute is 'dd'.

In the description of the other CollectPremium lifecycle, which handles collection from the benefits of an associated policy, we would specify the following.

- The entity to which this lifecycle is directly linked is always a POLICY entity.
- The *controlling influence* for this lifecycle is the PLAN entity pointed at by the Plan attribute of the policy.
- The *determining attribute* in the controlling influence is the PremiumSystem attribute.
- The *determining value* of the determining attribute is 'ap'.

So the function invocation:

START_LC ("policy", 1234, "CollectPremium") ;

will start the appropriate CollectPremium lifecycle according to whether the PLAN entity associated with policy 1234 has the value '*ap*' or the value '*dd*' for its PremiumSystem attribute.

Suspending a lifecycle

In some situations it is appropriate for a task to suspend an entity lifecycle. For example, if the holder of a policy applies to surrender the policy, then any current premium collection lifecycle should be suspended. Since the surrender may, in the event, not take place, it is also necessary to be able to resume the suspended lifecycle.

A lifecycle is suspended by execution of a function:

SUSPEND_LC (*entityclass, id, lcname*) ;

The lifecycle suspended is whichever lifecycle of the lifecycle family whose name is specified in the *lcname* parameter is currently active for the entity specified by the *entityclass* and *id* parameters.

When a lifecycle is suspended, no further tasks are performed until the lifecycle is resumed. A lifecycle is resumed by execution of the function:

RESUME_LC (*entityclass, id, lcname*) ;

If an entity is in state InStageN or AwaitingStageN with respect to a lifecycle, and that lifecycle is then suspended, the suspended state is SuspendedInStageN or SuspendedAwaitingStageN respectively. A lifecycle that has already failed cannot be suspended. When a suspended lifecycle is resumed, the state is restored to the state before suspension.

Cancelling a lifecycle

A lifecycle that is active, or has been suspended, may be cancelled. For example, on the death of the life assured, an active premium collection lifecycle must be cancelled rather than merely suspended.

A lifecycle is cancelled by execution of the function:

CANCEL_LC (*entityclass, id, lcname*) ;

When a lifecycle is cancelled, no further tasks of that lifecycle can be performed. The state of an entity with respect to a cancelled lifecycle is CancelledAtStageN, where before the suspension it was in state InStageN or in state AwaitingStageN–1. A lifecycle that has already failed cannot be cancelled.

Setting back a lifecycle

In some situations it is necessary to set a lifecycle back to a stage that it has already passed. This is most likely to happen where progress has been made through the lifecycle on an assumption that subsequently proves to be mistaken.

Consider, for example, a NewBusiness lifecycle for a life insurance policy in which the date of birth of the life assured was wrongly stated at data entry – perhaps by an honest mistake. When the birth certificate is subsequently obtained, the error is revealed. However, the ObtainBirthCertificate task may be relevant to a much later stage than the stage at which the original error was made. So the stages at which underwriting and premium calculation tasks are performed may be already completed by the time the correct information is known.

If the error in the date of birth is significant, it will be necessary to set back the NewBusiness lifecycle at least to the underwriting stage. It is necessary to recalculate the risk and the consequent premiums in the light of the corrected information. This can be done by executing the function:

SETBACK_LC (*entityclass, id, lcname, stage*) ;

in which the entity class and hidden ID and lifecycle family name are specified as before, and the stage parameter specifies the stage to which the lifecycle is to be set back. So for our NewBusiness example, the appropriate function invocation may be:

SETBACK_LC ("policy", 1234, "NewBusiness", "Underwriting") ;

The effect of executing the setback is as follows.

- All the original tasks in the Underwriting stage of the NewBusiness lifecycle for policy entity 1234 are placed in the *start* state.
- The policy entity 1234 is placed in the InUnderwriting state with respect to its NewBusiness lifecycle.
- Any tasks in stages after Underwriting are returned to the *null* state.

The general effect, then, is as if the lifecycle had never progressed beyond the point at which the Underwriting stage was started. However, there are many provisos that modify this general effect. They are the subject of the next section.

Backtracking

What is happening when a lifecycle is set back is often called *backtracking*. Some progress along a path has been made, and it has now become necessary to backtrack over that progress and start again from an earlier point.

Ideally, we would like the whole world to return to the state it was in when that earlier point was first reached, so that we can start again cleanly. Unfortunately, this is not in general easy to achieve, and we must pay careful attention to the difficulties that arise.

Side-effects

The difficulties centre around the *side-effects* of the stages so far completed. When a task is performed, it has a number of effects in the system, in the office, and in the outside world. These are its side-effects. For example:

- The value of an entity record attribute in the database has been updated. For example, the automatic underwriting task has set the value of the policy attribute RiskClass to *normal*.
- The performance of the task has been included in a summary report used by the office management. For example, there may be a monthly report on the proportion of risks underwritten in the *normal* class in the current year.
- An output has been produced and sent out to the outside world. For example, a letter has been written to a prospective life assured asking for a medical report. Or a cheque has been paid to a policyholder in response to a claim.
- Another lifecycle has been started, suspended or cancelled for the same or a linked entity.

Obviously, if we mean to return to an earlier stage in a lifecycle we must at least consider the side-effects of completed tasks, and what, if anything, we should do about them.

Classifying side-effects

We can classify side-effects into three classes.

- *Intolerable* An intolerable side-effect is one that must be somehow reversed or undone. If money has been paid to a policyholder in respect of a claim that subsequently proves to be unfounded or in some way inadmissible, the money must be recovered. If an incorrect value has been given to the Birth-Date attribute of a life assured, then that value must be removed and the correct value substituted.
- *Beneficent* A beneficent side-effect is one that should not be undone, because it would only require to be done again, producing exactly the same result. Suppose, for example, that in the NewBusiness lifecycle the task ObtainMedicalReport has been performed. This is a task in the Underwriting stage. Suppose also that the lifecycle must now be setback to the beginning of the Underwriting stage. However, repeating the task would be pointless: there is nothing wrong with the medical report that has already been obtained. A repetition of the task would simply produce the same result again.
- *Neutral* A neutral side-effect is one that is neither intolerable nor beneficent. For example, the erroneous calculation in the management report is a neutral side-effect. The calculated proportion is shown in the report only to two significant figures, that is, to the nearest 1 percent; it is regarded by management as background information only, and no decision is based on it; and it will be automatically corrected in the next report. No good has been done by the side-effect; but no real harm, either.

The appropriate treatment of each class of side-effect in setback is obvious. The intolerable side-effects must be undone. The beneficent side-effects should be preserved if possible. And the neutral side-effects may be either undone or preserved, whichever is more convenient.

Avoiding the intolerable

Unfortunately, handling side-effects is not always easy. The serious difficulties centre around the intolerable side-effects. Some intolerable side-effects simply cannot be undone.

Consider, for example, the CardUsage lifecycle of an Automatic Teller Machine. One of the tasks in this lifecycle is the dispensation of cash: notes are counted and dispensed through a slot to the customer. Cash dispensation is simply not reversible: the money once dispensed cannot be recovered. In a similar fashion, the side-effect of a task in an insurance policy lifecycle in which the policy document is sent to the policyholder is not reversible. If the premium has been paid, and the policyholder is in possession of the document, then the insurance company is on risk.

The point in both of these cases is that the reversal cannot be guaranteed. The ATM could display a message asking the customer to return the money by post or by inserting it into a slot provided for the purpose. The insurance company could write to the policyholder asking for the return of the policy document. In many cases, no doubt, an honest customer would comply; but there would be many in which a dishonest customer would prefer to take advantage of the error.

We must therefore design lifecycles so that intolerable and irreversible side-effects are not created. The latest point at which the setback could occur must precede the earliest point at which the intolerable irreversible side-effect could occur.

Of course, not all intolerable side-effects are irreversible. Entry of an erroneous value for the BirthDate attribute is intolerable; but it is easily reversed by substituting the correct for the incorrect value. An erroneous updating of an account balance is easily corrected by a compensating entry. If necessary, the compensating entry can be made by a manual task in which the human user determines the size of the compensation. For example, a bank error in a current account may give rise to all kinds of secondary charges for interest, for unauthorized overdraft, and so on. The necessary correction can most probably be judged better by a user than it can be calculated by the program for an automatic task. The bank simply needs a CompensationEntry task, and appropriate users authorized to perform it.

Task repetition

When the performance of a task is regarded as a neutral side-effect, it may be acceptable to allow the task to be repeated when the lifecycle is set back. But if the side-effect is regarded as beneficent, it will often be necessary to ensure that it is not repeated.

For example, in the case mentioned earlier, in which an erroneous date of birth causes set back of the NewBusiness lifecycle, the task ObtainMedicalReport produces a beneficent side-effect. It is therefore appropriate to ensure that the task is not repeated. This can be done directly in the lifecycle definition, by specifying that the maximum number of repetitions of this task is 1.

Backtracking lifecycles

In some cases it will be necessary to devise a special lifecycle, devoted to the purpose of identifying all the side-effects that have occurred since the point to which it is necessary to backtrack, and handling them appropriately.

Such a lifecycle will often need to make use of special techniques for handling side-effects. In particular:

- The retention in the database of historical information, along with details of the dates between which it was current. For example, a customer who complains in June about a faulty product purchased in January may expect a refund of the price paid and the supply of a sound replacement at the price that would have been paid in January.
- Provision and performance of special manual tasks to correct errors. These will often be decision tasks (D-tasks). For example, the manager of a bank must decide how to compensate an angry customer who has lost financially by the bank's erroneous failure to pay a cheque for which there were in fact sufficient funds in the account.
- Provision and performance of special automatic compensating tasks that calculate adjustments inverse to the adjustments made by intolerable side-effects. Sometimes this will be easier or commercially more acceptable than restoring an earlier state and recalculating forwards from there.

The first of these techniques – the retention of historical information – is especially important, and we will return to it in a later chapter on the subject of database implementation.

The shape of a lifecycle devoted to backtracking will often be rather like the shape of the original lifecycle over which backtracking is required, but in the reverse order. If the original lifecycle has stages StageA, StageB and StageC, in that order, the backtracking lifecycle will have stages StageCX, StageBX and StageAX, in that order, where each stage handles the side-effects of the correspondingly named stage in the original lifecycle. The reason, of course, is that if A, B and C have been performed in that order, then the required backtracking is to undo C, undo B and undo A, in that order.

Dataset Context of a Task

Entity datasets

In Chapter 5 we discussed the idea and structuring of datasets for tasks in a lifecycle. The example we used there is shown here again in Figure 6.1.

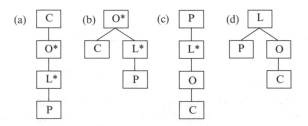

Figure 6.1   *Four dataset structures.*

Recall that these different hierarchical structures represent four different ways in which a customer entity (C), its orders (O), the order-lines (L) and the entities for the product (P) ordered in each order-line could be assembled into a dataset.

Each task in a lifecycle involving some or all of these entities is performed in the context of all or part of one of these dataset structures. For example, a task that calculates the price of the order must be performed in the context of dataset (a) or dataset (b). The task must have access to all the order-lines of the order, and the product ordered in each order-line, so that it can multiply the product prices by the quantities; and it must have access to the customer so that it can apply the discount rules that may depend on agreements made with the customer.

The contexts of datasets (c) and (d) will not do, because they do not make available all the order-lines of one order. The dataset (c) is concerned only with all the order-lines – whichever order they may belong to – in which a particular product P is ordered; and the dataset (d) is concerned with only one order-line.

Specifying datasets for tasks

The task is associated with one of the nodes of the dataset. For example, a task that calculates the price of an order is associated with an O node. The price can be calculated either in dataset (a) or in dataset (b), but the calculation must be associated with the single O node of (b) or with one of the O nodes of (a).

The dataset associated with a task can be thought of as a partial *view* of the database, and can be given a name. Using the full descriptive notation of the previous chapter, we might define the datasets (a) and (b) like this:

```
CustOrd = { 1 thecustomer: CUSTOMER [cust]
            2 *anorder: ORDER [ord] PlacedBy^
            3 *aline: ORDER-LINE [line] LineOf^
            4 theproduct: PRODUCT [prod] <ForProduct };
OrdCust = { 1 theorder: ORDER [ord]
            2 itscustomer: CUSTOMER [cust] <PlacedBy
            2 *aline: ORDER-LINE [line] LineOf^
            3 lineproduct: PRODUCT [prod] <ForProduct };
```

We could associate the order pricing task with either of these datsets. In the program for the task we would then refer to the entities in the datasets by their local names within the dataset. For example, in a task using the CustOrd dataset we could refer to *thecustomer*, to *anorder*, and so on. If the same task used the OrdCust dataset we could refer to *theorder*, to *itscustomer*, and so on.

Dataset independence

However, although both of these dataset definitions are perfectly satisfactory in themselves, and both offer the necessary access to entity data required by the pricing task, we should definitely choose the OrdCust dataset.

One execution of the pricing task is associated with one order node, and with other nodes that can be reached from there directly or indirectly – that is, with the customer and order-lines reachable from the order, and the products reachable from the order-lines.

The rule, then, is that we should choose the OrdCust dataset. We choose it because it has the natural root node for the task as its dataset root node. This does not mean that the task cannot be performed in the context of the CustOrd dataset. In the CustOrd dataset there are potentially many orders to be considered, but clearly the order pricing task can be initiated from any one of those order node instances.

Having chosen the OrdCust dataset as the dataset for the pricing task, we can quite easily detect, whether by human analysis or by a computer program, that the task can also be executed in the context of the CustOrd dataset. The necessary reasoning is as follows.

- The root node of OrdCust is the order node *theorder*. There is an order node (**anorder*) in CustOrd, that we may take as the starting point there.
- The CUSTOMER entity node *itscustomer* in OrdCust is found by following the PlacedBy pointer in the ORDER entity record; the customer node *thecustomer* in CustOrd is found in the same way.
- The order-lines and their associate PRODUCT entity records specified in OrdCust are similarly accessible in CustOrd.

Notice that the local names of the nodes are different in the two datasets. In CustOrd the CUSTOMER entity has the local name *thecustomer*; in OrdCust it has the local name *itscustomer*.

Data Interactions

Attribute references

In defining the program for a task we will need to refer to dataset entities, and to attributes of those entities. A reference to an attribute is written using a dot notation similar to the notation we used to refer to components of dataset domains in Chapter 3. So we may refer to:

itscustomer.InvoiceAddress.postcode

or to:

PRODUCT.UnitPrice

We should try always to use names that are as independent as possible of the associated dataset, provided that we avoid introducing ambiguity. The purpose, of course, is to make our data references fit into any feasible dataset context in which the task could be performed.

This means that we should use entity names in preference to role names when the role is played only by entities of the named entity class. So if only CUSTOMER entities can play the role [cust], we should refer to CUSTOMER and its attributes in preference to [cust] and its attributes. Of course, if the [cust] role could also be played by PURCHASER entities, it will be absolutely necessary to refer to the role name and to the role attributes.

We should also use entity names or role names in preference to local names. Local names should be used only when they are necessary to avoid ambiguity. This will be so only when the dataset contains two entity records of the same entity class, accessed by different pointer attributes. So, for example, in the dataset:

Policy = { 1 POLICY
           2 assuredlife: CLIENT <LifeAssured
           2 holder: CLIENT <PolicyHolder };

the local names assuredlife and holder are necessary because no distinct roles have (presumably) been declared in the entity model by which the two CLIENT entities in the dataset could be distinguished.

Defined attributes

The entity records and entity attributes in the database provide information about the outside world and about the history of the business interactions between the office and the people and organizations in the outside world. From the BirthDate attribute of a client a user in the office knows when the client was born; from the DeathBenefit attribute of a policy the user knows what the company has agreed to pay in the event of the death of the life assured; from the Quantity attribute of an order-line the user knows how many of the product the customer has ordered; from the RiskClass attribute of a non-standard policy the user knows what the underwriter has decided.

All of this information will be needed in later tasks, and none of it can be guessed or calculated. The attribute values must be explicitly provided by users and by people in the outside world so that they can be entered into the database. It all depends on observation and on the gathering of information in the world. We may call these attributes *observed* attributes, because ultimately they depend on observation.

There is another kind of attribute that we may also wish to store in the database. These are *defined* attributes. Their values are defined in terms of other attributes, and depend on observation only indirectly – only because those other attributes are observed attributes. Here are some examples of defined attributes.

- AgeNextBirthday of a client. Defined in terms of BirthDate of the client and TodaysDate.
- GrossPrice of an order-line. Defined in terms of Quantity of the order-line and UnitPrice of the product pointed at by the ForProduct attribute of the order-line.
- PoliciesHeld of a client. Defined as the number of policy entities in which the CLIENT entity is pointed at by the Policyholder attribute.
- ExpectedQuantityOnHand of a product. Defined as the cumulative total of the quantity received into inventory less the cumulative total of the quantity issued from inventory.

It is important to distinguish between observed and defined attributes. Defined attributes convey no information about the world beyond what is conveyed by the observed attributes in terms of which they are defined. The defined product attribute ExpectedQuantityOnHand, for example, does not provide information about how many of the product are now in stock. For that information it is necessary to visit the warehouse and count the products: that would give the value of an observed attribute that we might call CurrentProductCount. Probably it will be different from the value of ExpectedQuantityOnHand. Some of the stock may have been spoiled and some stolen.

Attribute definitions

To make defined attributes available for use in tasks, we must provide their definitions and decide how and when their values are to be calculated in accordance with those definitions.

There are essentially two strategies for definition. Either the value is calculated only when it is required; or it is calculated once, stored in the database, and recalculated whenever it changes. Here is an example of each.

- AgeNextBirthday of a client should be calculated whenever it is required. It is defined in terms of TodaysDate and BirthDate as follows:

AgeNextBirthday =
  IF (TodaysDate.month > BirthDate.month OR
    (TodaysDate.month = BirthDate.month AND
     TodaysDate.day $\geq$ BirthDate.day))
  THEN (1 + TodaysDate.year – BirthDate.year)
  ELSE   (TodaysDate.year – BirthDate.year)

- PoliciesHeld of a client is set to 0 when the client data is entered: this is the initial calculation. Subsequently it is incremented by 1 whenever a new policy is established for the client, and decremented by 1 whenever a policy held by the client is terminated.

The database mechanism may provide means for entering and using these definitions. Where it does not, the calculations can be treated as functions to be added to all the appropriate tasks.

Implicit state attributes

The possible states of an entity with respect to each lifecycle in which it can be involved are defined in the lifecycle definitions. They are directly accessible as the values of implicit attributes of the entity. The name of such an attribute is the name of the lifecycle, and its values are the values discussed in Chapter 4.

So, for example, if each car entity has a MajorServiceLC lifecycle, with stages Reception, Servicing and BookingOut, then implicitly each car entity has an attribute whose name is MajorServiceLC. The possible values of this attribute are '*InReception*', '*FailedReception*', '*AwaitingServicing*', and so on. There is an additional value '*null*', which is the value of the attribute for any car that is not currently involved in a MajorServiceLC lifecycle.

Rules and Functions

Some task elements are so simple that they can be captured completely in a single rule – that is, in a single statement. Such rules are worth recognizing as a category in their own right, because they can be used in many different tasks and introduced by suitable software into the texts of the programs for those tasks.

Wait rules

A common form of task is to wait for a stipulated period of time. For example, after providing a customer with full details of a contract, providers of financial services are legally obliged to allow the customer 30 days in which the contract may be reconsidered, and at the customer's absolute discretion, cancelled. Invoices usually allow a period at the end of which payment must be made; if no payment arrives, a structure of chasing tasks is begun.

Waiting may be conveniently regarded as a task to be performed. Usually it is in a task selection group with the customer action that may, or should, occur within the waiting period. Figure 6.2 shows such a task selection group.

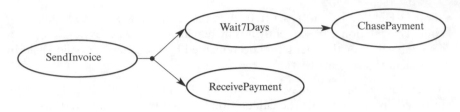

Figure 6.2   *A task selection group.*

Recall from Chapter 4 that if the ReceivePayment task is performed before the Wait7Days task, then the selection group has been executed. The Wait7Days task result will then be automatically set to *n/a* – non-applicable – and the ChasePayment task will not be executed. But if the Wait7Days task completes before ReceivePayment, then the ReceivePayment task result is automatically set to *n/a*, and the ChasePayment task will be performed.

For the Wait7Days task the rule specification is completely straightforward. We need write no more than

WAIT_DAYS (7) ;

to achieve a full description of the task. Notice that no dataset is required for this task element. It can be performed in any context, its connections to other tasks being specified entirely in the lifecycle definition in which it appears.

It is implicit in the WAIT_DAYS function that at the end of the waiting period the task result is set to *ran*, thus ensuring that any child tasks, such as ChasePayment in our example, will be spawned and performed next.

Check rules

Some tasks apply checks to the attributes of one or more entity records. Usually these are K-tasks (that is, checking tasks). Often the checks to be made will appear in many different tasks in many different lifecycles, and can be thought of as implementing standard rules of the business.

In the simplest cases, a check rule can be defined as an invocation of the function:

SIMPLE_CHECK (*attribute1, relation, attribute2, failurestate*) ;

For example, to check for a certain kind of life policy that the LifeAssured is at least 18 years old:

SIMPLE_CHECK ([life].AgeNextBirthday, ">", 18, "*failed*");

This invocation specifies that if the check fails the result state of the task in which it occurs is to be set to *failed*. Alternatively we could specify that an error record is to be created:

SIMPLE_CHECK ([life].AgeNextBirthday, ">", 18, "*ran*") ;

The error record is created by a task spawned by the task containing the check rule when it places itself in the *ran* state.

More complex checking can be done by defining a logical structure using the logical connectives AND and OR, and referring to that structure in a different function invocation. For example:

Pensionable = ((([life].AgeNextBirthday, ">", 65 AND
       [life].Gender, "=", "*male*")
    OR ([life].AgeNextBirthday, ">", 60 AND
       [life].Gender, "=", "*female*"));

COMPLEX_CHECK (Pensionable, "*failed*") ;

Set rules

Some simple business rules demand that particular values be given to certain attributes. For example, it may be a rule of the business that for a certain class of order payment is always required in seven days. In the appropriate stage of the lifecycle for an order of that class the rule can be enforced by a task that invokes a simple SET function:

SIMPLE_SET ([order].PaymentTerms, 7) ;

Following the patters of SIMPLE_CHECK and COMPLEX_CHECK, we may also have a more complex version for use when the value to be set is the result of a calculation from other attribute values rather than a simple constant.

Rule applicability

The applicability of a rule – or, more correctly, of a complete task – can be specified by the APPLICABLE_WHEN function. This function has a similar syntax to the SIMPLE_CHECK and COMPLEX_CHECK functions. For example, we might write:

APPLICABLE_WHEN ([life].AgeNextBirthday, ">", 18) ;

or:

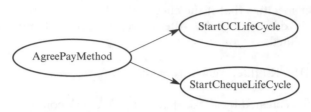

Figure 6.3   *Alternative tasks.*

Pensionable = ((([life].AgeNextBirthday, ">", 65 AND
                [life].Gender, "=", "*male*")
        OR ([life].AgeNextBirthday, ">", 60 AND
                [life].Gender, "=", "*female*"));

APPLICABLE_WHEN (Pensionable) ;

The meaning of this function is that if the check fails – that is, if the [life] is not at least 18 years old, or is not of Pensionable age – then the task result state of the whole task in which the invocation appears is automatically set to *n/a*.

Because rule applicability governs a complete task it cannot be used to choose between different parts of the same task. However, it can be used to choose between two alternative tasks without placing them in a task selection group. Figure 6.3 shows a simple structure of tasks.

The task AgreePayMethod sets an attribute PayMethod in an ORDER entity record to '*cc*' or to '*cheque*', indicating whether the customer wishes to pay for the order by credit card or by cheque. The task StartCCLifeCycle is defined as:

APPLICABLE_WHEN (ORDER.PayMethod, "=", "*dd*");
START_LC (..., ..., CCPayment) ;

and the task StartChequeLifeCycle as:

APPLICABLE_WHEN (ORDER.PayMethod, "=", "*cheque*");
START_LC (..., ..., ChequePayment) ;

After the AgreePayMethod task has placed itself in the *ran* state, both of the tasks StartCCLifeCycle and StartChequeLifeCycle are automatically placed in the *start* state. Both will be performed, but one of them will place itself in the *n/a* state when the APPLICABLE_WHEN function finds that it is not applicable.

The advantage of treating this kind of problem in this kind of way is, of course, that each of the two tasks StartCCLifeCycle and StartChequeLifeCycle is entirely independent of the other and of any additional alternatives that may be introduced later.

Output functions

Some tasks produce output that is highly standard. For example, form letters are of this kind. In an insurance company there are many letters, such as letters requesting a client to attend a medical examination, or asking for the production of a birth certificate, that recur in many tasks in many lifecycles. It is convenient to regard the extraction of the variable information for such letters as a common function.

Other output functions produce reports for use in the office. These functions can usually be programmed – or just simply defined – using the facilities of the database system. A report production task will be a TXO-task or an IMO-task.

Decision Tables

Sometimes a business rule is very complicated, depending on many different possible values of several attributes. For example, the discount applicable to an order-line may depend on the ProductGroup attribute of the product ordered, the Quantity attribute of the order-line, and the CustomerClass attribute of the customer. Often it is convenient to handle this kind of complexity by making a *decision table*, in which the different combinations of attribute values and the different results of calculation are laid out in a grid.

An example

Suppose first that we distinguish only two values of each attribute. The ProductGroup attribute has the values '*A*' and '*B*'. The Quantity attribute has a range of integer values, but in the discount calculation we will distinguish only '< 50' and '≥ 50'. The CustomerClass attribute has the values '*Major*' and '*Minor*'. The possible values of the resulting percentage discount are 0, 5 and 10. Then the decision table may be as shown in Figure 6.4.

Each column of the table represents a rule. For example, the rule represented in the first column is:

CustomerClass	Major	Major	Major	Major	Minor	Minor	Minor	Minor
ProductGroup	A	A	B	B	A	A	B	B
Quantity	<50	≥50	<50	≥50	<50	≥50	<50	≥50
Discount%	0	10	5	10	0	5	0	5

Figure 6.4 *A decision table.*

"An order by a Major customer for a product in ProductGroup A in a quantity of less than 50 receives a discount of 0%".

The advantage of a decision table is that the discount for any possible case can be found by checking the case against the rules until the rule that fits is found. There must always be exactly one rule that fits the case, because every rule is different, and there is a rule for every possible combination of values.

How many rules?

In the table shown in Figure 6.4, there are exactly eight rules because there are three attributes each having two values. There must be a rule for each possible combination of attribute values, and that means $2 \times 2 \times 2$ rules.

Eight rules is quite a manageable number, but we might have had three attributes with six, nine and seven rules. That would have meant $6 \times 9 \times 7$, or 378 rules. It would be impossible to show the table on one piece of paper, and much of the advantage of the decision table technique would be lost.

Indifference

A real business would probably not have 378 rules for allowable discount percentage. Probably they would have a much smaller number of rules, some of which would be very general rules, some would be more specific, and some would just be there to cover particular exception cases.

For example, the rules might be like this:

- Rule (a) The standard discount is 2%.
- Rule (b) There is no discount on orders of quantities less than 50.
- Rule (c) Major customers are allowed 10% discount on order quantities of 50 or more.
- Rule (d) The XYZ Company (customer number 1463) is allowed 7% on all orders of products in ProductGroup B.
- Rule (e) Minor customers are allowed 5% on orders of 50 or more of products in ProductGroup A.

We can represent these rules in another decision table. Figure 6.5 shows the table.

It differs from the table in Figure 6.4. It has an additional customer attribute (CustomerNumber) to cater for rule (d). The rule identifiers are shown at the heads of the corresponding columns.

The '–' entries indicate that the value of the attribute in that row is not relevant to the rule represented by that column. The rule is *indifferent* to the value of the attribute. All the rules are indifferent to the value of the CustomerNumber except rule (d).

	(a)	(b)	(c)	(d)	(e)
CustomerClass	–	–	Major	–	Minor
ProductGroup	–	–	–	B	A
Quantity	–	<50	≥50	–	≥50
CustomerNumber	–	–	–	1463	–
Discount %	2	0	10	7	5

Figure 6.5 *Another decision table.*

Rule overlap and precedence

This table clearly presents a difficulty. The difficulty is that the rules overlap: they are not mutually exclusive, as they were in the table shown in Figure 6.4. Every case comes under rule (a), which is indifferent to the values of all attributes. If the XYZ Company orders 45 of a product in ProductGroup B, that case will come under both rule (b) and rule (d).

The difficulty is resolved by recognizing that the rules are intended to be applied in a certain order of precedence. Rule (a), the standard discount rule, is to be applied only when no other rule is applicable. Rule (d) takes precedence over every other rule. But these are particular precedences for this particular table.

We can express the general principles of rule precedence in decision tables by considering the order of the attribute rows and the distinction between an indifferent entry ('–') and a specific entry (not '–'). The principles are then:

- Principle 1: Two rules x and y have equal precedence if in every attribute row either x and y both have specific entries or x and y both have indifferent entries.
- Principle 2: Rule x takes precedence over rule y if:
  - Principle 1 does not apply; and
  - the highest attribute row in which one rule has a specific entry and the other does not has a specific entry in rule x.

Applying these principles to the table in Figure 6.5, we can rearrange the attribute rows to satisfy Principle 2. The attribute row for customerNumber must be at the top, because Rule (d) must take precedence. The order of the remaining rows does not matter, because whatever their order Rule (a) will have the lowest precedence, and the other three rules, (e), (c) and (b), are mutually exclusive.

Now we may also rearrange the rule columns to show the precedence, so that the rules of higher precedence are on the left of the rules with lower precedence. (The rearrangement of rule columns does not affect the formal determination of precedence, but it makes the table easier to read.)

The resulting arrangement of the decision table is shown in Figure 6.6.

	(d)	(e)	(c)	(b)	(a)
CustomerNo	1463	–	–	–	–
CustomerClass	–	Minor	Major	–	–
ProductGroup	B	A	–	–	–
Quantity	–	⩾50	⩾50	<50	–
Discount %	7	5	10	0	2

Figure 6.6   *Arranging rows and rules in precedence order.*

To apply the decision to a particular case, we apply the leftmost rule whose entries are satisfied by the values in the case. This scheme embodies the intuitive recognition that more specific rules are exceptions to more general rules, and should therefore be applied in preference wherever possible.

A warning

The indifference and precedence scheme described here usually works well. But it relies absolutely on a certain assumption. This is that whenever two rules are applicable to the same particular case, one of them takes precedence over the other, allowing us to determine which rule to apply.

This requires that the specific entries for each attribute are mutually exclusive. If we allow overlapping specific entries – for example, both '< *50*' and '> *45*' as entries in the Quantity attribute row – we may be unable to determine the precedence between two rules in which they appear. Both may be applicable in a case where the value of Quantity is between 45 and 50, and there will be no way of deciding which to apply.

In the presence of overlapping entries whose precedence is not determined by the principles given, it may therefore be necessary to state the rule precedence explicitly. This can be done by numbering the rules. (It cannot be done simply by writing them in the required precedence order from left to right, because in the database representation each rule is a row of a database table, and there is no ordering among table rows in a relational database.)

Chapter Summary

In this chapter we have discussed the elements of programs for lifecycle tasks, but not those that concern the scheduling of workflow in the office – they will be the subject of the next chapter.

- Tasks must be able to set their task result states, and to start, suspend and cancel lifecycles. They do this explicitly by invoking functions (SET_RESULT, START_LC, SUSPEND_LC, RESUME_LC and CANCEL_LC) provided for the purpose.
- The lifecycle started by a START_LC function invocation will be one of a family of lifecycle classes. The particular member of the family chosen depends on the controlling influence and its determining attribute value.
- A task may also set back a lifecycle to an earlier stage. This is a form of backtracking, and requires a careful consideration of side-effects.
- Side-effects may be classified as *intolerable, beneficent* or *neutral*. Intolerable side-effects must be undone or annulled by a compensatory action. Beneficent side-effects should be preserved. Neutral side-effects may be either preserved or undone and then repeated, according to what is more convenient.
- Each task occurs in the context of some dataset, containing the records of the entities involved in the task. A task's dataset can be specified in such a way that the task will be partly dataset-independent. It will then be capable of being performed in different contexts.
- Some task elements can be regarded as *rules*. *Wait* rules, *check* rules, *set* rules and *applicability* rules were discussed in this chapter.
- Some complex rules can be expressed in *decision tables*. A decision table may have overlapping rules, the overlap being resolved by the notion of *rule precedence*. More specific rules take precedence over more general rules.

Questions

6.1 What kinds of business rule are there?

6.2 What are the parameters of a START_LC function invocation?

6.3 What must the members of a family of lifecycles have in common?

6.4 Why is backtracking often very difficult?

6.5 What are the three classes of side-effects? Which is the hardest to deal with?

6.6 How does the specification of task repetition in a lifecycle definition help in handling side-effects? Give an example.

6.7 Examine this dataset definition:

ProdSupp = { 1 PRODUCT [prod]
                2 SUPPLIER <Supplier

```
3 [buyer] <Responsible
2 BIN BinProduct^ };
```

To which entity class does the attribute BinProduct belong? The attribute Responsible?

6.8 Assuming the same entity model as in Question 6.7, define a dataset suitable for the task of finding the highest-value product for which a particular buyer is responsible.

6.9 Suppose that a task has two child tasks, A and B. They are defined as:

A: APPLICABLE_WHEN (ORDER-LINE.Quantity > 25);

... ...

B: APPLICABLE_WHEN (ORDER-LINE.Quantity < 40);

... ...

If both tasks are started, which will be performed? Does it make any difference if they are both in the same task selection group?

6.10 Suppose that the decision table shown in Figure 6.6 were changed by moving the CustomerClass attribute row to the top, above the Customer-Number attribute row. What difference would this make to the rule precedence? Find a particular case that would be affected by the change.

CHAPTER 7

Office Workflow

In Chapters 4 and 6 we discussed the definition of entity lifecycles, the arrangement of tasks within lifecycle stages, and the definition of programs for tasks. Inevitably, in doing so we found ourselves concerned with the interaction between the office and the world outside, because that interaction is the central theme of the entity lifecycles and of the conduct of the business.

But we have so far left untouched an important aspect of any office workflow system: the scheduling and management of the work done by users.

Scheduling Users' Work

For an individual policy, or an individual customer order, the basic sequence of events has already been determined by our lifecycle definitions: the implementation of a workflow system must guarantee to respect these lifecycle sequencings. But for the users and workgroups in the office there are still many choices, because they are not dealing just with one policy or one order. They are dealing with very many policies and orders, of which a considerable number will be active – that is, demanding attention – at any one time. The users can therefore turn their attention to one policy rather than another according to the way they decide to *schedule* their work. There is always a pool of tasks available.

The developer of a workflow system does not, in general, decide the scheduling of users' work in the office. The goal, rather, is to provide the means by which the users can make their own decisions, subject to some broad organizational constraints. Programs and tasks are structured into configurations appropriate to the different workgroups. This structuring is supported by an association of entities with business modules such as Claims or Deliveries: the New Business department does not handle Claims, and the Accounts department does not manage Deliveries to customers.

Within the workgroups there are further levels of workflow structure. Different individual users may have different competences, so certain tasks may be restricted to certain users personally. And different styles of working will demand menu structures that offer different arrangements of linked tasks.

Other considerations apply to automatic tasks. Here the scheduling is based entirely on considerations of operational convenience and efficiency (for such activities as printing), consideration of machine utilization and machine loading – especially for client–server and network systems where communication bandwidth may be at a premium – and response time.

It is not the role of the method to prescribe particular workflow designs. But we will discuss the considerations that should inform such designs, and the conceptual and implementation mechanisms that are available for realizing them.

The Workflow Problem

In the earlier steps of the development, we described the static model of entity classes and the dynamic model of task classes associated with the entity classes. Performance of individual task instances may be constrained by the availability of the necessary input data, and by the availability and willingness of an appropriate user to interact with the machine in the performance of the task. For individual task instances that are not freestanding – that is, that are positioned within an entity lifecycle – performance is also constrained by the current entity state with respect to its progress through the lifecycle.

But these constraints still allow a great deal of freedom. The order of performing individual freestanding task instances, and those individual lifecycle tasks that are in the *start* state, remains to be chosen. In particular, there is a very large scope for parallel performance of many task instances of many task classes. A large number of individual entities can be simultaneously involved in their lifecycles. Each one of those individual entities can be currently involved in many lifecycles. Within each lifecycle it is possible for two or more stages to be concurrently active (when each earlier stage contains an incomplete task that is not relevant until after all the other stages). And within one stage there may be several task instances currently in the *start* state. This situation is sketched in Figure 7.1.

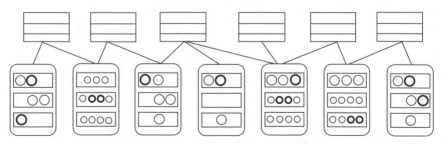

○ Task in start state, ready to perform
○ Task not in start state, not ready to perform

Figure 7.1　*Freedom for parallel execution of many tasks.*

All the heavily outlined tasks in Figure 7.1 are ready: they are in the *start* state, and can be chosen for execution. Tasks shown with a light outline are not ready to be performed. The freedom for parallel execution is that any or all of the ready tasks can be chosen and their performance can proceed in parallel, subject only to concurrency limitations of the database.

The workflow problem is to take advantage of this parallelism and to support an efficient and convenient way of working for the users in the office.

Task inhibition and stimulation

One way of looking at the workflow problem is to say that the lifecycle descriptions focus chiefly (but not exclusively) on the rules that *inhibit* task performance, while the workflow problem is to focus chiefly (but not exclusively) on the rules that *stimulate* task performance.

This distinction is comparable – but not identical – to the distinction between *safety* properties and *liveness* properties of a system. Safety properties state that nothing bad will ever happen – for example, that the goods will never be delivered before the customer credit check is satisfactorily concluded. Liveness properties which state that something good will happen eventually – for example, that once the goods have been delivered an invoice will eventually be sent to the customer.

System Action and Reaction

In respect of some tasks the office workflow machine can be *active* – that is, it can take the initiative in performing the task. For example, a data checking task may be an AP-task (an Automatic task, to be executed immediately following a Preceding task). The machine can take the initiative in performing this task as soon as the preceding task has been performed. Or it can perform the task later, when some internal condition is satisfied – for example, when there are at least ten such tasks waiting to be performed.

In respect of other tasks the machine may be *reactive* – that is, it reacts to an external stimulus. External stimuli arrive from other parts of the world with which it communicates directly. Figure 7.2 shows the lines of communication in a context diagram repeated from Chapter 1.

The machine communicates directly with the users in the office, with a legacy system, with the enterprise's Web site, and with a bank system that handles automated payments by Electronic Data Interchange. The external stimuli to the machine may therefore include the following.

- Incoming bank payment messages from the automated system.
- Incoming messages, perhaps in the form of records deposited in a shared database, from the legacy system and from the Web site.

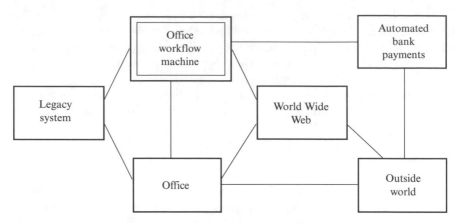

Figure 7.2   *Context diagram for an office workflow system.*

- Commands and requests issued by the office users in the form of menu choices, keyboard and mouse inputs, or any other mechanisms provided by the user interface.

Data entry for a bank payment received may be an XA-task (Automatic and eXternally stimulated). The machine can perform this task when the payment arrives by reacting to the input message that announces the payment. The treatment of an html form completed by a customer and received through the Web site may be similar. Underwriting for an insurance proposal may be an XM-task, and the machine can perform this task similarly by reacting to the keyboard input provided by the user engaged in the task.

Selective reaction

Although it is possible to construct the office workflow machine so that it is always ready to react to external stimuli from all sources, this would be unusual. More commonly the machine is constructed to react only selectively. Certain incoming stimuli are accepted only at certain times, and on certain communication paths. For example, the machine may accept the inputs associated with underwriting tasks only in the morning, and only from the terminals located in the underwriting department. The records deposited in the shared database by the legacy system may be ignored until they are all processed together after working hours.

   This selective reaction can go further. The machine can solicit inputs from users in the office. For example, it may be a business rule that every contract proposal that is not proceeded with must be reviewed by a senior user so that a decision can be taken whether further sales activity is appropriate. This review is a PMD-task: it becomes available for performance immediately following a preceding task – perhaps cancellation by the client; it is a manual task; and it requires a decision. Instead of merely providing the opportunity for task performance, by arranging to accept the inputs associated with the task, and then waiting for a user to provide those inputs, the machine can be arranged to remind the appropriate user in the appropriate department that the task is available and due for performance. A reactive task is being converted into one that is at least partly active.

Conditional action

Just as restrictions can be imposed on reactive task performance by restricting the machine's acceptance of certain input stimuli, so too restrictions can be similarly imposed on active task performance. Instead of allowing the machine to perform an active task according only to internal conditions of the machine, we can arrange for it to do so only when given permission by a user. Effectively, we are now converting an active task performance into a partly reactive performance, where performance of the waiting task is finally carried out only in reaction to receipt of the permission.

This kind of conditional action is particularly useful in controlling the production of printed documents. Cheque printing, for example, must be tightly controlled. The printer must be loaded with the appropriate stationery, and the production and subsequent handling of the cheques must be supervised by duly authorized users to avoid fraud.

A Data Model for Tasks

To understand the context in which tasks are performed, it is useful to make a data model. A simplified model of tasks positioned within lifecycle stages is shown in Figure 7.3.

There is one individual task instance for each task that has been performed in the system or is now available for performance. The TaskState attribute records its state, which is any one of *start*, *n/a*, *ran*, *failed* or *passed*. Tasks in the *null* state are not represented in the model.

Each task is associated with an individual stage of an entity lifecycle instance. The lifecycle instance is associated with a basic entity instance, such as a client or an agent or a policy. Each task is also associated, through its task-class, with a program and a dataset specification. The class of the basic entity must, of course, be the class of the root entity in the dataset associated with the task class.

This model is highly simplified in several respects, but it contains the main elements of the structure we will be concerned with in discussing how individual

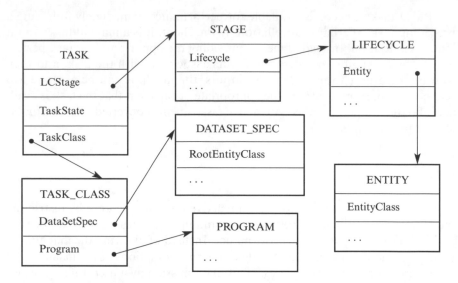

Figure 7.3 *Approximate entity model of tasks with lifecycle stages, linked entities, datasets and programs.*

task instances are to be selected for performance, how the appropriate balance of action and reaction may be chosen, and how groups of tasks may be formed for convenient execution at the same time.

Workgroup structures

One central consideration in arranging the workflow is that particular classes of task involve particular *workgroups* of users in the office. More precisely, particular lifecycle stages in a traditional office organization are associated with particular office departments; within the department, there will be particular users whose skills, knowledge or seniority are appropriate to particular tasks within each stage. In a more modern environment a workgroup is likely to correspond to a *team* that has responsibility for a coherent and significant aspect of the business.

This consideration leads us to confine the performance of certain tasks to terminals located in certain departments, and even to terminals associated with certain users.

It may be useful, in an environment where the workgroup and skill structures are sufficiently complicated, to hold this kind of information explicitly in a separate part of the database dedicated to control of the office workflow.

Figure 7.4 shows a structure of this kind. The association between task classes and the skills needed for the performance of the tasks in each class is many-to-many; so also is the association between skills and users possessing

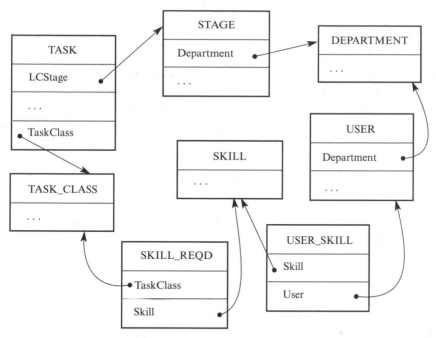

Figure 7.4 *Tasks, users and skills.*

those skills. That is why the link entities skill-reqd and user-skill are necessary. One instance of skill-reqd represents the necessity of one particular skill for the performance of tasks of one particular class.

Task Coordination

It will often be more efficient, either for efficient use of machine resources or to improve convenience and job satisfaction for the users, to coordinate the perform-ance of two or more tasks that might otherwise be treated completely independently.

Coordinating automatic tasks

Consider the example of cheque printing that was mentioned earlier. This demands the setting up of the appropriate stationery and the presence and attention of appropriate users. But the business constraints expressed in the life-cycle definitions treat each cheque individually. The lifecycle definition may say, for example, that the cheque for a certain type of insurance claim may not be printed before the claim has been examined and the written report of an author-ized loss adjuster has been received.

These business constraints on printing the cheque relate the task only to other tasks associated with the same claim or the same policy or the same client. But evidently it will be more efficient and convenient to wait until a number of cheques are to be printed, and then print them all in a single run. This will spread the cost of setting up the stationery and of bringing the authorized user into the printing room over many cheques, instead of incurring the cost separately, over and over again, for each cheque that is printed.

Stationery setup and user movement about the office are obvious and highly visible activities. Less obvious and visible are analogous activities that take place within the machine. To perform a task the machine must set up the program associated with the task, and it must assemble the dataset for the task. Just as in the case of cheque printing, there are reasons to spread these setup overheads over many tasks where it is possible to do so. The particular considerations for each case can be assessed only in the light of detailed knowledge of the internal workings of the machine.

Coordinating manual tasks

The coordination of manual tasks is both more subtle and more important than the coordination of automatic tasks. Consider, for example, the tasks involved in receipt of an order from a new customer. These tasks include:

- A data entry task, in which the details of the new customer are entered into the database.
- A checking task, in which the customer details entered in the database are checked against given criteria of plausibility, completeness and acceptability.
- Another data entry task, in which the details of the order are entered into the database.
- Another checking task, in which the order details are checked.
- A data entry task for each order-line.
- A checking task for each line, including checking the reference to the product ordered.

There are many possible ways of arranging these tasks. Here are some possible dimensions of the choice.

- Combine each manual data entry task with the automatic task of checking the entered details; alternatively, separate data entry from checking. The advantage of combination is the immediacy of feedback to the user entering the data being checked. A disadvantage is the interruption of the flow of data entry. Some users can enter data very fast and accurately, but need an uninterrupted period of concentrated data entry to do so. If the errors likely to be discovered by the checking are errors that cannot be corrected from the documents available to the user entering the data, there is little point in combining the two tasks.

- Combine the handling of the new customer with the handling of the new order; alternatively, separate them. A reason for separating them may be that the nature of the business demands an elaborate and specialized treatment of new customers, including negotiation of individual discount and payment terms. This may even be the responsibility of a different department from the handling of the order. A reason for combining them would be that the data for the customer and the order are both on the same document, as they would be in a mail-order system.
- Separate the checking (not the data entry) of the order-lines from the other tasks. In a business in which the products are made up to order, each order-line may contain quite an elaborate specification of the product required, and the checking of this specification may be best treated as a separate specialized task.

Considerations in task coordination

There are three central considerations in these choices. The first is the need for skill specialization and the allocation of specialized tasks to special groups of users.

The second is the need to balance the competing claims of different focuses and different spans of attention. It may be best to focus the user's attention for a relatively long time on one task type: this suggests that the individual tasks associated with the customer and order should be separated as much as possible. The user can then concentrate, for example, on entering the details of many new customers: the task program remains unchanged over a succession of many individual tasks. But it may be best to focus the user's attention on a dataset: on the new customer together with the new order and the order-lines that make it up. The user can then focus on this customer interaction and all that it involves, for as long as is necessary to handle it properly.

The third consideration is strongly related to both of the two others. It is the need to ensure that the jobs that each user is expected to do in the office are of a meaningful and satisfying size and complexity. Arguably, this consideration suggests that a larger job is always richer and therefore always more satisfying. Users can be left to reduce the size of their jobs if they wish to, provided that the system gives them that freedom at the user interface.

Menu Structure

In any interactive system, each user's freedom to configure different working patterns of jobs is reflected in the structure of choices available at the terminal. Typically these choices are made available in some kind of menu structure. Two simple tree structures of menus are shown in Figure 7.5.

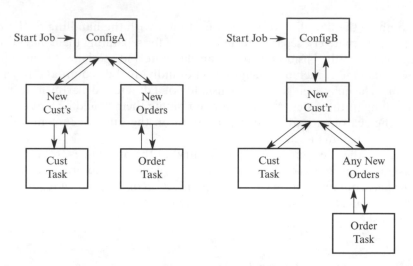

Figure 7.5   *Two menu configurations.*

In each structure, the job starts at the root of the tree. The leaves are screens for tasks, and the root and intermediate boxes represent menu screens. The arrows represent possible progression from screen to screen.

The main menu of configuration ConfigA offers a choice among NewCustomers, NewOrders and Exit. Choosing NewCustomers takes the user to another menu, which offers a choice between Customer and BackToMainMenu; similarly, choosing NewOrders brings up another menu offering a choice between Order and BackToMainMenu. The choices Customer and Order bring up the screens for the data entry task for a new customer and a new order respectively, and return to the NewCustomers and NewOrders menu when the task has been performed.

The main menu of configuration ConfigB offers a choice between NewCustomer and Exit. Choosing NewCustomer brings up the screen for the data entry task for a new customer; when the task has been performed the AnyNewOrders menu is automatically brought up. This offers a choice between Order and BackToMainMenu. The choice Order brings up the screen for the data entry task for a new order; when the task has been performed the AnyNewOrders menu is automatically brought up again.

Datasets and contexts

In the configuration ConfigA, the task of handling a new customer is separated from the task of handling a new order. Both tasks are available through the menu system, but the configuration offers two essentially disconnected modes: the NewCustomers mode and the NewOrders mode. The menu structure is

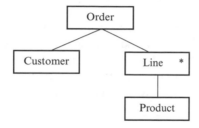

Figure 7.6   *A dataset structure.*

designed to make it easy and convenient to work for a period on a succession of customer data entry tasks, then for a period on a succession of order data entry tasks. It is less convenient to alternate between the two types of task.

When the user is handling a new order, it is done in an entirely fresh context, in which there is no record of any work done shortly before in handling a new customer. Of course, information about a previously handled new customer can be summoned from the database; but it is not automatically present in the context. The dataset for order data entry is essentially the dataset shown in Figure 7.6.

Using the menu structure of ConfigA, the user must rebuild the Customer part of the dataset for each new order to be entered, because there is no context – either in the machine or in the user's head – in which the relevant customer entity record is already present, even if that was the most recently entered new customer.

In ConfigB, by contrast, both of the data entry tasks are performed in the same context of a single choice in the NewCustomer menu. The data entry task for the customer leads on directly to the tasks for orders for that customer, so the order data entry task is performed in a context in which the most recently entered customer data is still current. Effectively, the dataset structure used is that shown in Figure 7.7.

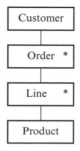

Figure 7.7   *A dataset structure.*

Supporting the Menu Structure

Different menu configurations will be appropriate in different circumstances, as briefly discussed in an earlier section of this chapter. But whatever menu structure is chosen to reflect the configuration of tasks in the workflow, it will be necessary to ensure that the user is supported by mechanisms that help to establish or maintain the necessary context for each task.

Handling hidden IDs

In making the basic entity model we relied heavily on the use of hidden IDs, automatically generated and assigned by the machine. These hidden IDs provide entity keys that are guaranteed to be unique, and thus remove a significant problem in the design and management of a database.

But hidden IDs are not directly readable or usable by humans. So the machine must keep the use of hidden IDs in the background. At the same time, it must provide the user with the ability to operate in terms of the familiar user keys such as Policy Numbers for policies, Product Codes for products, Account Numbers for accounts, and National Insurance Numbers or Income Tax File Numbers for people.

The required techniques are straightforward. The user keys appear as attributes in the entity records and in the records of any entities that refer to them. The association between a policy and its holder is then as shown in Figure 7.8.

For purposes of explanation only, Figure 7.8 also shows the hidden IDs, which are omitted from standard entity diagrams.

The attributes shown in parentheses are hidden IDs, and are not directly visible to the user. Internally, from the machine's point of view, the POLICY entity record is linked to the CLIENT entity record by the Holder attribute, which contains the

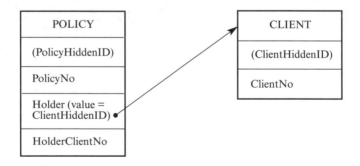

Figure 7.8　*Hidden IDs and user keys.*

value of the ClientHiddenID of the client who holds the policy. From the user's point of view, the Holder attribute is not directly visible. However, the Holder-ClientNo attribute of the policy is directly visible to the user, and has been declared in the data model as a primary key of the CLIENT entity class and a foreign key of the POLICY entity class.

When the user implicitly or explicitly requests the client record associated with a policy, the machine can then find it by means of the client's hiddenID, while at the same time guaranteeing to present the user with a client entity record whose ClientNo attribute has the value of the HolderClientNo attribute of the policy entity record.

When the user creates a new client record by performing a data entry task, the machine automatically generates and assigns a new value for its ClientHiddenId. The ClientNo value will be whatever the user has entered. The ClientNo attribute may or may not be a candidate key for the CLIENT entity record. If it has been declared in the database schema to be a primary key, the machine will not accept a value that is the same as the value of ClientNo in another CLIENT entity record already entered.

Uniqueness in the presence of change

It is often necessary to keep historical versions of an entity record, valid at different periods indicated by StartDate and EndDate attributes. To form a unique key it may be necessary to include these date attributes. We will return to this topic in the next chapter on Database Implementation.

Picking lists

Where a single task is to be performed for many entities successively, it will be convenient to present the user with a list of the available tasks, identified by the primary keys of the root entities of their datasets.

For example, consider the task of reviewing new business proposals that have been marked NPW (Not Proceeded With). If there are more than a very few of such proposals, it is clearly sensible for a qualified user to sit down at a screen for an extended period to examine a batch of them. The machine can readily select the proposals for which this review task is currently available, and present a list of them to the user for selection. This list may simply ordered, perhaps by the size of the proposal, on the grounds that the largest business opportunities merit the most immediate consideration. Alternatively, the list may be ordered by date, on the grounds that the business prospect cools quickly, and only early reviews are likely to produce good results.

Exceptional Task Initiation

It will often be appropriate to provide for exceptional initiation by a user of a task that is usually deferred for execution in a batch job. For example, a particularly important or particularly urgent policy endorsement may require to be printed at once instead of being deferred until the overnight printing job in which contract documents are normally printed.

To provide this kind of facility, it will be useful to allow the user to browse among all currently available tasks of all entities in the current dataset. Thus any task involving the policy directly – not merely the task of creating the endorsement record itself – or involving an associated premium or claim on the policy, could lead to an exceptional initiation of the endorsement printing task.

Another example of the use of exceptional initiation is the initiation of automatic checking of data just entered, when the standard default is to leave the checking to a later batch task execution.

Templates

The construction of on-line interactive programs, and batch programs, for an office workflow system can be largely systematized, or even mechanized. Quite apart from the advantage in reducing system development cost and time, a systematic and consistent approach to construction can ensure a consistent 'look and feel' for interactive programs and a consistent 'operational pattern' for batch programs which can be a major aid to efficient and convenient working.

There is a relatively small number of *templates* for on-line interactive and batch programs, and many if not all of the tasks to be performed can be fitted into one of these templates.

Data entry

The initial data entry that creates a new entity record in the database is an obvious candidate for consistent treatment. The entity model provides all the necessary information about the required entity attributes and their permissible values. The program to support the data entry task can be generated from this information.

Reference help

A component of many interactive programs is a *reference help* function. For example, a part of the data needed for a new order is the *reference* or identifier of the customer placing the order. This will be the primary key of the customer record and a foreign key in the order record. It will be visible to the user performing the data entry task.

It will be helpful to the user to show a list of selected attributes of customer entity records whose primary keys match whatever has been entered of the foreign key. For example, the CustomerName and perhaps PostCode attributes may be shown. Clearly, this facility should be provided with some care. It would be very inefficient and expensive to show the list of all potentially matching customers as soon as the initial character of the identifier has been entered: there will be far too many of them. One possible solution to this difficulty is to offer one of two help facilities according to what has been entered when the user indicates that the record is complete.

- Partial key reference help. If at least some minimum – say, half the correct number of characters – of the required identifier has been entered, then a list is displayed of selected attributes of the potential matches. The user then picks one. If none is the required customer, then the user may change what has been entered for the required identifier, and try again. One possible change of the entered data is to enter the whole identifier as '*' to invoke explicit search help.
- Explicit search help. If an asterisk '*' has been entered as the whole identifier, either originally or on failure of the standard reference help, a small screen is popped up in which the user can enter data into fields corresponding to attributes of the record sought – for example, CustomerName, BillingAddress and ShippingAddress. Entering complete or incomplete data values into any or all of these will trigger a search whose result will be a list of potential matches. Again, the user can pick one. If none is the required customer, then the user may change what has been entered for the required identifier, and try again.

'*' is a *wild card* value of the kind familiar in PC software. Some kind of 'wild card' feature is provided in most database systems. For example, it may be possible, in the language for data manipulation, to perform data retrievals such as:

```
SELECT ClientName, ClientNumber FROM CLIENT
WHERE CLIENT.ClientName LIKE 'SM%SON';
```

to retrieve the ClientName and ClientNumber attributes of all CLIENT entity records whose ClientName attribute begins with the two characters SM and ends with the three characters SON.

The reference help provided in a particular office workflow system will usually be strongly influenced by the 'wild card' feature available in the database system.

If the required identifier value is simply left blank, then this is treated as indicating that the value is unknown. This implies a null value for the user key, and an UNKNOWN value for the associated ID. The record can then be added to the database without its required customer identifier, with the appropriate null value for the CustomerNumber attribute. The absence of the required identifier will be detected in a later K-task in which the data is checked, and will become critical at the stage at which the checking task is relevant. This will be the stage at which the correct CustomerNumber is absolutely required for further progress in the lifecycle of the ORDER entity.

Finding available tasks

The use of a picking list discussed above, for finding new business proposals to review, is an example of another standard template. To generate a program corresponding to this template it is necessary only to specify the repetitive task to be performed, and the order in which the picking list is to be presented to the user.

The task points to the stage and hence to the lifecycle; and it also points to a dataset that has a root entity class. The required program offers the user the opportunity to perform the task for each entity in the root class for which the task is currently available.

Automatic tasks

Automatic tasks can be treated by use of a picking list in almost the same way as manual tasks. The list ordering need not be specified, but an additional criterion may be needed for picking the tasks to be performed. Effectively, this template allows the mechanized creation of batch or spooler jobs for which the functional content of the task to be performed on each item in the batch or spoolfile has been previously specified.

Batch job initiation

Just as the performance of a batch of successive manual tasks is initiated by a user choice from a menu, so the execution of a batch job of automatic tasks can be initiated by user choice from a menu. This would be appropriate for a job such as cheque printing.

A batch job of automatic tasks can also be initiated by the machine according to a *job initiation criterion*. For example, any of the following criteria may be appropriate, depending on the particular task.

- Initiate a batch whenever there are at least ten available tasks waiting.
- Initiate a batch whenever at least one task has been in the start state for at least 24 hours.
- Initiate a batch every Wednesday at 9 a.m.
- Initiate a batch as soon as there is any task at all available to be performed.

Workflow Reporting

The flexibility of an office workflow system of the kind we discuss here gives opportunities for some fine tuning and optimization of the system performance. The underlying technology, even of the dynamic aspects of the system, depends essentially on storing information about lifecycles and tasks in a standard kind of relational database. The records of lifecycle stages and states, and of task performance, should all include attributes to record the time at which each step in the entity progress through its lifecycles is taken.

It is then possible to extract the information needed to diagnose the cause of any defects in system performance, and hence to start looking for a way to improve the system. For example, the workflow reports may include the following.

- Throughput. The number of tasks of selected kinds performed by the system in a given period, or perhaps by particular workgroups or even individuals.
- Response time. The minimum, average and maximum time elapsing between two specified points in a lifecycle. For example: how long it is necessary to wait to obtain a medical report on a proposed assured life; how long elapses between original receipt of an order and delivery of the ordered goods; how long an insurance contract waits for a qualified underwriter user to perform a manual underwriting task.
- Lifecycle categories. What proportion of lifecycles of a particular class or family of classes exhibit a given pattern of task performance. For example, how many policies require manual underwriting? How many orders find themselves waiting for the customer credit check to be completed?
- Waiting lists. What is the average size of the queue of cheques waiting to be printed? Of orders entered but not yet cleared for delivery?

Effectively, there is no limit to the information that can be obtained about the performance of the system.

Chapter Summary

- By defining very small tasks as the building blocks of the system, we give ourselves the opportunity to schedule them in various ways.
- The order of tasks within lifecycles and stages is determined by the rules of business interaction. The order within the work of the office is determined by the design of the workflow.
- Broadly, the rules of business interaction say what must *not* happen at a particular point in the interaction, while the workflow says what *must* happen.
- Tasks are associated with lifecycle stages, and a lifecycle stage is often closely associated with a particular office department. Specialization is important in the performance of many tasks.

- Manual tasks can be formed into meaningful interactive jobs for users: for example, the entry of a new customer can be combined with the entry of the new customer's first order.
- The structure of an interactive job is reflected in its menu structure, and is also associated with the structure of the dataset needed to support its constituent tasks.
- There are a number of identifiable elements of interactive tasks. They can be formed into interactive jobs, and generated largely mechanically, in accordance with suitable *templates*.
- The operation of the system can and should be closely monitored to diagnose inefficiencies and inadequate service.

Questions

7.1 In discussing the menu structure we considered the relationship between customers and orders. In what kind of business would it be reasonable to consider new order data entry in the context of new product data entry?

7.2 What workflow constraints may apply to the performance of the task of cheque printing?

7.3 If two task instances are of the same class, must they be positioned in the same stage of the same lifecycle class?

7.4 Is a lifecycle class an appropriate focus for a user's attention? A lifecycle stage? A task class?

7.5 What kind of automatic task might usefully be scheduled from a user's menu?

7.6 A cheque arrives in the office accompanied by a handwritten note to say that it is 'payment of my monthly premium'. What help might the workflow system give a user in identifying the relevant policy?

7.7 Give three reasonable rules for the scheduling of automatic printing tasks in batches.

7.8 What is the most important criterion for grouping tasks to be chosen from the same menu structure?

7.9 Is reference help ever required for IDs? If so, when? If not, why not?

7.10 Why might a user want to browse among all the currently performable tasks of a dataset?

CHAPTER 8

A Database Implementation

For most computer system applications, different implementations are possible. In discussing the development of office workflow systems in this book we have been assuming an implementation in terms of an underlying database: in particular, a relational database.

Aspects of Database Design

In this chapter we will discuss some aspects of the design and structure of the system's relational database, and some of the techniques that allow a suitably designed and structured database to provide an efficient solution to some important problems.

Database for data and processes

The assumption of an underlying relational database has, perhaps, been most evident in the discussion of data modelling. In discussing entity modelling in Chapters 3 and 5, and the association of entity datasets with lifecycle tasks in Chapters 6 and 7, we often referred to the table and row structure of the database, and sometimes to relational operations such as join.

But paradoxically the underlying database implementation is even more significant in the process model than in the data model. Office workflow systems must satisfy the demands of process requirements from two sources. The *business interaction requirement* governs the ordering of events and tasks in the life of each entity of the outside world; and the *office workflow requirement* governs the ordering of events and tasks within the office itself. Both of these are subject to change. Business processes change as new products are developed, as business practices change, and as new statutory constraints are imposed. Office processes change as the product profile changes, as user expectations and competences change, and as new ways are found – perhaps by business process re-engineering – to improve office efficiency.

This combination of two different but interrelated process requirements, both separately changing, demands a system implementation that can handle process definition and execution in a flexible and robust way. The approach discussed in this book achieves this flexibility and robustness by using the database to represent as much as possible of the process definitions.

Production and plan databases

In this chapter we explain these ideas, and give a broad view of how both the entity lifecycle definitions and the chosen office workflow can be represented in data. In one sense these process representations become data in the database just like any other data, structured in tables and rows, and accessed by the standard facilities of a relational database system. But there are important conceptual differences between the business entity data, which we may call the *production* database, and the process definition data, which we may call the *plan* database.

We may make a further distinction within the process representations. The detailed specifications of tasks, and functions and rules within tasks, can also be represented in data. The part of the database in which they are stored may be called the *features* database. It contains the individual features from which process definitions are constructed.

Integrating explicit metadata

Some of the data modelling techniques we have discussed earlier, especially in the discussions in Chapters 5 and 6, lead naturally to an implementation in which we make explicit what is often called *metadata*, and add it to the database. For example, the possibility that one entity may play different roles, or that the same role may be played by entities of different classes, invite a somewhat unconventional implementation, in which metadata can be accessed and used when lifecycle tasks are being executed. This metadata, too, can be made explicit and integrated into the database.

Data and Programs

Building a computer-based system means ensuring that the computer behaves in accordance with certain constraints, and according to certain rules. It must calculate the sales discount in a certain way; it must generate management reports so that they present certain information in a certain format; it must offer menu choices in a certain structure to system users; it must apply certain rules in executing or permitting the tasks within a lifecycle.

A choice

In almost every case, we have a choice between implementing the behaviour we want in data and implementing it in program text. Suppose, for example, we want to carry out a trivial test: for a particular kind of sale, the tax calculation depends on whether the value of the ResidentIn attribute of the [purchaser] is the name of a country of the European Union. We can implement this test entirely in program text:

```
IF ( [purchaser].ResidentIn = 'United Kingdom' OR
     [purchaser].ResidentIn = 'France' OR
     [purchaser].ResidentIn = 'Germany' OR
     [purchaser].ResidentIn = 'Italy' OR
     [purchaser].ResidentIn = 'Spain' OR
     ...
   )
THEN {EU tax calculation} ELSE {non-EU tax calculation}
```

or we can implement it in data. To implement it in data we define an entity class COUNTRY, with an individual entity instance for each country of the world, and an attribute EUMember whose values are *yes* and *no*. The ResidentIn attribute of [purchaser] is then a pointer to a country. The check can now be:

```
IF [purchaser].ResidentIn → COUNTRY.EUMember = 'yes'
THEN {EU tax calculation} ELSE {non-EU tax calculation}
```

The test for determining whether a country is or is not a member of the EU has been moved from the program to the data.

An advantage of implementation in data

One clear advantage of the implementation in data over the implementation in program text is that it is easier to change. Broadly speaking, databases are designed to be easily updated, while programs are not. When a new country joins the European Union, it is much easier to update the COUNTRY entity record for that country so that its EUMember attribute now has the value *yes* than it is to change the program text.

This greater ease of change means that non-technical office workers can be responsible for determining which rules about tax calculation are appropriate for each country. Technical IS (Information Systems) staff need not be involved.

Going further

We could go further. If we add a TaxScheme attribute to the COUNTRY entity class, pointing to the appropriate tax calculation routine, then the check and calculation program text could be no more than:

PERFORM [purchaser].ResidentIn → COUNTRY.TaxScheme → TAXRTN(...)

where the dots in parentheses stand for the parameters of the tax calculation routine. The tax calculation routine to be performed is the routine pointed at by the TaxScheme attribute of the COUNTRY entity that is pointed at by the ResidentIn attribute of the [purchaser].

This version of our example goes much further than the previous version, because we are now moving towards the idea that the database contains the detail of what is to be done, while the program text contains only a more general mechanism for doing whatever is specified in the database. Now the non-technical office workers can be responsible for choosing the appropriate tax scheme for each country independently: the system is not even tied to the programmed rule that there is one scheme for EU countries and another scheme for non-EU countries. Without changing the program text at all we could easily arrange for any number of different schemes, each country using whatever scheme is appropriate to it.

Of course, there must be some program text to implement each of the schemes: the technical IS experts must still provide the tax calculation routines in the TAXRTN routine pointed at by the TaxScheme attribute of COUNTRY. These routines are in one sense a part of the database, because they are pointed at by COUNTRY entity records; but they are separate from the rest of the database because they are not in the form of entity records. There must also be a generalized program of some kind, to invoke the routines as required.

Figure 8.1 shows the resulting arrangement in a very informal diagram.

The database contains the entity records and the routines to be invoked. The generalized program can be quite general, perhaps not even containing anything specific to the particular system. If the database records contain enough

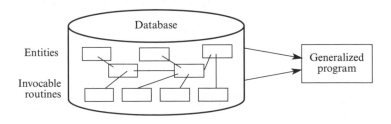

Figure 8.1   *Data and programs.*

information to tell it what to do, it merely invokes the routines according to what the database records demand. As we shall see, this is the foundation of a practical implementation of entity lifecycles. We will return later in this chapter to a more detailed and precise discussion of the relationship between data and program, and to the large structure of the database.

Classes and Individual Instances

Any database implementation of the kind we are discussing here will include records both for individuals and for the classes to which those individuals belong as instances. In some cases there may be records only for classes; in some there may be records only for individuals; often there will be records for both.

An example of class records only

A standard example in database systems is provided by *products*. For example, a supplier may sell many different products, and a manufacturer may manufacture many different products. Suppliers and manufacturers will usually find it necessary to have products as entities in their data models. The declaration of the PRODUCT entity may be something like this:

```
PRODUCT = {Name: name;
           Id: productid;
           Price: money;
           Description: longtext;
           FreeStock: number;
           ReservedStock: number;
           ReorderLevel: number;
           ... };
```

A very specialized supplier may have only a few PRODUCT entity records: one for Flanges, one for Widgets, one for Gadgets and one for Sprockets. When an order is received for 25 Widgets, the quantity 25 is compared with the value of the FreeStock attribute of the Widget PRODUCT record; if there is enough free stock, the order is allocated and eventually delivered. The next order, of course, may be for only one Widget, or for 32.

Why is this an example of having records only for *classes*? Surely the products are perfectly good *individuals*? From one point of view, that is true: one individual is 'Widgets'; another individual is 'Flanges'; and so on. But the supplier does not deal in those individuals. If you place an order by telephone, and say 'I want to order Widgets', the supplier will certainly ask you 'How many widgets do you want?' The individuals you are ordering are individual instances of the class 'Widget'. They are not the class 'Widget' itself.

We may ask: Why does the supplier not have a database record for each individual Widget? It's because the supplier and the supplier's customers regard Widgets as *fungible*. Individuals are fungible if they are interchangeable – if one will do as well as another for all practical purposes. Then all that is needed is to keep one record for the *class* of Widgets, and to use its attributes to store data about the *number* of Widgets in stock and on order.

The commonest example of fungibility is money. If you pay a pound to a shopkeeper for a box of chocolates, and then find that the chocolates are mouldy, you can demand your money back. But you cannot insist on receiving back the same pound coin that you gave the shopkeeper originally. For purposes of commercial transactions, money is fungible, so you can only ask for *a pound* back, not for the *same pound*.

The customer cannot ask the supplier for a *specific* Widget – say, the Widget that came off production line 3 at 12.15 yesterday. The order must be for *any* one Widget, or for *any* 32 Widgets.

An example of both class and individual records

However, if Widgets must be treated like parts for aeroplane engines, the supplier – in this case, no doubt, the manufacturer – will also want to have a record in the database for each individual *item* – that is, for each individual widget. For safety reasons, every widget is individually identified: in the event of a breakdown, it is then possible to trace the manufacturing and supply history of the widget involved in the breakdown, and to discover where the failure occurred. The same is true of flanges, gadgets and sprockets: they are all items, and all individually identified and tracked.

The data model might then look something like Figure 8.2.

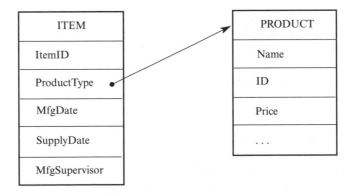

Figure 8.2   *Classes and instances.*

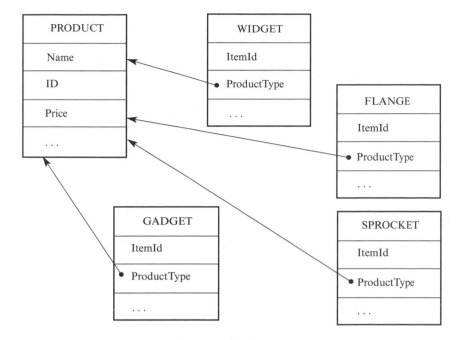

Figure 8.3 *Classes and instance classes.*

All information about the individual items is in the corresponding item entity records; the information about the classes they belong to is in the product records.

If the information to be stored about the individual items depends heavily on the product class of the item, then it may become necessary to have different entity classes for the individual items of the different products. This would be very cumbersome, as can be seen from Figure 8.3.

This data model is cumbersome because it has a separate entity class for each of the four product classes. If the manufacturer adds a new product class, brackets, it will be necessary to add:

- a new entity *record* to the PRODUCT entity class, whose attribute values will hold such information as the price of brackets; and
- a new entity *class* to the data model, whose individual entities will have attribute values such as the manufacturing date of an individual bracket instance.

It would be far preferable to be able to add only the new entity record to the PRODUCT entity class: adding or changing an entity record is much easier and simpler than adding or changing an entity class, because it does not affect the data model at all. In making the data model it is an important objective to make it as robust and stable as possible with respect to foreseeable developments of the business.

The Large Structure of the Database

A powerful conceptual aid to achieving the stability and robustness we want is to think of the data model as defining a structure of three parts: the *production* database; the *plan* database; and the *features* database. This division into three parts is not a formal structuring; it will often be found that a particular database table may be assigned to one part or another depending on the current purpose and point of view. But it is often very helpful in considering questions that arise in data modelling.

Production, plan and features

The three parts can be characterized in the following way.

- The production database contains the data that records the conduct of the business from moment to moment. Every interaction between the office and the outside world will result in adding a record to the production database or in changing attribute values in an existing record there. For example, when a policyholder pays a premium, records in the production database are updated to reflect the event and the consequent change in the mutual obligations between the enterprise and the policyholder. One of these records would probably be the policy record itself, and another the premium record.
- The plan database contains the data that records in detail the plans according to which the business is being conducted. Here the word plan is being used largely in the sense familiar in the financial services industry – the sense in which it is used in phrases such as *pension plan*, *investment plan* or *Personal Equity Plan*. So in the premium payment example, the policy has been written and operated under the rules of a certain Plan. The Policy record contains a Plan attribute, whose value is a pointer to the Plan entity record in the plan database. The Plan entity record contains information about eligibility (this kind of policy is not available to people under 18 years of age), premium payments (payment must be monthly by direct debit), tax rules (a certain part of the benefit is treated as capital repayment and is not taxable) and so on.
- The features database contains the definitions of the features from which the plans are constructed. These definitions may take the form of routines that are expressed in the programming language and can be directly invoked by programs, or of data records that can be interpreted by programs. For example, the tax rule in the policy plan specifies that a certain part of the benefit is treated as capital repayment. In the PLAN entity record the BenefitTax attribute may be a pointer to a routine that can be invoked to perform the appropriate calculation. Or it may be a pointer to a record containing details of the required calculation such as the fraction of the premiums paid that is

deemed to be investment, and the maximum fraction of the final benefit that can be treated as capital repayment. Or it may, perhaps, be a pointer to a record from which a complete decision table can be retrieved.

Relationships among the database parts

The relationships among the parts are, in general, implemented by pointer attributes. Figure 8.4 shows the relationships in the policy example.

Even with all three parts in place, the database is still entirely passive. It provides the information about what has happened, in the production part; it provides the plan according to which it happens, in the plan part; and it provides the features that compose the plans, in the features part. But there is no engine to drive the activity, and the database contains nothing that directly demands any activity. We will look more closely into this when we come to discuss the representation of tasks and lifecycles later in this chapter.

Ownership and responsibility

An office workflow system is usually a large system, with many parts and aspects. The responsibility for looking after and maintaining the system must be explicitly assigned. This assignment also has an ownership aspect. The people responsible for a part of the system have an obligation to look after it and keep it current. They should also think of themselves as the *owners* of that part of the system: that is, as the only people who are entitled to change it.

The operational users in the office are clearly responsible for the operation of the production part of the database. As they engage in the business interactions between the office and the outside world, their involvement in the tasks that make up those interactions necessarily involves them in using and updating the production part of the database.

It is useful to recognize also another category of users, whom we may call *strategic* users. These users are responsible for ensuring that the plan part of the

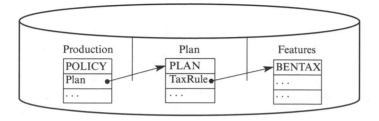

Figure 8.4   *Production, plan and features database parts.*

database evolves appropriately to reflect the changes in the rules for conducting the business. In a life assurance company, therefore, these users will be involved in adding or updating records in the plan part of the database whenever new plans are devised that the enterprise wants to offer to prospective customers, and whenever the rules for existing plans are changed by legislation or industry regulation.

The features part of the database remains, essentially, the responsibility of technically expert people, whom we may call *technical expert* users. Some of them may be in a separate Information Systems department, some may be in the office along with other production or strategic users.

As a general rule, features that are implemented as routines in the programming language are likely to be the responsibility of people in the Information Systems department. But in some cases these routines can be generated mechanically from specifications entered in the form of data records. These records are accepted by a software tool that produces the required routines without further user intervention. *Business expert* users in the office may well be able to enter these specifications and so to generate the routines.

A View of Lifecycles and Tasks

In Chapters 4 and 6 we explored the definition of lifecycles and tasks. In Chapter 7 we discussed their arrangement into a convenient flow of work for the users in the office. The underlying implementation depends on representing them in the database, with exactly the division into production, plan and feature parts that we have been discussing above.

In this section we will discuss the data model representation of lifecycles, tasks and workflow jobs. First, each of the three will be discussed separately, and then the complete picture will be shown in which their relationships are made explicit.

Lifecycles and stages

Lifecycles illustrate the production and plan parts of the database very directly. The START_LC function invocation described in Chapter 6 starts an individual lifecycle instance. This individual instance conforms to a lifecycle plan in just the same way as an individual life assurance policy conforms to a policy plan.

The conformance of an individual to its associated plan is found again at the more detailed level of a lifecycle: each lifecycle stage instance conforms to the stage plan, in which the task structure of the stage is defined. Figure 8.5 shows a simplified data model view of lifecycles and stages.

The production part contains records for lifecycle instances and stage instances, and the plan part contains records for lifecycle and stage classes. Each instance record contains a pointer attribute Class, pointing to the class to

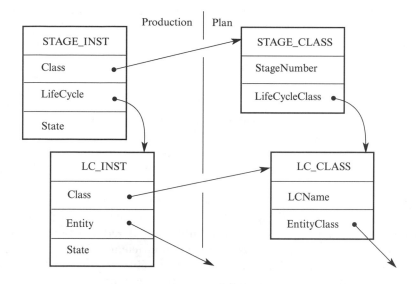

Figure 8.5 *Classes and instances of lifecycles and stages.*

which the instance belongs. The instance records contain State attributes whose values indicate the progress through the lifecycle instance. It is necessary to have a State attribute for each stage as well as for each lifecycle, because a lifecycle can be engaged in more than one stage at a time, when an incomplete task at an earlier stage is relevant to a later stage.

Each stage instance belongs to a lifecycle instance, as indicated by its Life-Cycle attribute; and each stage class similarly belongs to a lifecycle class. Each lifecycle class is associated with an entity class, and each lifecycle instance is associated with an entity instance. Naturally, the entity instance must belong to the class with which the lifecycle class is associated. Incidentally, we may note that the constraint – that the entity instance must belong to the entity class – is not expressible in the data model notation.

In a similar way, there is a constraint that the lifecycle instance associated with a stage instance must be of the class associated with the stage class. However, here there is some redundancy. A lifecycle instance cannot exist without at least one stage instance. So the value of the Class attribute in the lifecycle instance can always be determined from an associated stage instance: the value of the attribute is the value of the LifeCycleClass attribute in the corresponding stage class. Instead of going down and along (from STAGE_INST to LC_INST to LC_CLASS) in Figure 8.5, we go along and down (from STAGE_INST to STAGE_CLASS to LC_CLASS).

We could eliminate the redundancy from the model shown in Figure 8.5, perhaps adding a cardinality expression to the LifeCycle association of STAGE_INST to show explicitly that a lifecycle instance must have always at least one stage instance. But this kind of redundancy is useful: it can often make the data model easier to understand. The association between LC_INST and LC_CLASS is clearer if it is shown directly.

Access efficiency

There are also important considerations of efficiency that should not be ignored. The fewer pointers that must be followed to extract or process a piece of information, the quicker it can be done. The direct pointer from LC_INST to LC_CLASS gives a much faster path than the path via STAGE_INST and STAGE_CLASS.

Strictly, it would be more proper to separate the conceptual data model, in which considerations of efficiency play no part, from the physical data model, which shows how the database has been implemented and how the conceptual model has been distorted by considerations of efficiency. But in the kind of system we are concerned with in this book it is sensible to have one data model only, and to show this kind of optimization in that data model.

Tasks

Like lifecycles and stages, tasks have instances and classes. Because some tasks are grouped into task selection groups, as explained in Chapter 4, it is convenient to treat every task as if it were a member of a task selection group. A selection group containing only one task is exactly equivalent to that task.

Figure 8.6 shows the data model for tasks and selection groups. In the plan part, each task class is associated by its Group attribute with a group class. A task selection group class can have many parent task classes, and a parent task class can have many child tasks; so the link entity PARENTAGE is used to record this many-to-many association. Each selection group instance, however, can have only one parent task instance; so the association between parents and children for instances is provided by the Parent pointer attribute of the task selection group instance.

Task programs and workflow jobs

Each task class is associated with a task program: that is, with the executable or interpretable program that contains the detailed instructions for executing the task. These detailed instructions include the details of the dataset structure that must be present for any execution of the program. But individual tasks cannot be executed without being placed in the context of an interactive or batch workflow job. The resulting structure is shown in Figure 8.7.

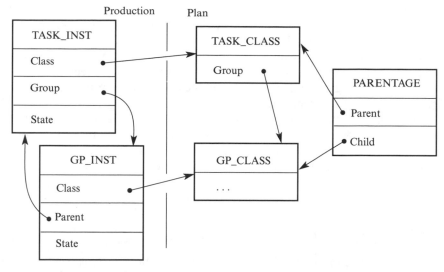

Figure 8.6   *Classes and instances of tasks and selection groups.*

A workflow job may be of a batch job class or an interactive job class; the Job-Type attribute indicates which it is. It is associated with an executable job program that is invoked by a user at a terminal, or by the operating system of the machine. For an interactive job, the job program is based on a structure of menus from which the user chooses the task programs to perform. Whether interactive or batch, a job may incorporate more than one task program; and one task program may form a part of more than one workflow job. This many-to-many association is therefore represented by the link entity class PGM_CNTXT.

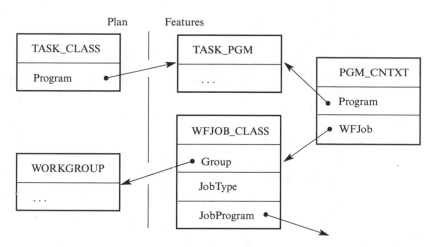

Figure 8.7   *Tasks, task programs and workflow jobs.*

Each workflow job is associated with one particular workgroup of office users. In the case of a non-interactive batch job, this may be the workgroup that is responsible for invoking the job when it should be run: for example, a group in the finance department will be responsible for invoking the cheque-printing job. Some batch jobs may be automatically scheduled for execution by the machine's operating system; in such a case, the associated workgroup would be identified as the system scheduler.

Notice that task programs and workflow job classes are regarded here as belonging to the features part of the database. There is no instance entity corresponding to a task program, because all the information about an individual instance of its execution is held in the task instance record in the production part of the database.

Execution relationships

We can begin by considering the execution of a freestanding task, such as data entry for a new customer, that is not a part of any lifecycle stage.

The task program for the task is incorporated in a workflow job, as shown in Figure 8.7, and invoked as a part of that job by a user. When the task program runs, it creates a task instance record of the appropriate task class, as shown in Figure 8.6. At the end of the task, it invokes the START_LC function, as described in Chapter 6. This creates an instance of the requested lifecycle, in the form of a LC_INST record associated with the appropriate production customer entity, and an instance of the first stage of the lifecycle, as shown in Figure 8.5.

Lifecycle stages and task selection groups are associated as shown in Figure 8.8, which ties together the partial models of Figures 8.5 and 8.6, by linking task selection groups to lifecycle stages.

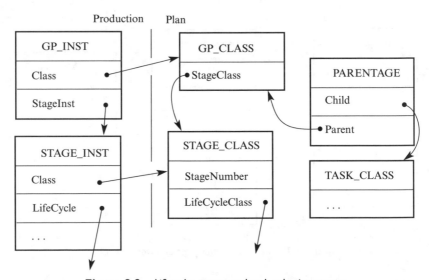

Figure 8.8   *Lifecycles stages and task selection groups.*

Each task selection group class is associated with one lifecycle stage class. When an instance of the stage is started, an instance of each of its original task selection groups is started. That is, a GP_INST record is created, with the value start for its State attribute. An original task selection group is a group that has no parent task; as shown in Figure 8.8, this means that there is no PARENT-AGE record associated with the task selection group by its Parent attribute.

When the selection group is started, an instance of each of its tasks is started. The production database now contains a record for each task of each original task selection group in the first stage of the lifecycle. These tasks are now in the pool of tasks available to be performed.

Advantages for Workflow and Lifecycles

There are important advantages to be gained by implementing tasks, lifecycles and workflow in a database form. The most significant of these advantages are technical uniformity and robustness.

Technical uniformity

An office workflow system necessarily depends on a database implementation for the production data about the progress of the business interactions. It is advantageous to use the same technology for other purposes in the system to which it is suited.

Technical uniformity exploits the experience and knowledge gained in one area to make both development and operation easier in other areas. Both the Information Systems experts who are responsible for development, and the strategic office users who are responsible for the plan parts of the database find themselves dealing with a familiar technology. Of course, for the Information System experts there may be some programming to be done in extending the repertoire of available features from which plans can be constructed. But the technology of defining and executing lifecycles is the technology of updating a relational database, no different from the technology used in executing business interaction tasks.

Robustness

Relational database technology has achieved a good level of robustness in operational use. The concept of a *transaction* allows updates to be structured into atomic units. That is, each transaction either completes its updates as specified or else has no effect at all. This property of atomicity is an essential safeguard against failure of a communication network, failure of a client–server connection, or other system failures.

Because the implementation of tasks and lifecycles uses the database technology, the progression of business interactions can be thought of as a series of database transactions, enjoying this property of atomicity. The pool of tasks to be performed, represented in the database records for task, selection group, stage and lifecycle instances, is as robust as the production data of customers, policies, clients, orders and all the other information about business interactions.

Effective Dates

In an office workflow system it is important to recognize and cater for the constantly changing environment in which the business is conducted. The rules imposed by legal regulation and industry standards, and the development of new products and new ways of doing business, all mean that the process model underlying the system is subject to constant alteration.

A requirement example

This constant alteration introduces a major complication into the system. Not because of the changes themselves, but because changes must usually be applied selectively. For example, legislation may require a new report to be returned to the tax authorities in respect of a certain kind of life assurance policy, but only for those policies that were taken out after a certain date. After that date, the system must deal both with policies for which the report is required, and with policies of the same kind for which no report is required.

Possible solutions

There are two obvious ways of satisfying this requirement.

- A new lifecycle class can be introduced. There are now two lifecycle classes for the same aspect of the same product, which is inconvenient but not apparently disastrous. All the tasks which formerly executed the function invocation

  START_LC (*entityclass*, *id*, "OldLifeCycle")

  are changed so that they now execute the function invocation

  START_LC (*entityclass*, *id*, "NewLifeCycle").

  The new lifecycle contains the additional tasks necessary to provide the required report. When a further change is required to the lifecycle, yet another new lifecycle can be introduced, and the starting tasks changed so that they execute

    START_LC (*entityclass*, *id*, "NewNewLifeCycle")

and so on for each required change.

- The additional tasks for the report are added to the existing lifecycle, but are protected by an applicability condition. For example:

APPLICABLE_WHEN ([policy].StartDate, ">", 31/12/90)

The report is produced only when the policy start date is later than 31 December 1990.

Difficulties

Both of these attempted solutions are unsatisfactory. The second is unsatisfactory because the definitions of lifecycle tasks become more elaborate with each change. There is no obvious point at which an elaboration can be undone – in the illustration above, when the applicability condition can be dropped. Task definitions therefore become encrusted with successive increments of complexity, and there is a gradual deterioration in the intelligibility (and therefore in the maintainability) of the system.

The first attempted solution is unsatisfactory for a more subtle but more compelling reason. Even after the newer version of the lifecycle has been introduced, it may still be necessary sometimes to start an earlier version of the lifecycle. There are two major causes of this necessity.

- Backtracking. In a backtracking situation it may be necessary to restart an entity lifecycle by cancelling the old lifecycle and starting a completely new one. But, of course, the version to be started is the version that had been originally started, not the new one that has superseded it.
- Communication delays. Communication between people and organizations in the outside world and the office is often subject to delays. Postal delays are an obvious case in point; and delays can be introduced by mistakes in handling incoming paper documents within the office itself. A client whose proposal form is sent in good time before the stated deadline will not be willing to receive the new version of the policy if it is less advantageous then the old version that had been promised.

A general solution

A general solution can be provided to these and similar difficulties. The solution has two parts.

First, every record in the database contains a DateEffective attribute. The value of this attribute is a pair of dates, StartDate and EndDate. The validity of the record is restricted to dates between these start and end dates. This technique is used without exception – for production data records and for all lifecycle and task class and instance records equally.

Second, the execution of any task program takes place in a context in which there is a defined variable ProcessingDate, whose value can be set by a function invocation in the program text. The meaning of this variable is that the task is performed as if it were being performed on the given processing date. Any record accessed by the task is automatically checked to ensure that its validity, as given by its start and end dates, covers the processing date.

It is therefore relatively straightforward to perform any task in the context of the database as it would have been on the specified processing date. When the mislaid proposal, for example, is eventually found, it can be processed exactly as it would have been processed had it not been mislaid. The lifecycle started after cancellation and backtracking is started as it would have been started on the original starting date.

Which date?

In fact, the problem is more complex than this. When we are concerned with a significant event in the outside world – for example, the death of the life assured of a policy – we must distinguish three dates. First, the *event date*: the date on which the event actually occurred. Second: the *booking date*: the date on which an input signalling the event arrived at the machine. Third: the *processing date* discussed above.

Determining the correct choice of processing date may be quite difficult. Suppose, for example, that a client of a financial services company telephones an order to buy certain shares. The system is temporarily unavailable, so the order is noted on paper. By an error it is not input to the system until two days later. In the intervening period, the share price has changed, and a new Stock Exchange accounting period has begun. What should be the processing date? In complex cases of this kind it may be necessary to devote a large decision table to specifying the appropriate rules.

Implementing Roles

The treatment of entity roles, discussed in Chapter 5, can be implemented quite readily in the database environment.

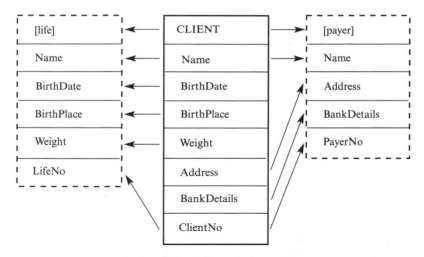

Figure 8.9   *Entity and role attributes.*

Explicit roles

A role of an entity can be thought of as a defined selection of its attributes. For example, a CLIENT entity may play the [life] role of the LifeAssured in one policy, and the [payer] role of the PolicyHolder in another. For each role, only a selection of the CLIENT entity attributes is needed. For example, BirthDate, Birthplace and Weight are needed for [life] but not for [payer]; BankDetails is needed for [payer] but not for [life].

The appropriate selections of the CLIENT entity attributes may be as shown in Figure 8.9. (Figure 8.9 is not a data model diagram: it is only an informal diagram to show which attributes are required in each role.)

The textual declaration of roles, and the way in which the renaming of attributes (such as ClientNumber in the example) may be declared is explained and discussed in Chapter 5. In implementation terms, the example may be easily expressed in a SELECT statement of SQL. For the [life] role we may write:

```
SELECT  Name, BirthDate, Birthplace, Weight, ClientNo
   INTO  :Name, :BirthDate, :Birthplace, :Weight, :LifeNo
   FROM  CLIENT ...
```

and for the [payer] role we may write:

```
SELECT  Name, Address, BankDetails, ClientNo
   INTO  :Name, :Address, :BankDetails, :PayerNo
   FROM  CLIENT ...
```

In each case the SELECT statement specifies both the required subset of entity attributes and the necessary renaming of some of them: for example, ClientNo in CLIENT becomes LifeNo in [life].

Floating roles

The case of floating roles is a little harder to implement cleanly. A floating role is a role that may be played by entities of different classes, as shown in Figure 8.10.

The attributes of the [seller] role are renamings of attributes taken from the BROKER and SALESPERSON entity classes. To deal with the fact that a pointer to a [seller] may point either at a BROKER entity record or at a SALESPERSON entity record, we need a special table called the KnownEntities table. Each record in the KnownEntities table contains the name of an entity class of the data model. So there will be, for example, a KnownEntities record containing the name "Broker", and another containing the name "Sales-Person", as well as one for every other entity class. Each record of the KnownEntities table, of course, has a hidden ID in the usual way.

Any pointer attribute that points to a seller – for example, in an entity record such as a policy record – consists of four parts.

- A pointer to the record for the individual BROKER or SALESPERSON, whose value is the hidden ID of the individual's entity record.
- The user key of the individual BROKER or SALESPERSON.
- A pointer to the relevant record in the KnownEntities table – the record containing the name "Broker" if the seller is a broker, or the record containing the name "SalesPerson" is the seller is a salesperson.
- The user key of the KnownEntities table record.

This is enough information to allow the floating role to be processed as if it were an entity class, with explicit tests in the program coding for the different entity classes that can play the [seller] role.

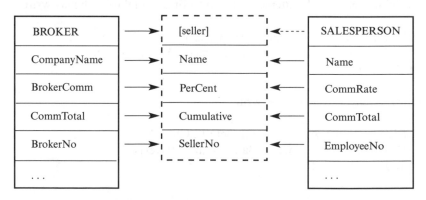

Figure 8.10   *Entity and role attributes.*

A complete table of all [sellers] can be formed by SELECT statements and the UNION operator. For example:

```
SELECT  Name, CommRate, CommTotal, EmployeeNo
  INTO  :Name, :PerCent, :Cumulative, :SellerNo
  FROM  SALESPERSON ...
UNION
SELECT  CompanyName, BrokerComm, CommTotal, BrokerNo
  INTO  :Name, :PerCent, :Cumulative, :SellerNo
  FROM  BROKER ...
```

Special Pointer Values

A well-known problem with relational databases is the treatment of *null* attribute values. A null value can arise from any of the following causes.

- The information is not yet available. For example, when the information for a new insurance prospect is first entered, some of the desired information will be available and some will not. It is necessary both to provide a place to put all the information that is available and to allow the lifecycle to go ahead – typically, to a checking task – with some kind of null value for information that is missing.
- The individual entity instance considered does not have the attribute in question. For example, Figure 8.11 shows the association between managing and managed employees in a company. If the management relationship is not allowed to be circular (that is, no employees may manage themselves, either directly or indirectly), and there is only a finite number of employees in the company, then there must be at least one employee who does not have a manager. For that employee the ManagedBy attribute must have some kind of null value. Since it is an association attribute, whose value is the hidden ID of an employee entity, an appropriate value is NONE, the ID of a special employee record.
- The individual entity instance may have an entirely non-specific value. For example, if we implement decision tables – as we should – in the database, then an indifferent entry, corresponding to a '–' entry in the displayed form of the decision table, has an entirely non-specific value that should be represented by some kind of null.

Figure 8.11   *An association with a null value for at least one entity.*

It is convenient to provide for all of these cases, and to distinguish them from one another. For non-association attributes, such as BirthDate, this can be done by choosing special values of the domain that do not otherwise occur. For example, a date of 00-00-0000 can indicate that the date of birth is unknown, and 00-00-0001 that it is indifferent.

For association attributes we prefer to provide special records in each database table corresponding to the different kinds of null: an UNKNOWN, a NONE, an ALL and an ANY. Each of these special records in each table has its own hidden ID, which is the value of any pointer attribute that points to it. This technique can simplify what can otherwise be an awkward problem of handling conventional null values in a relational database.

Chapter Summary

The technology of a relational database management system provides a good foundation for implementing an office workflow system. In particular:

- It allows behaviour to be implemented in data rather than in program text, and therefore to be more readily changed when the need arises.
- It allows a reasonable implementation of individual instances and classes, sufficient for the needs of the kind of system we are considering here.
- The large structure of the database can be regarded as a structure of three parts: *production*, *plan* and *features*.
  - Production data is the operational data from business interactions.
  - Plan data represents the rules according to which the business interactions take place.
  - Features are the units of functionality from which plans are built.
- Tasks, task selection groups, stages and lifecycles can be implemented in data records, both as class definitions and as individual performance instances. There are important advantages of this technique, including robustness and technical uniformity.
- For an office workflow system it is important to handle changes in the business rules explicitly. Each record in the database should have an explicitly stated period of validity, expressed as start and end dates.
- Unknown or irrelevant values of association attributes can conveniently be treated as pointers to special records. A special record of each kind must be added to each database table.

Questions

8.1   Should the KnownEntities table be regarded as a part of the production, plan or features database?

8.2 Must every entity record in the production database be associated with a record in the plan database?

8.3 For what part of the database might a strategic user be responsible? A technical user?

8.4 Who is entitled to change a plan record? A feature record?

8.5 In what record is the result state produced by executing a program stored?

8.6 When would the processing date of a task be earlier than the booking date of its input?

8.7 What does the property of atomicity guarantee?

8.8 Why is the KnownEntities table required?

8.9 In implementing a role by the SQL statement:

```
SELECT   Name, Address, BankDetails, ClientNo
  INTO   :Name, :Address, :BankDetails, :PayerNo
  FROM   CLIENT ...
```

what is the purpose of the INTO clause?

8.10 Why might it be important to think about the attribute values of the CLIENT entity record pointed at by the pointer value NONE?

CHAPTER 9

Project Structure

In the earlier chapters of this book the development method is described as a sequence of phases: making the data model to reflect the information needed to run the business; making the process model to capture the lifecycle and task structure of business interactions between the office and the world outside; defining the content of each task; structuring the tasks from the point of view of the flow of work in the office; and implementing the system in terms of a relational database.

A Larger View

This sequence has an internal coherence, but it must be modified in various ways to give a practical project structure. The method as described provides only the core of technical development activities. In a practical project attention must be paid to some larger considerations that will have an important impact on the project structure. Broad goals, such as user ownership of the system and involvement in its development, may demand a particular approach to the activity of discovering and capturing the established or desirable rules of business interaction. Risks, such as the risk of unreliable operation or erroneous system outputs, must be weighed. In some projects they will lead to a different emphasis in some technical activities, or the use of additional or different techniques.

In this chapter, some of these larger considerations and their implications are discussed, and some additional techniques are explained. The focus is primarily on the implications for the technical content of the project activities. The goals and risks discussed in this chapter are by no means a comprehensive catalogue. Rather they are a representative sample, intended to indicate the kind of consideration that must be taken into account in planning the project structure.

The central theme of project structuring is placing project resources – especially the developers' time and effort – where they are most needed.

Goals and Risks

Naturally, it is necessary in planning a development project to pay careful attention to the project goals, and to plan the project so that they will be achieved. It is also useful to consider a complementary idea – the idea of project risks. When we consider a goal, we are paying attention to some desirable thing that we are trying to achieve; but in considering a risk we are paying attention to some undesirable thing that we are trying to avoid.

To some extent, a risk may be just the obverse of a goal. The risk that the project will be late is the obverse of the goal of completing the project on schedule, and the risk that the office users will be unable to use the system effectively is the obverse of the goal of ensuring that they are competent in its use. But there is more to it than that. Goals tend to be broader and more general, but risks should be more specific and more sharply focused on the particular project and its particular possible outcomes. Think of the analogy of car driving. When you drive a car you should have safety as a goal; but you should also be looking for particular risks – for example, when you are passing a line of parked cars you should be aware that one of the cars may pull out unexpectedly into your path, or that the driver's door of one of them may be opened suddenly. So you drive more slowly, and leave enough room for a door to open without causing a collision.

Boehm's spiral model

Barry Boehm has put forward a model of development projects in which the project is seen as a spiral of many turns. The first turn is concerned with the system concept phase, the second with the system requirements phase, then design, and so on. In each turn of the spiral the first step is to determine the objectives of the phase, then the second step is a risk analysis, in which the risks specific to the project are assessed for likelihood and severity, and a plan made to deal with each one.

The spiral model is explained in 'A Spiral Model of Software Development and Enhancement'; Barry W. Boehm; *IEEE Software* May 1988. It is well worth getting a copy of this paper, if you can, and reading it thoughtfully.

Project goals

Some important project goals are commitment, ownership, timeliness and robustness.

- *Commitment* The broad goal of an office workflow system is to support the work of the users in the office. Almost every function that the system provides is for the assistance of the users, and can operate only by virtue of their interaction: most of the substantial tasks in a typical system will be manual – they will be M-tasks, not A-tasks. The success of the system therefore depends crucially on the willingness of its users to play their part, and on their commitment to its successful operation. This is why the project should be regarded as a joint project between the users and the developers. A joint activity – discovering the main tasks and entities – is discussed in a later section of this chapter.

- *Ownership*   Users' commitment to a system must also rest on the users' perception that they *own* the system: that is, that it is in a large measure their own creation and their own responsibility; that its development has been a joint project between them and the technical information systems staff; that the view of the business it embodies is their own view, and not a view imposed on them by outsiders. One particular area in which user ownership can be made very immediate is in the definition of many of the rules of the kinds discussed in Chapter 6.

- *Timeliness*   Almost every project must be completed according to a definite schedule. In some cases the schedule may be very tight indeed, especially where it is designed to meet an imperative commercial objective such as the creation of a new branch of the business. Where the business is already well understood, it may be possible to adopt a fast-track project plan, and this kind of project is discussed in a later section of this chapter.

- *Robustness*   An office workflow system is always central to the activities of the enterprise, and must be robust. Robustness means that the whole system can be relied on to be available for use, and that it will not cease to operate because of minor equipment failures. To a significant extent achievement of this goal of robustness is ensured by the underlying technology of the relational database mechanisms, especially the structuring of system function as a set of many independent atomic transactions. Incremental development can also contribute valuably to robustness by ensuring that increasing reliance on the system comes only with increasing experience of its use. Some points on incremental development are discussed in a later section of this chapter.

Specific risks

The effort to be devoted to dealing with a particular risk depends on its severity. The severity of a risk can be thought of as the product of two factors: How likely is it that the bad thing will happen? and: How bad will it be if it does?

In a safety-critical system, the risk of failing to shut down the nuclear power plant, or the risk of administering a massive overdose of X-rays to a patient being treated by the medical radiotherapy machine, may be very small in the sense of being very unlikely to happen; but the consequences will be so bad if it does happen that these risks must be regarded as extremely severe. Their treatment therefore demands the application of virtually unlimited resources.

In an office workflow system, by contrast, the consequences are rarely catastrophic, but the likelihood of their happening may be quite high. Some typical risks are the following.

- *Building the wrong system* It is often easy to overestimate how well the existing system and its operation are understood. Even when the economic justification for the development project is well understood, rushing too quickly into the implementation of an ill-understood system can produce a system that fails to meet the needs of the business in several respects. The basic treatment for this risk can only be a carefully fostered relationship between the business expertise of the users in the office and the analytical and technical expertise of the professional IS developers. An important technique here is the use of discovery sessions, which are discussed in a later section of this chapter.

- *Unmaintainability* As time passes after the initial introduction of the system, modifications will certainly be needed to meet changing business requirements, the introduction of new products, and new regulations. The chief problem in maintenance is traditionally one of uncertainty: no-one dares to change the existing system because no-one is quite sure how it works or precisely what it does. This risk is somewhat reduced by the loosely-coupled structure of tasks within stages of lifecycles. But it is still necessary to pay explicit attention to the risk by recording enough information for crucial aspects of the behaviour of the system to be clearly understood. This topic is discussed later in this chapter in a section on documentation.

- *Unforeseen situations* No matter how carefully the tasks and lifecycles are designed, they will not handle every possible sequence of events in the outside world. Because the world is informal, and because the individuals who interact with the office are human, no absolute limit can be placed on what may happen. Situations will therefore arise that have not been foreseen, for which the system has no specific defined response. This risk can be dealt with both by working to reduce the number of such unforeseen situations, and by providing general escape routes to handle them. An analysis technique is discussed later in this chapter for discovering otherwise unforeseen situations, and a technique for establishing a sufficient set of general responses that can be used to handle them.

- *Erroneous outputs* Because developers are not infallible there is always a risk of erroneous results: for example, the system may produce incorrect documents. This risk is particularly severe where backtracking is involved, because setting back a lifecycle, or cancelling and restarting it, may take place in many different contexts, and it is not trivial to ensure that all the possible contexts are considered.

Technical Constraints and Freedoms

The method presented in this book has been described as a sequence of phases. This sequence is far from sacrosanct, and must be expanded and modified in the light of the assessment of the project goals and risks and how best to deal with them. But it does reflect some technical constraints in the order of development. These constraints are discussed in this section.

Development dependencies

Some phases of a development depend for their input on the results of earlier phases. For example:

- Workflow structuring and tasks. The workflow structure is a structuring of the tasks to be performed by users. For sensible structuring it is necessary to consider several aspects of each task. For example, the task content must be considered so that it may be offered to users with appropriate skills. The dataset of the task must also be considered so that tasks with related datasets can be grouped where that is desirable. And the arrangement of tasks within lifecycle stages must be considered so that immediately consecutive tasks can be offered to the user if that is appropriate. This dependency of the workflow on the tasks means that it is not possible to structure the workflow before the tasks have been defined and assigned to lifecycle stages.
- Entities and attributes. Attributes are tied to entities; for example, a name attribute may belong to a client entity or a broker entity; an amount attribute may be the amount of a benefit in a policy entity, or of a monthly premium in a policy entity, or it may be a total amount in an invoice entity. It makes little sense to talk about attributes in the absence of a set of recognized and understood entities. In the data modelling phases, therefore, it is necessary to consider the entities before the attributes.
- Entities and lifecycles. Lifecycles are tied to entities: each lifecycle instance involves an instance of some entity class. Identifying this entity class is an essential element in understanding the purpose and content of the lifecycle. For example, a lifecycle for servicing a car must be understood to be tied to an instance of the car entity class; it would have either a completely different sense, or no sense at all, if it were tied to a car owner, or a service garage, or a service mechanic. It is therefore necessary to consider the entities before the lifecycles, or at least in conjunction with them.

These orderings form constraints on the project structure that should always be respected. However, it is important to recognize that development can (and should) be iterative at many levels, and this iteration leads to some modification of the ordering at the most detailed level. For example, consideration of a proposed entity attribute may lead to recognition of a previously ignored entity class; and consideration of the workflow structure may lead to recognition of previously ignored tasks.

Freedoms

Not all relationships between the contents of different phases and activities are so tightly constrained. In general, for example, there is a circular relationship between data and process models: the process model is defined in terms of operations on the data; but the data is defined in terms of what is necessary to support the process model.

Another notable example is the relationship between tasks and lifecycles. It is perfectly possible to define all – or most – of the tasks first, and only after that to position them in lifecycle stages. It is equally possible to define the lifecycle stages first, and only after that to identify the tasks that make them up.

Top-down

Notice that this kind of freedom does not give a general permission to describe aspects of the system in a top-down fashion. Top-down descriptions are permissible where the subject matter to be described is already in existence and is already reasonably well known. That is why, for example, it is often acceptable to describe a lifecycle in terms of stages before identifying the constituent tasks. The stages are already known from the existing business practices, and from the existing practice within the office. It is therefore reasonable to describe the lifecycle of a contract in this kind of way:

> 'First it is dealt with by the New Business department; then it goes to the Underwriting department; then ...'

This is perfectly reasonable. The audience for the statement knows what the New Business department is, and what the Underwriting department is. The terms are already well-defined. But it would not be reasonable or helpful to describe something entirely new, in the course of invention, in this kind of way:

> 'First it is dealt with by the Stage 1 tasks (I don't know what Stage 1 is, or what the tasks are, but we'll come back to that later); then it goes to the next stage – let's call it Stage 2 (I don't know what that is either); then ...'

It is not reasonable or helpful to use a top-down sequence of describing anything new because such a sequence gives a description built on sand. The terms used have no clear meanings at the time they are used, and will be subject to what are sometimes called *semantic drift* and *semantic conflict*. Semantic conflict occurs when different people attribute different meanings to the same word. Semantic drift occurs when one person uses the same word in gradually changing meanings over a period of time. Semantic drift and semantic conflict are common problems in many kinds of system. In typical office workflow systems they need scarcely occur at all, and it is gratuitously harmful to introduce them into the development.

User Commitment and Discovery

An important technique for obtaining and strengthening user commitment to the system is to involve the users from the very beginning in the process of *discovery*. Discovery is finding out the system requirements by finding out the details of the business interactions between the office and the world outside.

We have assumed in previous chapters that the rules and patterns of business interaction are already well established and well known. They are fixed by legislation, by the customs of the business sector, and by the established practices of the enterprise and its customers. But the knowledge of these established rules and patterns is most often possessed by the users, not by the technical information systems staff. This knowledge – like most kinds of human knowledge – may be distributed among many users, and nowhere recorded in a systematic written form.

This situation offers both a need and an opportunity for cooperation in building both the data and the process models.

Early discovery sessions

If the whole business area of the project is not already very well known to the developers, it is often wise to conduct some early discovery sessions with selected users. For each particular topic, such as New Business, or Endorsements, or Underwriting, experienced users from the appropriate department should be requested to take part in a discovery session. The central purpose of the session is for the users to instruct the developers, not *vice versa*. There should therefore be no more than two developers at most in the session, one of whom should act as a facilitator: that is, should ensure that all the users are stimulated and enabled to take an active part, and should exercise enough control over the session to keep it focused on its purpose.

The purpose of an early discovery session may be, for example, to create a list of candidate entities and tasks in the part of the business area in hand. Simply asking users to provide such a list by spontaneous generation of ideas does not usually work. It is therefore necessary to start with something to focus attention and thought. A good candidate for this role is a tentative context dia-

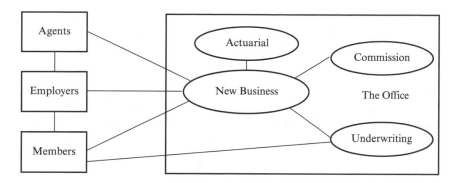

Figure 9.1   *A dataflow context diagram.*

gram, in which the world outside the office, and the office itself, have been broken down into smaller parts.

One or two outline diagrams of this kind were shown in Chapter 1 (Introduction); a variant of those diagrams could be used, or the kind of context diagram that is used as the top level of a Structured Analysis dataflow diagram. Figure 9.1 is an example.

Using a context diagram

It is important to understand that the diagram shown in Figure 9.1 has no formal meaning. Its purpose is to help the participants in the discovery session to make a reasonably complete list of the tasks involved in the business area – which in this case is New Business.

The starting point is the identification of the business area, the classes of individuals with which it interacts in the world outside, and the other departments or areas within the office with which it communicates. The diagram in Figure 9.1 shows that the New Business department communicates with the Underwriting, Commission, Actuarial and Finance departments, and interacts with Agents, Employers and Members. At this point, there are no arrow heads on the lines that indicate communication and interaction: each line merely indicates that there is some kind of communication between the parts it connects.

By cooperating in making this initial diagram, the users are stimulated to think purposefully about the interactions and communications that occur in their work. Then further detail can be added, by identifying the particular messages and documents that pass in either direction. It is a good idea here to maintain a numbered list of the message and document types, and to write the numbers, together with arrowheads indicating the direction of message sending, on the lines of the diagram, adding further lines where necessary. In this way it is possible to achieve two useful results.

- The users participating in the session become enthusiastic contributors to the list of messages and documents, and so strengthen their commitment to the system being developed.
- The list created is a useful starting point in identifying the tasks to be performed by the users in the area being discussed.

The resulting decorated diagram will look something like Figure 9.2, although in a realistic case it would contain more communications than are shown there.
    The associated list of communication messages may be as follows.

(1)   The department requests underwriting of a life from the Underwriting department.
(2)   The department informs the Commission department of new business and the associated commission rates.
(3)   Employers send proposals either directly or through an agent.
(4)   The department requests and receives rates for group life schemes from the Actuarial department.
(5)   Various chasing and follow-up letters are sent out by the department.
(6)   Responses are received to various follow-up and chasing letters.
(7)   Employers send cancellation notices to the department.
(8)   Prospective members send application forms to the department to join a scheme.
(9)   The Underwriting department sends requests for medical and other information to prospective members.
(10) Prospective members send requested information to the Underwriting department.
(11) The Underwriting department quotes terms for insuring a life in accordance with a request previously received from the department.

Notice the extremely informal nature of the diagram and the list. Neither the selection of information nor the manner in which it is represented are precisely

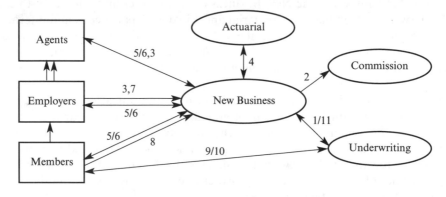

Figure 9.2   *A decorated dataflow context diagram.*

consistent. But this is not important. The diagram and list do not form a part of the formal project documentation: they are above all aids to discovery, and to motivating the participants at the discovery meeting. The interaction between participating users leads to a very efficient process of discovering what is sought – here, classes of outside world entities, and interactions between the department and those entities and between the department and other departments of the enterprise.

Later discovery sessions

Almost any stage of the project at which information is needed about the conduct of the business can make use of a discovery session of this general kind. The need for information creates a need – better viewed as an opportunity – for involving the users in the development and increasing their commitment.

Here are some examples of possible further discovery sessions:

- A session to identify all the types of form sent to and completed by clients, medical practitioners and other people. The sending and receipt of these forms will become tasks in the system.
- A session to identify the information needed by office users to handle the completed forms when they are received. This information leads to the identification of the datasets for the associated tasks.
- A session to identify lifecycles by identifying recognizable 'matters' in the existing user view of the arrangement of work. A 'matter' is often the subject of a separate paper file in an office where the existing organization of work is based on largely manual procedures.

The crucial characteristic of a successful discovery session is the active role of the users. They are not watching the developers at work; they are not even helping the developers with their work. They are doing the work themselves, with a little encouragement and help from the developers.

Total User Ownership

The work done in discovery sessions is essentially informal. It would be inappropriate in these sessions to demand the degree of precision necessary for the detailed specification of the data model and for the programming of tasks. But there is one important area in which users can, and should, be given full control over a formal part of the system.

This is in the specification of business rules for tasks. In Chapter 6 a number of simple types of rule were discussed. Some of them should be specified directly by users, who then become the owners of those rules, and responsible for ensuring their correctness in the event of business changes. For example:

- *wait* rules, in which the office waits a specified number of days for a response from the outside world before taking a certain action: for example, waiting for a 30-day 'cooling-off period' during which the policyholder is legally entitled to repudiate the contract.
- *check* rules, which specify whether certain attribute values are acceptable in a certain case: for example, whether a certain type of policy may be issued in respect of an assured life who is less than 18 years old.
- *set* rules, which specify mandatory values for certain attributes in certain circumstances: for example, the number of days of grace allowed for premium payment in a certain type of policy may be fixed at 10.
- *applicability* rules, which specify when a certain task is applicable: for example, that a task that starts a ChequePayment lifecycle is applicable only when the payment method for the order is marked as '*cheque*'.

User specification of all or most of these rules is an important contribution to economy in development resources, because they know best what the rules should be. At the same time, it provides the basis for ownership and fosters their commitment to the system.

Speed of Development

Most projects are scheduled according to the needs of the business – especially the competitive – situation. Meeting the schedule is an obvious goal, and can justify some acceleration of the development process. But it is important to recognize that acceleration of development brings attendant risks: especially the risk that the system will be of poor quality and will damage the enterprise by inconvenient or faulty operational behaviour. There is also the risk that it will prove expensive or even impossible to maintain when requirements change (a later section in this chapter returns to this point in discussing documentation).

A fast-track project

The basic notion of a fast-track method is to eliminate some development phases that seem to offer too little benefit for their cost. Methods that lead to database implementations always invite the creation and use of fast-track versions, because data and process modelling can always be viewed as activities of 'analysis' or 'specification' that can be dispensed with when the schedule is pressing. The method discussed in this book is particularly prone to this approach, because so much of what is done leads in the end to the construction of the database implementation.

In Chapter 8 some aspects of the database implementation were discussed. It was shown there that lifecycles and task structures, and entity roles, and workflow job structures, can all be represented in terms of a relational database. They can therefore all be expressed in terms of a database schema and a population of records conforming to the schema. In a fast-track project it is possible, in the extreme case, to develop the whole system in those terms: the only tool the developers need is the software to support the entry and population of a schema.

In some projects this fast-track approach may be a feasible option. The essential precondition is that the specification of the system – the underlying data and process models, both in their large structures and in their smallest details – must be thoroughly well understood by everyone involved, including both the developers and the users. This understanding may be present for various reasons.

- The system to be built is a direct re-implementation of an existing mechanized system that works well, is thoroughly understood, and is to be faithfully reproduced in the new system.
- The system to be built is an implementation of an existing set of models. These existing models may be either:
  - a generic system that happens to require little or no tailoring for the requirements of the system to be built; or
  - a set that emerged from a very careful and detailed Business Process Reengineering project that has been thoroughly discussed and criticized, and is now accepted by everyone in the office.
- The system to be built is trivially simple to understand, in a business where the central demands on the system are response time and throughput of a small set of simple transaction types.

These conditions will rarely be satisfied. From the point of view of a risk analysis, it is important to remember that the great disasters of systems development come from too much speed and too little precision. There have been failures due to too much precision and too little speed, certainly; but they are almost always smaller failures, with less serious consequences.

What might be called a semi-fast-track project can be based on a strong emphasis on early discovery sessions at the expense of the more formal modelling stages. These discovery sessions can be conducted over an intensive period, and can give a fast route to at least a first approximation of the required data and process models, which can then be expressed in database terms.

Incremental development

Another way of modifying the pace of development is to adopt an incremental approach, delivering a succession of increments to the system by which it grows from a small and simple core to the full-blown system.

One great potential benefit of an incremental approach is that it helps to familiarize the users with a new system. This is particularly important where users have had little or no previous experience of computer-based interactive systems, and need time to become familiar with their operation.

We may note that this lack of familiarity with interactive computer-based systems is becoming rarer and rarer, as the use of computers at home becomes more and more common. The problem is likely to shift slightly, to a need to make interactive business systems look more and more like whatever games or web-surfing software are in common use by young people.

A database implementation is helpful here again. Once the basic entity model has been defined, with a reasonable population of attributes for the entities, it is easy to generate the programs for a number of tasks automatically. For example:

- Tasks for basic data entry of each entity class.
- Tasks for navigating through datasets, defined in the database as partial views.
- Tasks for updating entity records.
- Tasks for displaying or printing tied roles – that is, projections of entity data in the form of selected attributes.
- Tasks for entering values of pointer attributes, with automatically generated assistance for finding and choosing valid foreign keys ('reference help').

Documentation

Documentation of a system may be defined as a collection of descriptions that do not form a part of the operational software itself. So a lifecycle diagram showing stages and tasks is documentation, while the same information expressed in a database schema is not. Traditionally, documentation is a bugbear of software developers. Often it is ignored altogether; often it is hastily produced in a grudging and perfunctory last step before the developers are released from their bondage to the project.

There are several important points about documentation that should be grasped before it can be assigned its proper place and weight in a project.

Documentation for understanding

Documentation is not an end in itself. The sole purpose of documentation is human understanding.

Developers need to understand what they are creating while they are creating it. For them, documentation must be an aid to accuracy and to creative thought. This is the reason for using diagrams to represent data and process models, rather than the database schemas into which they can, and will, be converted: the diagrams are simply easier to work with and to understand, and they can suggest ideas and questions in a way that even an equivalent textual representation of the same information can not.

Users need to be able to understand what the system means in business terms. Does the system provide for policyholders who have lost their policies? Does it provide for customers who want to cancel one line item of an order but leave the rest intact? What rules does it embody for the payment of commissions? What information is stored about policyholders?

After the system has been in operation and requires to be changed, both users and developers need to understand what the effect of any proposed change will be. If the maximum length of a line of address is increased from 25 to 30 characters, what entity attributes will be directly or indirectly affected? What print formats will need to be changed?

The same documentation is unlikely to serve all these purposes of understanding, because different people are asking different kinds of question. So the place of documentation in the project should be seen not as one large question, but as many smaller questions. And, of course, each document itself should aim not to give a huge complete description that answers every question about everything, but a small and clear description that answers one question about one thing.

Automatic documentation

Some useful documentation can be produced automatically. For example, some database development environments can produce schema diagrams automatically from the textual form of the database schemas. Some can produce what is often called an 'impact analysis', in which the impact of a proposed change to the database scheme definition is explicitly followed through and reported. The attraction of using automatic documentation tools is, of course, that producing the documentation costs almost nothing.

But there is no point in automatically produced documentation if it does not serve the purpose for which it was produced. In particular, it is a mistake to think that automatically produced documentation can serve the purposes of developers during the early creative phases of a project that is building a completely new system. For such purposes, the human act of producing the documentation is itself the carrier of a large part of its benefit. By contrast, developers faced with modifying a large existing system that they do not understand may be well served by the kind of documentation that can be produced automatically from the implemented system.

Documentation choice is risk-oriented

Choices about the production and use of documentation in a project should, in general, be based on risk analysis rather than goal analysis. The risk of making the wrong choice is primarily the risk of finding that necessary understanding is hard to obtain, that important questions cannot be readily answered. This is what happens in the classic cases of systems that become impossible to maintain because no-one understands them.

Because documentation choices are risk-oriented, the documentation activity should be seen as a collection of available techniques for managing identified risks, not as a general requirement to be satisfied in a standard manner. The focus of the risk analysis must be: What questions may be asked? By whom? How bad will it be if they cannot be easily answered? What documents would allow them to be answered?

The decisions that will flow from risk analysis should determine the following.

- What documents are to be produced in the development stages to describe the data and process models, the tasks and the workflow structures?
- What software support should be provided for deriving documents automatically from the development products to answer specific questions that may arise?

Incompleteness Risks

A particular kind of technical risk in any system is that the system will be incomplete: that is, that essential functionality has been omitted. This is important enough to merit a brief discussion here.

Trivial and serious incompleteness

Sometimes an incompleteness risk is relatively insignificant. For example, if a system fails to produce addressed envelopes for letters that require them, it is straightforward if somewhat irksome to produce the envelopes by some other means – even on a typewriter if necessary – while waiting for the deficiency in the system function to be repaired.

Sometimes the risk is serious. For certain kinds of incompleteness, there is a risk that unforeseen circumstances will leave the system in a state that cannot be tolerated for business or legal reasons but also cannot be repaired in any sure and reliable way. For example, insurance and other financial sector systems are the target of frequent fraud; at the same time they are subject to stringent auditing requirements. A fraud may not be discovered until a late stage, after many tasks have been performed, creating a tangled web of consequences that can neither be accepted nor be easily unravelled. A system of this kind that does not have provision for dealing with late-discovered fraud is seriously incomplete.

Identifying incompleteness

A valuable aid to identifying incompleteness during development is a suitably organized discovery session. Incompleteness is an entertaining topic to explore, because it involves questioning every assumption, and this is like playing an amusing game. Experienced users are by far the best people to identify incompleteness in a system description, simply because they will have seen enough unexpected happenings to know that there can always be more.

Simple techniques may be used in such a discovery session. In particular, it is very useful to encourage the participants to look at every significant interaction from the point of view of the individuals in the world outside. Because an office workflow focuses on supporting the work of the users in the office, there is a danger of failing to consider what could happen at the other end of each interaction. What if the policyholder is away on holiday? What if the dog eats the policy document? What if dealing in the shares is suspended?

It is also useful to try to match up every communication with its response. For example, in the group insurance new business system area roughly sketched in Figure 9.2, we might ask why the communication numbered 8 in the diagram evokes no response. Prospective members send application forms to the New Business department to join a scheme, but apparently receive no response.

Finally, because there will be some residual incompleteness in even the best system, it is essential to provide means to detect and handle unforeseen situations during system operation. A notable example is a regular workflow report showing situations that may be evidence of incompleteness:

- *Stalled tasks*   Any task that has been waiting in the start state for more than a certain length of time may be in danger of never being executed at all. The important case from an incompleteness point of view is waiting without time limit for an X-task such as a response from the outside world – perhaps from a client – that never comes.
- *Task class profile*   If no instances of a particular class of task have been performed within a certain period, this may simply reflect the current profile of task activity. But it may instead reflect a failure in the design of the system to schedule tasks of that class or to make them available to office users for performance. This is likely to apply to I-tasks, where the initiative lies within the office. The system may be failing to give users the opportunity to perform the tasks.

Handling incompleteness

The main technique for handling the incompleteness that remains when the system goes into operation is to provide tasks and lifecycles that can restore the system to an acceptable and consistent state. The definition of these tasks and lifecycles will rely heavily on the techniques for handling backtracking, discussed in Chapter 6.

It is reasonable, in a system where the risks and penalties of incompleteness are high, to devote a project phase specifically to the design and provision of such restoring tasks and lifecycles.

Chapter Summary

The outline sequence of stages implied by the method must be adapted and filled out to give an appropriate structure for the particular project in hand.

- The choice of project structure should be based on an assessment of the goals and risks for the project.
- Goals are positive: they are broader and more general. Risks are negative; they are more specific than goals.
- A central goal in any office workflow project is user commitment to the system. This can only be achieved by involving the users as leading participants in the development.
- The technical content of the method stages imposes some major constraints on the ordering of development activities. But it also leaves some substantial freedoms.
- A vital additional activity in many projects will be discovery sessions. The output of a discovery session is informal; the chief purpose is to involve the users in identifying all the elements of the business and the interactions it involves.
- A project plan can be oriented towards the fastest possible development; it can also be oriented towards incremental development and delivery. The latter is valuable for user familiarization with the system.
- Documentation activities should be chosen in response to identified risks, and documents should aim to answer specific questions rather than to provide complete descriptions.
- A specific project phase devoted to identifying possible sources of incompleteness and to dealing with them is often justified.

Questions

9.1 How many entity classes might there be in the data model for a medium-size office workflow system? How many attributes for a typical entity class? If the whole data model is to be shown on one piece of paper, how big would the paper have to be?

9.2 Identify three risks that you think might be important in a development project.

9.3 Sketch a lifecycle for New Business, handling a simple life assurance proposal. Now sketch a lifecycle for the same interaction, seen from the proposer's point of view.

9.4 What is the technical purpose of a discovery session? What is the motivational purpose?

9.5 How can you deal with the possibility that the system will encounter unforeseen situations?

9.6 What kinds of task program can be automatically generated from the data model?

9.7 Is it possible to define all the tasks completely before defining any lifecycles?

9.8 Describe three questions you might want to be able to answer from a data model.

9.9 Why must tasks be defined before workflow?

9.10 When would you consider adopting a fast-track project structure? What would the main work in such a project focus on?

Appendix I Glossary

Note Words shown in italics in a glossary definition are themselves the subjects of other glossary entries.

A-Task
    An *automatic task*.

ANY
    A special value used in place of a *null value* for an *association attribute*.

Association
    A link between two *entity instances* of the same or different *classes*.

Association Attribute
    An *entity attribute* whose value is an association of the entity with another entity of the same or a different class. For example, the LifeAssured attribute of a POLICY entity has a value that associates the policy with a CLIENT entity. Also referred to as a *pointer attribute*, because it points to the other entity.

Attribute
    A property of an *entity*. An attribute has a *value*, drawn from the *domain* of the attribute. For example, the attribute Premium of a POLICY entity has a value drawn from the domain **money**.

Automatic Task
    An automatic *task* is one that does not require any interaction between the machine and a user. For example, sending a reminder letter for an overdue bill may be an automatic task.

Backtracking
    Returning to an earlier point in time to reprocess transactions that have proved to be incorrect. Suppose, for example, that an erroneous debit is made in a bank account offering interest compounded monthly. When the error is discovered four months later, it is necessary to return to the point at which the error was made, correct it, and recalculate the interest from that point to the present.

Backtracking Lifecycle

A *lifecycle* devoted to handling *backtracking*. That is, to determining and dealing with the *side-effects*, and restoring the desired state of affairs.

Beneficent Side-Effect

A *side-effect* that is useful, and need not therefore be undone (or compensated for) when *backtracking* to an earlier state.

Booking Date

The date on which the input for a task was received by the *machine*.

Business Module

A major area of responsibility in the business conducted by the *enterprise*.

Business Rule

A rule of business that forms a part of a *task* definition. For example, that the policyholder of a type-3 policy must be over the age of 18. The types of business rule include *set rules*, *wait rules* and *check rules*.

Cancel

To terminate the progress of a *lifecycle*.

Candidate Key

A column, or combination of columns, in a relational database table, that can serve as a *key* to the rows: that is, no two rows have the same key value.

Cardinality

The cardinality of an association or relationship is its 'how-manyness'. For example, *one-to-one* and *many-to-one* are cardinalities.

Cardinality Expression

A precise expression specifying how many *entities* at one end of an *association* can be associated with one entity at the other end. For example, the number of ENGINE entities associated with one AEROPLANE entity is (1-4, 6, 8).

Check Rule

A *business rule* that certain checks should be applied to certain *entity attributes*.

Class

A collection of distinct identifiable individuals sharing certain characteristics. For example, the *entity* class POLICY is a collection of distinct identifiable individual POLICY entities, sharing the characteristics that they all have Policyholder and Premium *attributes*. The *lifecycle* class CLAIM is a collection of distinct identifiable individual CLAIM lifecycles, sharing the characteristics that they all have Notification, Assessment and Payment stages.

Classification Entity

An *entity* whose purpose is to provide information about associated entities by describing the properties of a *class* to which they belong. So, for example, an INVESTMENT-PLAN entity may describe such properties as limits on the invested capital, tax regime, interest payments and repayments of capital. An INVESTMENT-CONTRACT associated with the plan would have those properties. Each individual INVESTMENT-PLAN entity therefore effectively defines a class whose members are the INVESTMENT-CON-TRACTs associated with the plan.

Composite Domain

A domain whose *values* are *composite values*: that is, they are not atomic or elementary, but are made up of more elementary values. A composite domain is also called a *datagroup domain*.

Composite Value

A *value* that is made up of more elementary values. For example, a **date** is made up of a **day**, a **month** and a **year**. A domain of composite values is called a *composite domain*.

Context

The parts of the world that are involved with the system. In particular, the *office* with the *users*, the *outside world* and the *machine*.

Context Diagram

A diagram showing the parts of the *context* and their intercommunication.

Controlling Influence

An *entity* that is associated with another entity, and determines the choice for it of the appropriate *lifecycle class* from a *lifecycle family*.

D-Task

A *task* that consists essentially of making a decision. For example, deciding whether to admit a large claim against a policy.

Data Model

A *model* that concentrates on the properties that remain unchanged over time and the individuals over which those properties hold. For example, a description in terms of *entities* and their *relationships* is a data model.

Datagroup Domain

See *Composite Domain*.

Dataset

The set of data associated with a *lifecycle* or *task*. It consists of the database record for the *root entity* (the entity to which the lifecycle or task is most closely linked), and other entity records directly or indirectly associated with the root entity.

Date-Effective Attribute

A *composite attribute* that marks a database record with a *Start Date* and *End Date* to define the period during which it is valid. This allows an efficient and convenient application of different rules and plans to lifecycles that have the same type but began at different times. It can also greatly simplify the difficulties of *backtracking*.

Decision Table

A table laying out the distinct combinations of circumstances for a complex *business rule*.

Decision Table Rule

A column in a *decision table*, specifying a rule that applies in a particular combination of circumstances.

Defined Attribute

To be distinguished from an *observed attribute*. An *attribute* whose *value* is defined in terms of observed attributes. For example, the AgeNextBirthday attribute of a CLIENT entity is defined in terms of the client's BirthDate attribute and TodaysDate, which are themselves observed.

Dependent Entity

An *entity* is dependent on another if it cannot exist without the other. For example, an ORDERLINE entity cannot exist without an ORDER entity in which it is a line.

Discovery Session

A session involving experienced business users and one or two system developers, in which the users are stimulated to explore their knowledge of the business and make it explicit.

Domain

A set of *values* of the same kind. For example, **money** is a domain whose value are money amounts such as £252.16 or £1.27; **date** is a domain whose values are dates such as 10 July 1997 or 25 December 1999.

Domain Declaration

A textual representation of a *domain*, showing its name and the representation of its *values* by a database *type*. For a *composite domain*, the structure of its values is shown.

Dynamic Model

A *model* describing how some part of the world changes over time by the occurrence of events. A *process model* is a dynamic model. An example of a dynamic model is a collection of *lifecycle* definitions, which describe the arrangement of task performances in the successive stages of the lifecycle.

E-Task
    A data-entry *task*, such as entering the information about a new customer into the database.

EDI
    Electronic Data Interchange: the electronic transmission of data to implement atomic commercial transactions such as bank debits and credits.

End Date
    The date up to which the information in a database record is valid. Part of the *Date-Effective attribute* of the record.

Enterprise
    The organization that owns the *office*, and on whose behalf the office conducts the business.

Entity
    An entity is an identifiable individual belonging to an *entity class*. For example, John Smith may be an entity belonging to the entity class CLIENT.

Entity Attribute
    See *Attribute*.

Entity Class
    See *Class*.

Entity Declaration
    A textual representation of the properties of an *entity class*.

Entity Diagram
    A diagram used to represent all or part of a *data model*, in which each *entity class* is represented by a box, with its *attributes* represented by stripes in the box.

Entity Instance
    See *Instance*.

Entity Lifecycle
    See *Lifecycle*.

Event Date
    The date on which an event occurred in the *outside world*: for example, the date of death of an assured life. This may be significantly earlier than the *booking date*.

Failed
    When a *task* has been performed, but has failed, it places itself in the *failed* state. For example, a customer credit checking task that finds the customer's credit is not good places itself in the *failed* state.

Family
See *Lifecycle Family*.

Features Database
The part of the database containing definitions of the features from which the business plans in the *plan database* are constructed. Feature definitions may be program texts, or data records that can be interpreted by programs.

Floating Role
A *role* that may be played by *entities* of different *classes*. For example, the role of [dwelling] may be played by a HOUSE, FLAT, BOAT or CARAVAN entity.

Foreign Key
A *key* occurring in an entity record as an *association attribute*. Also used to denote the value of an association attribute.

Freestanding Task
A *task* that is not positioned within a *lifecycle,* but can occur at any time. For example, a *data-entry task* for a new CUSTOMER *entity* would be a freestanding task, because the new customer may be quite unrelated to any existing entity or lifecycle.

Function
A piece of program that can be thought of as a unit, and can be embodied in (or invoked from) the program for a *task*.

Hidden Key
See *ID*.

I-Task
An internally initiated *task*. That is, one initiated by a user in the *office*, not by a person or organization or system in the *outside world*.

ID
An automatically allocated hidden identifier. Every *entity* – that is, every row in every table – in the system has an ID, which is the value of a hidden ID *attribute*. The ID is also referred to as a *hidden key*.

Indifferent Entry
An entry in a *decision table rule* for an *attribute* indicating that the rule is to be applied regardless of the *value* of the attribute. The entry is represented by '–', which is not regarded as a *specific* attribute value.

Initiate
The *machine* initiates a *task* by placing it in the *start* state, so that it is ready to be performed. A *user*, or a person or organization or system in the *outside world*, initiates a task by causing an event that involves or demands performance of the task. For example, a policyholder may initiate the ReceiveBirthCertificate task by sending her birth certificate to the *office*.

Instance

An instance of a *class* is an individual of that class. For example, John Smith and Jane White may be instances of the entity class CLIENT.

Interaction Sequence

An interaction sequence is a sequence of events in which the *office* interacts with a person or an organization in the *outside world*. For example, a small interaction sequence may consist just of the sending of a letter by the office and the sending of a reply by the recipient. Large interaction sequences may involve several people or organizations in the outside world.

Intolerable Side-Effect

A *side-effect* that must be undone (or compensated for) when *backtracking* to an earlier state.

K-Task

A data-checking task. Typically, checking the data entered by an *E-task*.

Key

A value uniquely identifying a row of a relational database table.

Lifecycle

A lifecycle is a major *interaction sequence*. A lifecycle is always associated with a *root entity*.

Lifecycle Dependency

A constraint between two *lifecycle classes*, referred to as the master and dependent lifecycles. It specifies that no instance of the dependent lifecycle class may progress past a certain point unless the instance of the master lifecycle class for the same *entity* has reached a certain *stage*.

Lifecycle Family

A collection of *lifecycle classes* for a single *entity class*. All members of the family have the same lifecycle class name. The choice of the appropriate lifecycle class is determined by the *controlling influence* for the entity for which the lifecycle is to be started.

Lifecycle Stage

The largest subdivision of a *lifecycle*. In general, progression through the stages of a lifecycle is sequential, each stage finishing before the next stage begins. But this progression may be modified by *backtracking*, and by some *parallel processing* of stages.

Lifecycle State

The state of a lifecycle is the extent to which it has progressed through its *stages*. Lifecycle states are named from the stages: for example, InStage3, AwaitingStage5, SuspendedInStage4, and so on.

Link Entity Class

> An *entity class* whose purpose is to represent a *many-to-many association* or an association with more than two participants. Each instance of the link entity class represents a link between two or more associated entities. For example, each instance of MARRIAGE represents a link between two PERSON entities.

M-Task

> A *manual task*.

Machine

> The machine is the part of the system composed of computer hardware and software. It may be distributed, consisting of several machines linked by a network.

Manual Task

> A manual *task* is one that requires interaction between the *machine* and a *user*. For example, entering information from a handwritten letter is a manual task.

many-to-many Relationship

> A *relationship* between *entity class* A and entity class B is many-to-many if it can associate one A entity with many Bs, and one B with many As. For example, the relationship **teaches** between TEACHER and PUPIL entities in a school is a many-to-many relationship, because each TEACHER teaches many PUPILs and each PUPIL is taught by many TEACHERs.

many-to-one Relationship

> A *relationship* between *entity class* A and entity class B is many-to-one if it can associate many A entities with the same B, but each A with at most one B. For example, the relationship **MemberOf** between PUPIL and CLASS entities in a school is a many-to-one relationship, because many PUPILs are members of the same CLASS, but each PUPIL is a member of only one CLASS.

Method

> A systematic way of doing anything. In particular, of developing systems of a certain kind.

Method Phase

> A conceptual phase in the development method, not necessarily corresponding to the recognizable phases of a practical project. The method phases are: the Entity Model phase; the Business Interaction Model phase; the Business Tasks Definition phase; and the Office Workflow Definition phase.

Model

> A is a model of **B** if there is some important description that is true of both of them. The common description is often also spoken of as a model. For example, a data model is a description both of certain aspects of the world outside the *machine*, and of the arrangement, structure and content of the

database records inside the machine.

N/A

See *Not-Applicable*.

Neutral Side-Effect

A *side-effect* that is neither *intolerable* nor *beneficent*. It can be accepted or undone, whichever is more convenient.

NONE

A special value used in place of a *null value* for an *association attribute*.

Not-Applicable

A state of a *task*. When a task is started but finds that it is not applicable to the situation in hand, it places itself in the not-applicable state. Tasks in a *task selection group* that are not executed are placed in the not-applicable state. Also called the *n/a* state.

Null Value

A specially-chosen value of an *entity attribute* that is used when no specific value can be assigned to the attribute, either because it is not known, or because no specific value is applicable to the particular entity concerned.

O-Task

A *task* that produces output. For example, sending a letter inviting renewal of a motor policy.

Obligation

A mutual legal or moral bond that commits two parties to interact over a period in a certain way. For example, when a customer places an order the enterprise becomes obliged to supply the goods at some point in the future, and the customer becomes obliged to accept and pay for them.

Obligation Entity

An entity that represents an *obligation*, such as a PENSION entity, or a MORTGAGE entity.

Observed Attribute

An *attribute* whose value for each *entity* that has that attribute can be determined only by observation of the world. For example, the BirthDate attribute of a CLIENT entity can be determined only by observation of the world – or, equivalently, by relying on information provided directly or indirectly from such observation. To be distinguished from a *defined attribute*.

Office

The part of the *enterprise* that conducts the enterprise's business with the *outside world*.

one-to-many Relationship

A one-to-many *relationship* is a *many-to-one relationship* viewed in the other direction. The relationship **MemberOf** between PUPIL and CLASS entities in a school is a *many-to-one relationship* (many PUPILs are members of one CLASS). Viewed in the other direction, the relationship **HasMembers** between CLASSes and PUPILs is a one-to-many relationship (one CLASS has many PUPILs).

one-to-one Relationship
A *relationship* between *entity class* A and entity class B is one-to-one if it can associate each A entity with only one B, and each B with only one A. For example, the relationship *governs* between GOVERNMENT and COUNTRY entities is a one-to-one relationship, because each GOVERNMENT governs one COUNTRY and each COUNTRY is governed by one GOVERNMENT.

Original Task
An original task is a *task* that is automatically started when its containing *lifecycle stage* is started. All the original tasks of a stage can be performed in parallel.

Outside World
The world outside the *office*, with which the *enterprise* conducts its business. For example, for a mail order company the outside world would include at least its suppliers, customers, customers who are also catalogue agents, credit card companies, banks, and the Post Office and other delivery services.

Owner
The owners of a part of a system are the people who are responsible for it and are entitled to change it.

P-Task
A task that is *initiated* immediately following a preceding task.

Parallel Processing
Simultaneous progression through two or more *lifecycles* or other processes. For example, a policy may be simultaneously progressing through a lifecycle for premium payment and a lifecycle for claim assessment. A single lifecycle may be simultaneously progressing through two *stages*, where an incomplete task in the earlier stage is not *relevant* until after the later stage. Within one lifecycle stage different *users* may be simultaneously working on two tasks.

Passed
A state of a *task*. When a task has been performed, and has succeeded, it places itself in the *passed* state. For example, a data checking task that finds no error in the data places itself in the *passed* state.

Phase
See *Method Phase*.

Plan Database
The part of the database containing details of the plans according to which the business is conducted. For example: pensions plans in a life assurance

company, or discount plans in a selling organization.

Pointer

The value of an *association attribute*. It is equal to the *ID* of the associated entity, and can be usefully thought of as pointing to it.

Pointer Attribute

See *Association Attribute*.

Primary Key

The *key* of an *entity* record that is the most important from the point of view of a *user* of the system: that is, the most effective and most commonly used.

Process Model

A model that describes the arrangement and sequencing of events over time, and the consequent pattern of changes in state. For example, a *lifecycle* description is a process model.

Processing Date

The date on which a *task* is considered to be performed. This will usually be the actual date of performance. But in some circumstances, especially when *backtracking*, it may be an earlier date.

Production Database

The part of the database containing data that records the conduct of the business. For example: policy records in an insurance company.

Ran

A state of a *task*. When a task has been performed, but its purpose has not been completed, it places itself in the *ran* state. For example, the task of writing a letter places itself in the *ran* state so that a further task can receive the expected reply. When a task is placed in the ran state, it automatically *spawns* all of its *subtasks*.

Reference Help

Interactive on-screen help provided for the purpose of finding the record of a particular *entity*. For example, entering the first few characters of a CLIENT's name may produce a display of all CLIENTs whose names begin with those characters.

Relationship

An association between two *classes*, by which individuals of one class are associated with individuals of the other class. For example, PlacedBy is a relationship between ORDER and CUSTOMER *entity classes*, in which each ORDER entity is associated with exactly one CUSTOMER entity. A relationship may be *one-to-one*, *many-to-one* or *many-to-many*.

Relevant

A *task* is said to be relevant to a *lifecycle stage* when that stage may not be started until the task is complete. For example, the task ClearCheque may be relevant to the lifecycle stage ReleaseGoods. The stage to which a task is relevant may be separated from the stage in which it appears by one or more intervening stages. These intervening stages can therefore progress without waiting for the task to be completed.

Resume

To permit a *suspended* lifecycle to continue to progress.

Role

A role is a part played, or a position occupied, by one *entity* in relation to others. For example, a CLIENT *entity* may play the role of [policyholder] in relation to a POLICY *entity*.

Role Definition

A textual definition of a *role*. It specifies the *classes* of *entity* that may play the role, the *attributes* of those entity classes that are required for the role, and the renaming of those attributes. For example, the role of [payer] can be played by a CLIENT entity; it requires the client attribute BankDetails; and it renames the attribute BankAccount.

Root Entity

The *entity* primarily involved in a *task* or *lifecycle* is said to be the root entity for that task or lifecycle.

Rule

See *Business Rule, Decision Table Rule*.

Rule Precedence

A scheme for allowing two or more *rules* in a *decision table* to apply to the same circumstances, and determining which rule should apply in any particular case by an order of precedence among rules.

Selection Group

See *Task Selection Group*.

Set Rule

A *business rule* stipulating that a certain *attribute* of an *entity* should be set to a certain *value*. For example, that the ContractStatus attribute of a certain kind of POLICY entity should be set to 'fully-paid' on the 30th anniversary of its commencement date.

Side-Effect

An effect of the execution of *tasks* in a *lifecycle*; especially, an effect of a task over which it becomes necessary to *backtrack*. Side-effects may include updating the database, producing outputs, and impact on the progress of other lifecycles.

Spawn

A *task* is said to spawn a *subtask* if the subtask is automatically started when the task reaches the *ran* state. The subtask may consist of a *task selection group*.

Specific Entry

An entry in a *decision table rule* for an attribute indicating that the rule is to be applied only when the attribute has the specific value given in the entry. The rule is not *indifferent* to the value of that attribute.

Stage

See *Lifecycle Stage*.

Start

A state of a *task*, in which it is ready to be performed. For example, an original task is placed in the *start* state when its containing *lifecycle stage* is started.

Start Date

The date from which the information in a database record is valid. Part of the *DateEffective* attribute of the record.

Static Model

A *model* describing the fixed properties of some part of the world: that is, the properties that do not change over time. A *data model* is a static model.

Strategic User

A strategic user is a *user* who is responsible for, and *owns*, a part of the *plan database*.

Subclass

A subclass is a *class* entirely contained in another class, which is a *superclass* with respect to the subclass. For example, the *entity* class MANAGER is a subclass of the entity class EMPLOYEE: every MANAGER is also an EMPLOYEE.

Subtask

A subtask is a *task*, or a *task selection group*, automatically started when a certain task is placed in the *ran* state.

Superclass

A *class* of which another class is a *subclass*. For example, the *entity* class EMPLOYEE is a superclass of the entity class MANAGER: every MANAGER is also an EMPLOYEE.

Suspend

To suspend a lifecycle *instance* is to prevent it from progressing until it is subsequently *resumed*.

T-Task

A *task* that is *initiated* at a predetermined time. For example, at the beginning of every month, or when the LifeAssured reaches the age of 65.

Task
A task is the smallest meaningful unit of work. For example, a task might be writing a letter asking for sight of a birth certificate, or receiving a premium payment.

Task Class
See *Class.*

Task Classification
The classification of *tasks* according to: how they are initiated (*I-task*, *P-task*, *T-task*, *X-task*); how they are performed (*A-task*, *M-task*); and their content (*D-task*, *E-task*, *K-task*, *O-task*, *U-task*). The full classification of a task is formed by one prefix chosen from each group: for example, a TMD-task.

Task Pool
The pool of *tasks* that are available for performance at any one time, either by *users* (for *manual tasks*) or automatically by the *machine* (for *automatic tasks*).

Task Selection Group
A group of *tasks* that are *spawned* as a single *subtask* of a task that is placed in the *ran* state. The tasks of a selection group are related by mutual exclusion. When the group is spawned, all the tasks of the group are started, but only one of them can be executed: the first task of the group that reaches the *ran*, *passed* or *failed* state causes all other tasks of the group to be placed in the *not-applicable* state.

Technical User
A technical *user* is one who is sufficiently technically expert to be responsible for, and to *own*, some part of the *features database*.

Tied Role
A role that is not a *floating role*. It is tied to a single *entity class*: that is, it can be played only by entities of that class.

Top-Down
A technique of approaching a topic as a hierarchical structure, dealing with the top level first and then successively lower levels until the bottom level is dealt with last. Top-down is a reasonable approach to describing something that already exists and has a single dominant hierarchical structure; it is not an effective approach to inventing or designing something new.

Type
A restricted kind of *value* in the computer for which the underlying database mechanism and programming language provide a representation and a set of operations. For example: Integer or Character(n).

U-Task

A *task* that updates the information in the database but does not create any new record.

UNKNOWN

A special *value* used in place of a *null value* for an *association attribute*.

User

A person working in the *office*, whose work is supported by the system being developed.

User Key

A *key* that is convenient for human use, such as a National Insurance Number, a Client Number or a motor car registration number.

Value

A particular individual element from an appropriate *domain*, corresponding to a particular *attribute* of a particular *entity*. For example, the value of the Height attribute of the entity John Smith may be 175cm, which is an element of the **humanheight** domain.

Wait Rule

A *business rule* stipulating that the office must wait for a certain period of time before performing some *task*. For example, 10 days must be allowed to elapse after the due date for an invoice payment before sending the customer a reminder letter demanding payment. A wait rule may be implemented by a separate task that waits for the stipulated period after it enters the *start* state and then automatically places itself in the *ran* state.

Workflow

The flow of work in the *office*. That is, the pattern of performing *tasks* by which the *users* conduct the business of the *enterprise*.

Workflow System

A system of the kind whose development is discussed in this book.

Workgroup

A group of *users* in the *office* who work on similar or related *tasks*. Often equivalent to a team as defined by a Business Process Re-engineering exercise: for example, a team to handle New Business in an insurance company.

X-Task

An externally *initiated* task. That is, a task initiated by a person or organization or system in the *outside world*, not by a *user* in the *office*.

Appendix 2
Diagrammatic Notations

In this appendix the diagrammatic notations used in the book are illustrated and explained. Some very informal *ad hoc* notations used only once or twice are omitted. See, for example, Figures 3.1 and 4.11.

Context Diagram

Problem context diagram

A problem context diagram shows the relevant parts of the world for a problem, their connections and the machine that is to solve the problem.

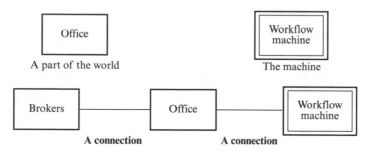

Figure A2.1

Two parts of the world and the machine are connected. The Brokers are connected to the Office; the Office is connected to the Workflow machine; the Brokers are not connected to the Workflow machine. The connections may be of any kinds.

Dataflow context diagram

A dataflow context diagram shows parts of the world outside the system of interest, and parts of the system of interest, and their connection by dataflows.

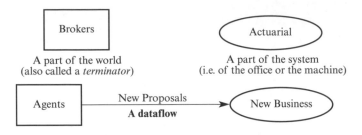

Figure A2.2

In a dataflow context diagram all connections are regarded as flows of data. A dataflow may be named or otherwise identified (e.g. by a number).

Entity Diagram

An entity diagram shows entity classes and their attributes and associations. It may also show roles. An entity diagram need not be complete: it may show only selected entities and selected associations.

Entities and attributes

Figure A2.3

An entity class named POLICY, with an entity attribute named Benefit, another attribute named CommenceDate, and unspecified further attributes (...).

The entity class name is always in the top stripe; but the order of the attributes is not significant.

Association attributes

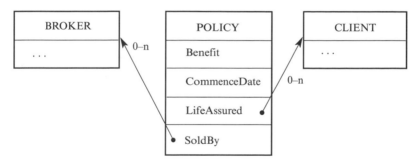

Figure A2.4

Each POLICY entity has a LifeAssured attribute associating it with one CLIENT and a SoldBy attribute associating it with one BROKER. Each CLIENT is associated with 0–n POLICY entities by their LifeAssured attributes; each BROKER is associated with 0–n POLICY entities by their SoldBy attributes.

Tied roles

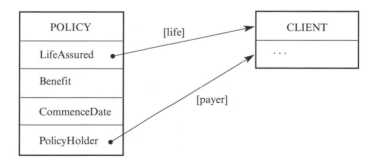

Figure A2.5

A CLIENT associated with a POLICY by its LifeAssured attribute plays the [life] role; a CLIENT associated by the PolicyHolder attribute plays the [payer] role. These are tied roles: they can be played only by CLIENT entities.

Floating roles

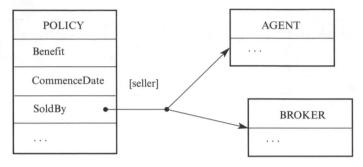

Figure A2.6

The [seller] role is a floating role: it may be played by an AGENT entity or by a BROKER entity.

Dataset diagram

A dataset is a hierarchical structure of entity records used in the performance of a task. The links in the structure show how one record can be reached from another using entity association attributes.

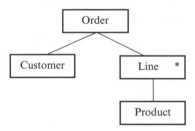

Figure A2.7

The root of the dataset is an Order entity record. From an Order record one Customer and zero or more Line records can be reached. From a Line record one Product record can be reached.

Lifecycle Stage Diagram

A lifecycle LC1 with three stages Stage1, Stage2 and Stage3, occurring in that order.

T is a task in Stage 1.

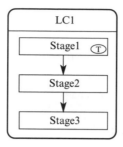

Figure A2.8

External control of lifecycle

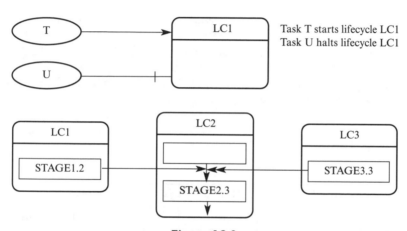

Task T starts lifecycle LC1
Task U halts lifecycle LC1

Figure A2.9

Stage2.3 of LC2 must not start until the linked LC1 has reached its Stage1.2 and *all* the linked LC3s have reached their Stage3.3.

Task Diagram

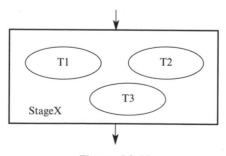

Figure A2.10

Tasks T1, T2 and T3 are independent original tasks in lifecycle stage StageX

Independent subtasks and selection groups

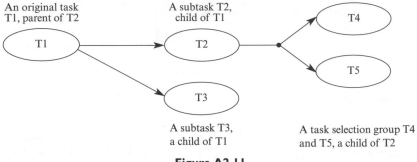

An original task
T1, parent of T2

A subtask T2,
child of T1

A subtask T3,
a child of T1

A task selection group T4
and T5, a child of T2

Figure A2.11

Subtasks T2 and T3 are mutually independent. Tasks T4 and T5 are in a selection group, so only one of them can be performed.

Decision Table

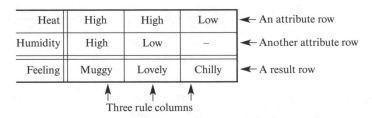

Heat	High	High	Low	← An attribute row
Humidity	High	Low	–	← Another attribute row
Feeling	Muggy	Lovely	Chilly	← A result row

Three rule columns

Figure A2.12

This decision table has two attribute rows (Heat and Humidity), one result row (Feeling) and three rule columns. The entry '–' for the Humidity attribute in the third rule is an *indifferent* attribute value; all other attribute values shown are *specific*.

Appendix 3 The LogicWare Environment

As the Preface explains, the method described in this book grew out of the creation and use of a development environment called LogicWare. The design and implementation of LogicWare was begun in 1988 by Beta Computers, a small software house in Scotland specializing in software solutions for major companies and other software houses. Beta is now a part of the Sherwood International Group of companies.

Sherwood's work is focused on business systems, with a particular emphasis on business process engineering. The goals of the LogicWare project were initially very simple: to provide an in-house tool set that would help to deliver large-scale business systems faster and more reliably. After several experiments, the original LogicWare development team of Kenny Cockburn, Peter Neilson, Colin Gordon and Graham Twaddle devised an initial approach that would help companies to re-engineer their business processes in a very practical way. The process descriptions and designs were recorded in a business-oriented repository that could be used by end users, designers and developers alike. Development of LogicWare has continued since 1988, and the LogicWare tool set now consists of several interrelated tools, including a run-time system.

The first versions concentrated on program generation from the repository. One of the tools, the *Logical Database Encapsulator*, provided an easy interface for the construction of relational database schemas. It supported the kind of entity modelling described in Chapters 3 and 5, including the mapping of the entity model into the relational schema and the treatment of roles, datagroup domains and derived attributes. A second tool, the *Autocode Processor*, generated program code in the 4GL associated with the database system. Some of the programs were generated from templates – for example, data entry and query programs; others were generated by fitting code automatically derived from the repository into a framework provided explicitly by the programmer.

The lifecycle basis of the business processes was treated next. The structure of lifecycles as sequences of stages was modelled in the repository, the information being entered in the same way as the business data model, using the

Logical Database Encapsulator and programs generated by the Autocode Processor. This uniformity between the handling of data and the handling of processes proved to be a source of considerable power and simplicity. The subsystem for populating the repository with lifecycle structures grew into a tool in its own right, called the *Workflow Tool*.

The Workflow Tool quickly developed to handle task structures within lifecycle stages. This kind of information was normally gathered as a part of an exercise in business process re-engineering, and it was natural to enter it into the repository in the same style as the larger lifecycle structure. The repository came to include information on task and subtask structures along with ownership and other business information. A graphical tool could then be used to diagram any of the business processes within the company, and also to produce a printed procedure manual such as those used in ISO 9001. Dependencies between separate lifecycles – such as the requirement that policy cancellation should halt premium collection – were also recorded, and these dependencies could then be handled within the process definition model.

Information about business processes was typically captured and recorded in workshops with the end users. The resulting repository data, suitably formatted and presented by diagramming and other tools, was treated as the definitive business requirements documentation and given both to the business people and to the system developers.

An important rule evolved at this stage: the task structure within the system must precisely reflect the tasks identified by the business users. Each task must exist in its own right in the given order, and the progress of work in execution must be identified in accordance with the defined lifecycle stages and tasks. The developers were therefore strongly discouraged from re-interpreting the business requirements and overengineering their solution. This was considered paramount, as Sherwood wanted to keep a one-to-one correspondence between the task requirements and the programs that implemented them. This correspondence would contribute to cutting down the confusion that often arises between what users want and what the IT department later provides.

The Workflow Tool focused attention on the details of task programs, including effective dates, the type of standard template to be used for each task, the common functions that could be shared among tasks, the possibilities for generic programs to implement several different tasks, and the opportunities for parallel task execution. The development and refinement of these concerns went hand in hand with the development of the *Workflow Engine*, which provided the basis of the run-time environment for task execution.

Interestingly, business users proved much readier to examine the detail of business processes than the detail of business data. For some reason that is not at all clear, business users are enthusiastically ready to immerse themselves in the details of a processing task, but are inclined to think rather vaguely – one might more charitably say 'abstractly' – about data. The idea of a dataset associated with a task corresponds quite well with what they like to call 'a business object'; the details of attribute values and domains seem unimportant.

This is not, of course, the only advantage of the dataset concept. The approach allows data in the relational model to be involved in more than one 'business object' at the same time. For example, client information can be in a claim object at the same time as it is in premium collection or reporting object.

In general, the data requirements for a task dataset are a combination of stored data and derived data. In the repository, the dataset is represented as including this stored and derived data, and also any parameters needed for derivation, such as the date to be used for calculating a derived AgeAsAt value.

All this information is stored by the Logical Database Encapsulator. In addition to providing a convenient interface for entering this business-oriented information, it also dealt with the implementation detail of the data structures, including attribute domains, cardinalities, hidden IDs, and specifications of database *joins* and *filters* for constructing task datasets.

At this point the repository was capable of storing both a business process model and a business object model. The next area of business definition that required both modelling and recording in a formal manner was the business products and practice.

Business product information was reasonably easy. From the data viewpoint, the actual data used by the business could be stored and then abstracted into a class structure from the bottom up. The specific versions of business entities explained by the users could be abstracted to give generic versions of these entities.

At the same time, anything that was likely to change could be treated as a data object. One example was the recognition of many of the entities populating what eventually came to be known as the *plan database*. Another example was the increasing treatment of look-up codes as entity classes. An attribute domain whose values were frequencies, with *monthly* and *yearly* as its current possible values, would be extracted into a separate entity class FREQUENCY. Attributes such as PremiumFrequency, which had been normal attributes, now became association attributes, pointing to a FREQUENCY entity.

This approach strengthened the checking that could be done purely by using database integrity rules. But it could not deal with business rules that could not be reduced to referential integrity: for example, such rules as: 'The age of the life assured must be greater than 18 if they wish to take out a pension', or: 'New business can be written only if the risk in the area concerned does not exceed the capital left to cover this area of risk'.

Such rules were not easy to implement in data alone. They might involve more than one table or view, expressions involving very complex derived data, or data-driven *joins* with dynamic *filters*. They could not be implemented using simple database triggers and stored procedures. Solving this problem led to the development of another tool: the *Business Rules Processor*.

The approach taken was based on rules of the kind used in the Mycin expert system for diagnosing and treating bacterial infections of the blood. Mycin's rules are of the form: 'If these conditions are true then perform these actions'. The Business Rules Processor stores business rules of this form in the repository, and links them to the tasks within the workflow system. Originally there were only *check* rules, in which the only permitted actions were to accept or reject the data presented to the rule. As time went on the scope and style of the rules were expanded to include *set* rules (which could set data values in entity records) and *action* rules (which could execute almost any function that could be defined in the database, including the functions for starting and stopping lifecycles and tasks). This flexibility in rule definition has proved very valuable, especially in certain complex applications such as medical underwriting.

A further development in the treatment of business rules justified a separate tool: the *Decision Table Processor*. These decision tables were frequently best used where the business users could define a standard outcome with some exceptions to the rule, and the factors were quite numerous. This made it simpler for the end users not to have to think about rules based logic that covered every case: a decision table that could be developed incrementally by adding rules and exceptions successively was all that was needed.

Thus the tools provided the following repository functions:

- Workflow Tool:
  - Process models
  - Process dependencies
  - Task parallel processing model
  - Process ownership
  - Task ownership

- Logical Database Encapsulator:
  - Object model
  - Object map to relational data structure
  - Roles of base storage entities
  - Derived data definitions
  - Data dependencies between data elements

- Business Rules:
  - Business Product rules repository
  - Business Practice rules repository
  - Use recording of rules
  - Ownership of rules within the business community

- Autocode Repository
  - Use of datsets within application programs
  - Use of data elements within screens and applications
  - Use of entities and roles within an application

Holding all this information in the repository allows the system to produce *impact analysis* on changes to a business requirement all the way through to the lines of application code, calculation code and business practice and operation. This is invaluable as it provides not only application software impact but also business impact, a crucial requirement for rapidly changing businesses.

Finally the LogicWare tools use the above repositories to write application code that is solid, robust and easy to change. At the same time, the run-time workflow engine can deal with parallel deployment on SMP machines (and in the future possibly MMP machines), allowing the business users to exploit parallel processing and in very scaleable yet easily changed applications.

Scaleability tests have shown even on a small 4×486 cpu machine the system can easily reach 700 transactions per second for a single task. This allows much easier implementation of high-volume complex systems. Because the parallel processing techniques have been implemented in the LogicWare tools, they are much more easily exploited by a development team.

Applications developed in the LogicWare environment include the best-selling life and pensions administration system Amarta. Amarta is provided as a best practice business model for running large-scale life and pension systems. Typically, the model within the repository is tailored and adapted to suit a client's own products and practice. The code generation tools can generate up to 80% of all the code required to produce a full application. Current implementations of LogicWare are for Oracle and Informix databases.

Index

A-task 71, 186
access efficiency 172
accessing a dataset 111
action rule 27, 226
active system behaviour 145
AD-task 82
ALL special ID 60, 114, 182
Amarta system iv, ix, 227
ANY special ID 60, 114–5, 182
AO-task 87
AP-task 145
APPLICABLE_WHEN function 135–6, 177
associated entity 89, 92
association 19, 45, 48, 218, 154
    attribute 20, 42, 67, 96, 113, 219–20
association, optional 113
    three-way 58–9
atomic value 52, 46
atomicity of update 175
attribute categories 55
    definition 56, 132
    domain 106
    in role 44, 103, 106, 179, 180
    order 218
    reference 27, 130
    row 139, 222
    value 20, 46, 49, 67, 222
attribute value, specific 222
attribute, association 19–20, 42, 67, 96, 219–20
    defined 131–2
    derived 56
    determining 123, 141
    entity 18, 37, 39, 51, 54, 106, 112, 188, 218
    fixed 55
    ID 42, 50
    observed 131–2
    pointer 44, 47, 57, 60, 62, 102, 112, 131, 169, 196

repeated 46
variable 55
visible 154–5
authorized user 147, 150
Autocode Processor 223
    repository 223–6
automated bank payments 9–10
automatic documentation 197
    task 15, 25, 70, 72, 144–5, 149, 155–6, 158, 175
AwaitingStageN state 22, 80–1, 86, 90–2, 124, 133

background program 16
backtracking 24, 34–5, 117, 125, 141, 177–8, 187
    lifecycle 127–8
backtracking, handling 199
basic entity model 38, 115
batch job 156, 158, 172–4
beneficent side-effect 117, 126–7, 141
Beta Computers 223
Boehm 185
booking date 178
BPR *see* Business Process Re-engineering
British Computer Society ix
business 3
    area 191
    competitiveness 33
    department 8
    expert user 170
    interaction 4, 12, 81, 159, 161, 182, 190
    interaction phase 17, 20–5, 35
    module 143
    object 224–5
    obligation xi, 4
    Process Re-engineering ix, 8, 16, 31, 54, 162, 223–4